TEX SMITH'S
HOW TO BUILD REAL HOT RODS

by LeRoi Tex Smith

Motorbooks International
Publishers & Wholesalers ®
Printed in USA

First published in 1988 by Motorbooks International Publishers and Wholesalers Inc. PO Box 2, 729 Prospect Ave. Osceola, WI 54020 USA

Motorbooks International is a certified trademark, registered with the United States Patent Office.

Printed and bound in the United States of America

The information in this book is true and complete to the best of our knowledge. All recommendations are made without any guarantee on the part of the author or publisher, who also disclaim any liability incurred in connection with the use of this data or specific details.

We recognize that some words, model names and designations, for example, mentioned herein are the property of various manufacturers. We use them for identification purposes only. This is not an official publication.

Library of Congress Cataloging-In-Publication Data

Smith, LeRoi
    How to build real hot rods / Tex Smith.
    p.   cm.
    Includes index.
    ISBN 0-87938-338-0
    1. Hot rods - Design and construction. I. Title
TL236.3S65 1988
629.2'28--DC19   88-31186
                       CIP

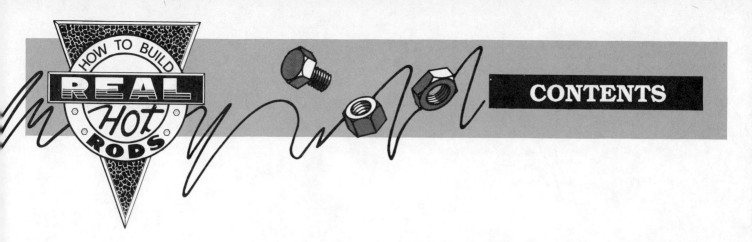

CONTENTS

This book has been in the "possibles" for about ten years now. But what kicked it overcenter was a comment Wally Parks made to me during the spring of 1987. We had been talking about the modern state of hot rodding, particularly as it applies to drag racing, and Wally paused thoughtfully. "You know," he mused, "it really was great back on the dry lakes when we were still young, back when we were building real hot rods. Cars were made of a mixture of mechanical pieces. Guys weren't afraid to try something different, and we just bolted things together to see if it would all work."

To see if it would work. I've since reflected on my own hot rodding background, and that has truely been the catchall. I've been doing this crazy thing called hot rodding all these years, mostly just to see if some zany idea would work. And as I consider what other car enthusiasts have told me, the same thread of truth holds sway everywhere. When we pause long enough to think about it all, isn't that the very foundation of the automotive industry? Of airplanes? Boats? Spaceships? sophisticated engineering ultimately enters the picture, but at the outset, it is merely curiosity and the glimpse of a need.

I like to believe that every hot rodder follows his own drummer. I like to believe it, but I don't. Far and away, the great majority of hot rodders are followers. Not necessarily cookie cutters, but followers down the path of least resistance. I do it myself. If I have a particular area I'm working on, and I remember a magazine article, or remember the name of someone who has done a similar job, I'll consult them. I still build _real_ hot rods.

So, tell me. Exactly what is a _real_ hot rod? Here is a question that begs definition, simply because we can find no two people who agree completely on what a real hot rod is!

For me, it is a matter of personal taste. A hot rod or a custom car can really be called a personalized vehicle. A real hot rod is whatever the builder/owner wants it to be. But, since I have yet to find a hot rod that the builder/owner is totally and completely satisfied with, I must wonder if there is anywhere a finished real hot rod. Sort of like the cat chasing its tail.

A real hot rod can be in any one of the myriad guises that we find within this fascinating hobby. It can be a drag car or a near restoration. It can be a wild and radical custom or a traditional roadster/coupe/sedan. It can be a pro-streeter or a muscle car. It can be a truck or a three-wheeler. It can have 500 cubic inches or 1.5 litres. It can even be a cookie cutter look-alike. It can be anything, as long as it is a direct expression of the builder's individuality.

We must also consider exactly who the real hot rodder is.
The person with the car. I have been building hot rods and customs for too many years now, yet I have never been able to perfect the construction expertise of someone like John Butera or Roy Brizio or Magoo or Winfield. I do the best I can, and try to become better. Were I a professional builder, welding and cutting and designing every day, I would become better. Instead, I am like practically all hot rodders, doing my hobby as a part time pasttime. I suppose I can be described as a

real hot rodder. I have a friend who does not weld or cut or grind. He isn't very good at it, so he has the work hired out. He bolts together things, and does what maintenance he can. I think he can be described as a real hot rodder.

In one sense of the word, we are both builders, one directly, one indirect The cars I build reflect my own desires (as well as my craftmanshipshortcomings!) The cars my friend has built reflect his own desires. In a way, the person who buys a ready made rod might also be called a real hot rodder, but only if that person continues in the hobby, and is not in it just to keep up with neighbor Jones.

The fatal mistake that so many veteran and neophyte rod enthusiasts make is in trying to create a (or have created, or buy) a vehicle that everyone (or most everyone) will like and admire. Building a vehicle to satisfy someone else somehow misses the mark. The nation's car makers try this each and every year, and so far they haven't succeeded. When the rod builder decides to have the machine that he/she wants, and everyone else can stick it in their ears, then that builder is going to come very close to creating a real hot rod.

In a strictly humorous gesture, I often chide contemporary rodders with the claim that a real hot rod has no top, is painted in primer, and has no fenders or hood. Not at all true, of course. Back in the "good old days" if we could have afforded a great paint job, we would have had one. We needed fenders, but we wanted to look like race cars. And, in California at least, the roadster was considered the most sporty of body designs. Not unlike the convertible of today. The cars we had then have somehow become the standards of today. Not because of any kind of engineering superiority.

In those early days at the SoCal dry lakes, the Southern California Timing Association (SCTA) would not allow coupes and sedans to run. The general response was that if a person wanted to race a real hot rod, he could go to the nearest junkyand and buy a roadster body for $15! Some of the early four cylinder veterans claimed that the Ford flathead V8 simply was not a real hot rod motor. Now, years later, I hear the same kinds of things said about fiberglass and the modern four cylinder engines.

I hear people say that no one builds real hot rods anymore. I hear others say that unless the car looks like something from the 40s or 50s, it isn't a real hot rod or custom. Somehow or other, nostalgia forgets that if we had the things of today back then, the cars of back then would look like the cars of now. Don't let anyone ever convince you otherwise...the modern hot rod and custom is a far better vehicle than we were creating 30 and 40 years ago. And, it is just as much a real hot rod as those early attempts were.

A lot of this has to do with how we used those early rods and customs. Back then, I don't recall a single person who had the luxury of building a car "on the side". We drove those vehicles, usually every day. When we made a modification, it was done late into the evening or over the weekend, because we couldn't tie up our transportation for any length of time. Today, we start a project and it never sees the light of necessity until the day we roll it (fully painted and upholstered) out the garage door.

Lately, there has been a creeping virus of Show Rod-itis working its way into hot rodding. There is an increasing emphasis on price of the vehicle, rather than an appreciation of the car for what it is, or does. Part of this value drive has been generated by the restored car hobby, where vehicle dollar worth has come to overwhelm vehicle utilization worth. Investment has overcome pleasure of use. The street driven rod or custom cannot stand alongside a non-driven show car, so guess which car is perceived to have the most value.

In such an economy, street driven hot rod values also begin to escalate, and change is bound to take place. Quality built rods and customs of today command a higher price than their restored contemporaries. Many of these vehicles are purchased by people who know little or nothing about cars. They only remember what their peer group in high school considered super, so they buy one now, years later. Hopefully these people come to realize exactly how special is the vehicle they own, and hopefully they come to make a long term committment to the hobby. Unfortunately, a lot of these people were "into" Corvettes and Vans before they discovered rods. These are the people most attracted to show rods.

Don't misunderstand me. I love show rods, because they are superb examples of rolling sculpture. But they are not street rods, or street machines, or street customs. While lots of them may look bad, with their pro-street image, neither are they race cars. They are idea cars. they are dream cars. On the same level of interpretation as the cars created every year or so by the world's manufacturers of mass transportation. This doesn't mean a show rod is any less a real hot rod, it only means that we need to remember the context in which such a vehicle is created. It is for show, and in that respect, it is true to itself.

Dave Lukari has a phrase that sums it all up quite well, "Real hot rodding is not mega-bucks...it is mega-ingenuity!"

Throwing dollars at a car does not necessarity make it a real hot rod. And dollars don't automatically disqualify such a car. Many of the so-called high-tech cars are true masterpieces. Not exactly practical, but masterpieces nonetheless. I should point out here that the phrase high-tech is not at all appropriate. Precious few of these vehicles have any kind of high or advanced-age technology involved. They have advanced craftsmanship.

We get into problems when we try to lump all of our hot rodding interest together. It just doesn't work well.

Just as a true dual-purpose hot rod doesn't work well. If we build a street rod, then try to do well at the nostalgia races, we usually lose. To a car that is more racer oriented. Same with a show car. While we may have fun with such a car, we can't normally be totally successful at either end of the equation. For most rodders, having fun with the car is what it is all about. This might be the fun of racing, or of driving across country, or of showing. Such a car, the one that gives true and honest pleasure, is a real hot rod or custom.

In the end, we must define a real hot rod as a very personal thing. It is what we each want, and not what we think someone else wants. And, friends, that is what makes hot rodding so much fun in the first place! See you down the road somewhere.

LeRoi Tex Smith
Publisher/Editor

CHAPTER 1

What To Build

It well could be that the most difficult part of any hot rod or custom building project is deciding upon <u>what</u> to build. This is a decision that can, and does, have a direct bearing upon practically every aspect of the project, from cost to labor to parts availability to pride in the finished product. Too often, this is also the most overlooked part of the entire process.

I did much of the engine swap articles while I was at Hot Rod magazine in the 50s and 60s. During that time, nearly every letter we received on this popular subject said something like, "I have this 800 cubic inch Zoom-O straight twelve engine and I'd like to put it in my Crosley sedan...Essentially, the writer already had access to an engine, and perhaps some kind of chassis was handy. No planning, just how to get results. That is much the way many rodders are introduced to their projects... beginner and old hand alike.

For the beginner, it is one of two approaches. Aunt Maude has this old 1952 Plymouth four door.....Or, all the magazines show the pieces advertised to build a car just exactly like the one on the cover! For the old timer, it too often is trying to find the kind of car that was always wanted...Or, all the magazines show the pieces advertised to build a car just exactly like the one on the cover!

The first thing to decide when beginning a project is exactly what is wanted. Then, what is needed. Then, what is really practical, given the circumstance of talent/money/vehicle design. And finally, what is available. It will be surprising, when some real thought is given to this process, exactly what kind of project evolves.

If you make up a list of what is wanted, the list will probably evolve into what is really desirable, and what might be acceptable. When you throw in what is needed, things change a bit. If the rod is to be a second or third car, you might start thinking of what would work best for you. Give mom the family sedan that you have been using, and think of a really useful rod. Something that will do for commuting, or for your work. A pickup truck, perhaps, or a four-door luxury type sedan (to impress the boss and clients). When you start thinking in terms of need, rather than want, the selection process can skew around a bit. Now, add what is practical. A 500 cubic inch big block with a GMC supercharger is not the best thing in the world for commuting. And it needs tender loving coaxing that might not be what your boss or client thinks is keen. If the rod is to be a second car for the wife to drive, then it had really better be practical (and dependable, with a huge capital D).

After you have narrowed your list of potentials, you have to throw in what is available to you. Much of the country is in a state of biodegradeability. Simply put, the vehicles disappear over time, thanks to rust. In parts of the midwest and east (both the U.S. and Canada), finding a car in good shape that is more than 10 years old is something of a miråcle. That isn't as big a problem in much of the west, and a few areas such as North Carolina. What is available depends entirely upon how much you want to spend in getting it to your front drive. You can find lots of old cars in the Rocky Mountain states, in excellent condition, but getting them to your garage door is going to cost money. Yes, you can combine a vacation trip and take along your car trailer, thus reducing the cost to minimal. And sometimes you can find a way to transport such a vehicle via a friend. But be honest when figuring what this will cost. You might want to get such a vehicle from a local "dealer", if you will actually end up saving money.

Here's an example: A friend came by the house recently with a trailer load of good rod bodies and frames. Two 1932 Ford Tudors, and two 1934 Ford Tudors. Several 1932 frames, and miscellaneous parts were tucked here and there. He had bought them all over in South Dakota (where that dealer had hauled them from Canada!), and he was enroute to his home in California. He figured that with a minimum amount of body work here and there, plus some primer, he would get about $3800 each for the popular Deuce bodies, a similar price for the '34s. So, a rodder in that immediate area might actually be better off paying such a price, than travelling 2000 miles to buy such a body for a couple thousand dollars. Do some homework first.

Interestingly, many rodders (newcomers and experienced alike) tend to overlook really sound building projects right in their own backyard. A few years back, I stopped at a gas station enroute to the Street Rod Nationals in St. Paul, Minnesota. The young attendant admired my 1948 Chrysler and said, "Boy, I'd like to find something like this to build up!" My reply was, "What about that 1947 DeSoto setting out back of the station." The fellow could only see that my car was shiney, he couldn't see the dusty relic out back as being the same.

So, a big part of deciding on what to build will involve looking into the habit of looking everywhere for dead vehicles. Behind garages and back of barns, in gulleys and tucked away in community alleys. Even in used car lots. Recently, I visited a friend during a rod run, and when following him home, I noticed a 1957 Nash sitting forlorn in a weedgrown field. Right alongside the main street. When I mentioned it to my friend, he dismissed the car as having "always been there". When I looked the Nash over closely, I noted that it was indeed the top of the Nash line, and a very desirable model. It was entirely complete. The upholstery was good enough to be used, all glass was perfect, and the chrome trim was excellent. Here was a car that could be turned into an outstanding ride for very little money. All it needed was imagination. An engine swap of some kind, probably a later model rearend, and disc front brakes. Add some good big/little tires, then give it a wild paint job. Leave all the chrome in place, and the machine would be dynamite. Probably for a total cost of under $3000.

No, That Nash would not be just like the other cars. Not even remotely. But it would be a real hot rod. Daring to experiment, to be different, is what hot rodding is all about.

So, when you start looking at your rod building list, you start to see that you might possibly want to turn things around. The list might should read; 1)What is available, 2)What has potential out of what is available, 3)What you really need, and finally 4) What you want.

Almost always, when a person builds something that is out of the ordinary, he doesn't realize how popular the car can really be. He doesn't think that he might be starting a trend, or being on the leading edge of hot rodding. Just take a look at how strong a following has developed around Ford's "ugly duckling" 1937/1938 models. A few years ago you wouldn't

---

"Interestingly, many rodders (newcomers and experienced alike) tend to overlook really sound building projects right in their own backyard."

---

see more than two or three at all the rod runs in a season. Now, people are falling over themselves trying to find good building material. Because someone dropped the front of one in the weeds, and painted the distracting chrome pieces. Suddenly the ugly Ford had become high-tech.

When deciding what to build, especially if you are a first-timer, or relatively inexperienced, don't think that you must have a 1932 or 1934 Ford. It isn't prerequisite to have a 3-window coupe, or a car with 500 cubic inches. Instead, start looking at available cars and trying to see their potential.

Five years ago, I advertised in Old Cars Weekly newspaper (OCW, Iola, WI 54990. That's all the address needed. This is a restoration oriented paper that reaches 90,000 subscribers a week, a lot of them hot rodders.) for a 1960 Chrysler. I only got two responses, but one was a car out in Tacoma, Washington. It was a New Yorker hardtop, in driveable condition, but with a bent rear quarter panel. Price was an economical $500. This was the same body style as the 300 letter series car, with big fins and lots of chrome. It was a luxury car for its day, and with the 413 cubic inch engine, it had performance.

I bought the car and delivered it to an acquaintance who does custom bodywork and paint. The body was straightened, some minor rust areas fixed, and then some of the chrome was removed. Not all, but lots of extraneous stuff, including all Chrysler identification. The car was painted with the German Sikkens two-part system, bright Porsche red. Police car wheels were installed, along with Sears radials. The result was a car with well over 100,000 miles on it, but it still ran (runs) great, and it is extremely popular with the contemporary crowd. High school and college kids think it looks super, with the tall fins and bright color. Hot rodders admit that here is one "big" car that looks right.

I have just rebuilt a hot 440 engine and TorqueFlite (from Gary Dagle) for the car, and this winter will install a 1973 Satellite (Plymouth) rearend and front disc brakes. When I am finished totally rebuilding the car, which we anticipate will run about 140 mph at the Bonneville salt flats, I will have less than $2000 invested. And not a lot of time, because I started with a piece that was in decent condition.

In this case, I was lucky. I got what I wanted to build, although there weren't a lot available in response to my ad. I have since spotted dozens of similar cars, left to die. The car was something I needed, since my everyday transportaion was going back to the lease company, and it certainly did have potential. I know, it isn't a '57 Chevy or a Mustang or a 1935 Ford roadster. But it is a hot rod, in every sense of the word. It is unique.

I keep looking at it, and I think how neat it would be to mold in the headlights, and french the great taillights, and smooth off the door handles, etc. Here is a car that could be a wild mild custom as well as a pure hot rod.

It isn't difficult finding something neat to build into a real hot rod, but it does take some mental imagination. And some practical thought. A few years ago a young man came to me asking about fixing up his four door 1956 Chevy. I cautioned him at the time that he could do it, but not to expect any good resale from the car. He would put more into the rebuilding process than what he could sell the car for. He persisted, and sure enough, two years later he found that he could get only a fraction return on his money investment (not counting the labor). The car was nicely done and it would haul, but it was a four door. A little more patience on his part, looking for a hardtop or two door post, and he would have realized his investment, and probably a profit.

Getting your money back out of a project should not be the sole deciding factor in what you decide to build, however. This 1960 Chrysler of mine will not bring a big resale price. It is a hardtop, best of the line. But, it is a Chrysler. I really don't care, because I built the car to drive. I don't have a huge amount of time or money in the project, so I don't have to think of resale.

I might think about this differently, in the case of an older project I have underway. I'm building a dollar-a-pound roadster project for our HOT ROD MECHANIX magazine. This is a 1931 Ford roadster body on a set of highly remodeled 1932 Ford frame rails. I am putting a ton of time and effort into the car, although total finished cost will be somewhere around $1500. Yes, one thousand five hundred. When the car is finished, it will be worth several thousand dollars, simply because it is a roadster. I have available a great 1928 Dodge four door sedan. If I built this car, no matter how little I spent in construction, it would not bring as much resale. It could be a Willys or a Durant or a Whatzit, and this would remain the truth. If the sedan were a four door 1932 Ford, it would be a different story, however.

So, being practical about what you decide to build includes the determination of how much money you want to invest/recoup. You don't want to just pour money into something that is not going to have a value, unless that value is pure self satisfaction.

After you have decided that a particular vehicle is what you want to build, and you have one located, inspect it in the harsh light of reality. The best method is to make a written list of everything on the car that must be repaired. If the car is really reaching back in age, you can almost assume total reconstruction. In such a case, say a 1932 Ford body, you might be better off to get a new fiberglass unit. Be honest with yourself. If the upholstery in the later model is a bit shabby, expect a full upholstery job. At around two grand minimum. The paint is surely going to be changed, and engine/trans replacement is probable. You make the list, and wince at the results.

One of the very best ways to get into a project is to buy something that has been started (and not butchered beyond saving). This is what many of the most experienced rodders do. As a good rule, many builders start a project, but lose interest after they have done all the grunge work, such as chassis, and brakes, and steering, etc. They have been working on the car for a year or more, and it just doesn't seem to be getting anywhere. So they lose interest. Right at the point where the car will start to go together and begin to look like something.

Quite often, you can buy such a project at a really good price. Usually it will be more expensive than a similar un-worked-on car, but you are getting the vehicle with all the ugly work already finished. And you usually get a good engine and transmission, plus a lot of parts, at the friendly price. Such a basket case may take a while to sort out, but you will be way ahead of the game with the car.

The bottom line is to build a car that you want, or at least think might make an interesting vehicle. If you think of it as being practical and something with potential, chances are that other people will think the same...after you are finished. You can build a complete oddball, or a duplicate of other cars in town. Just as long as you do it your way, and for your own purposes, you will create a real hot rod.

Looking in the Country

by Carl Brunson

This very complete '48 Ford two door sedan sits on a frame, but the engine and entire undercarriage has been removed. All the car is still intact, including interior trim and dash, a few minor items have been removed over the years by author Brunson for other Ford projects.

While the four door sedan might not be the most popular of building material, something such as this Buick ('55 or '56) could be turned into a great rod. It would be different, and it does have potential as a strong runner, with Buick V8 power.

I'm a bodyman/painter by trade, but an incureable old car scrounge by hobby. I just happen to live in the Rocky Mountain area, where we still have lots of tin laying around, in the towns as well as on the farms and ranches. And, the tin is in good shape, because we don't have big rust problems.

Recently, I carried my camera on one of my weekend outings. There aren't as many complete cars around as I would like, but by combining several different finds, it is usually possible to come up with a total unit. Of course, the later the model car, the more complete it is likely to be. Recently I've gotten in the habit of picking up potential building material, such as grilles, or fenders, or bumpers. This begins to make quite a pile at the house, but it is also great swapping material. Sometimes, the best find of the day will be a hood emblem or a taillight bezel. I brought home enough 1935-36 Ford parts last summer to build one complete car.

When I'm out scouring the countryside, the biggest prob-

lem is in finding the vehicle owner. Rule number one out in this country: Just because something looks abandoned doesn't mean there is no owner. I start by asking at nearby ranch houses, or sometimes a person who is working a field. Many times the people tell me where other old cars are located (way back on the land where it can't be seen from the road), and almost always they just give me the relic

The very best old car spotting times in the west are early spring and late summer. Before the grass gets high, and after the fields of grain have been harvested. I've included some photos I took just to show what is available within 30 miles of my home. Lots of building stuff, from very early to very late.

When friends from the East come visiting, I always suggest they bring along some kind of trailer, and some tools. Very useful are a jack, come-a-long, vise grips, hammer, and chisel. These in addition to regular screwdrivers and wrenches/socket sets.

When looking at cars to build, it is best to start with the most perfect piece possible. This '53 Chevy two door has good glass and only minor body dents, much of the chrome trim is still excellent. All this would be in favor of fixing the car up.

The popular 1957 Chevrolet is still very much in evidence on western farms, but lots of them have been picked over for trim and similar small parts.

Never seen are the hot Oldmobiles of the Fifties and Sixties, although there are a few Olds fanatics building such cars as rods. During years to come, a car such as this will become extremely rare as a rod or custom, now is the time to pick one up.

The station wagon, particularly the two door, is almost totally overlooked in rodding and customizing, but a car such as this Ford Ranch Wagon would be excellent for either type of machine. Here, the glass has all been broken, which would be a determining factor in starting on it as a project.

Shoebox Fords (1949-53) have been gaining in popularity with rodders and customizers in recent years, there seem to be thousands of them laying in American and Canadian fields and back yards. These cars can be either mild or wild rods or customs, and they take just about any kind of engine swap very well.

Discarded parts of cars are everywhere in the nation, not just in the west, but there is less rust to be concerned with in the less humid climates. This MoPar front end section has been laying in the grass for two decades and would need practically no work to make perfect again.

Early tin, especialy non-Ford items, is abundant in most of the nation, but be careful when selecting such a vehicle for a project because it might have a wooden body framework, and that means a lot of extra basic work (and cost).

Looking in the City

by Eric Pierce

A couple hundred yards from a freeway, but accessible only through a backyard, this Model A Sport Coupe is very good. We left our name and phone number, just in case it might come up for sale.

All the good rod building material, so we've heard it said, is gone from most easily-accessible locales. All that's left is someplace in the outback of Idaho or Montana. Carl Brunson has shown what is in the immediate vicinity of his Idaho home, and through the years Tex Smith has shown us literally thousands of good builders laying discarded around the backroads of the nation. While some might accuse this author of being somewhat skeptical by nature, I think there is suffecient evidence to support the notion that there is still plenty of good tin inside the nation's city limits...regardless of opinions to the contrary.

So, camera in hand and self-restricted to the city limits of my own hometown, I set about spending a day in search of urban vintage tin. It is important that the reader understand that, unlike most town and cities across America, my hometown is fairly new. Just a scant 30 or so years ago, it was nothing by ranches and brush. If, I figured, I could find a significant amount of VT in such a newly-established community, finding even more buildable stuff in an older town should be even easier.

In an urban setting, camoflage seems to be the most often encountered element of old car hunting. Unlike the more rural areas, where abandoned cars are usually left where they die, city cars (regardless of their rodding or restoration potential) get towed away. Sometimes rather quickly. Keeping America Beautiful obviously starts with removal of old cars. Or so city officials seem to think. So, we started our search by

looking for urban camoflage...and we found old cars.

In looking for any kind of old car to build, one must be something of a detective, using clues to discover the likely spots where tin may be stashed. A disembodied Ford front axle, for example, led me to a long-stalled rod project 1940 Ford sedan. An obviously long unused early Ford pickup truck parked at the street curb (how it escaped the zealous city fathers is unknown!) helped identify an old-time rodder with a long-abandoned and partially disassembled coupe in the backyard. Where there's one old car or even part of one there is usually more.

For want of a better term, Backyard Peeping can also be very rewarding. Binoculars from higher ground, or just cruising up and down residential streets can be very rewarding. Electric and gas meter readers are great sources of information. When you do find something interesting lurking in a backyard, be sure to obtain the owner's permission before going farther. Saves greatly in mental and physical wear and tear.

As the photos illustrate, we had a very productive day in terms of vintage tin found. And, we had a great time finding it. All the gold may be in California (or Idaho and Montana), but there's still plenty of good tin right in your own backyard. As overheard at Carl Brunson's shop a couple of years ago, "Hey, that's a great 1936 Ford Tudor. Practically no rust, and really complete. Where'd you find it?" Carl's reply, "Oh, I got it from a guy back in Massachusetts!"

Just after finding this 1940 Ford Standard, author came in contact with the owner's dog!

This 1940 Ford Delux Tudor was in a trucking company yard for years, tracking down the owner was a task. But Mike Rangel did it and now owns the car.

Urban tin relies on camoflage to remain intact over any length of time. This straight and primed 1935 Ford pickup cab and bed has been in sight for years in an equipment rental yard. Never hurts to ask.

Auto body shops sometimes sport half-finished projects that have been shoved aside. Shop owners and workers are also good leads when looking for a project to build.

Frames and frame sections often are free for the taking, and are valuable as repair material. Good for trading, so don't pass it up.

The western states are full of cars from the 40s and 50s and 60s. These do not rust, and they go begging for a nice home.

While not always true, a good rule of thumb is that where there is one. there are usually more. This early Ford pickup lead to a former project rod.

And here's our "diamond in the junkyard". This 40s era Chevy is a full custom, complete with boattail. This is a for real early custom of unknown heritage, quietly awaiting someone to love. If you're interested, contact Eric Pierce via HOT ROD MECHANIX magazine, PO Box K, Driggs, Idaho, 83422.

CHAPTER 2

Frames

The automobile frame has but one function. It is the platform to which powerplant, suspension, and body components attach. How well, or how poorly, the frame works on a hot rod is generally a matter of original vehicle design and intended use. For the hot rodder, it is vital to understand the original intent of the frame and vehicle, since this will have an almost absolute bearing upon whether or not an original frame can/should be used, how it should be used, and what modification may be required.

Perhaps the very best example of this particular problem of frame selection and modification occurs frequently in rodding, because so many early Fords are built into rods. The model T and model A cars are popular vehicles to rod. But there is considerable difference in the frames of the two, although basic frame/suspension design is the same. In fact, this very basic frame/suspension design holds true with Fords through the 1948 model year.

In this early Ford chassis approach, the frame and body are created to pivot on a centerline of the suspension, as seen on a line drawn through the center of the vehicle front to rear. This is a direct carry-on of earlier horsedrawn carriage practices. Therefore, what a rodder does to such a chassis,

An automobile frame, whether for the passenger car or the racer, is nothing more than a platform to hold suspension and engine/body.

Frames at right show the typical Ford Model T at top, the improved Model A in the middle and the beginning of the V8 era with the 1932 Ford at bottom.

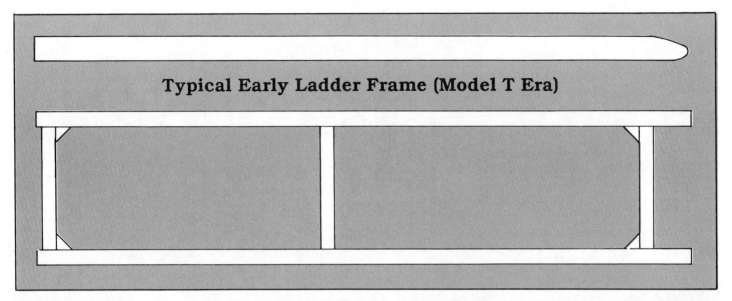

Typical Early Ladder Frame (Model T Era)

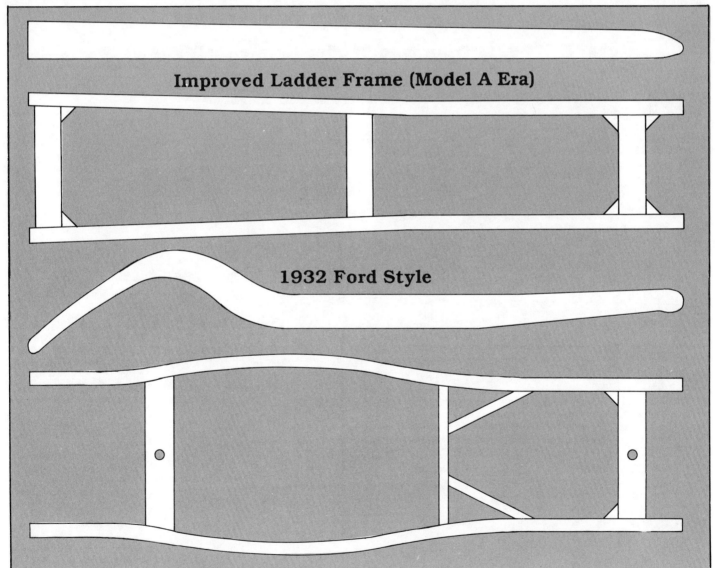

Improved Ladder Frame (Model A Era)

1932 Ford Style

during modifications, has a direct bearing on the frame.

Because the Model T Ford was a very lightweight vehicle, the frame was equally minimal. It was a simple ladder type design (as was the following Model A frame), with two nearly parallel side rails connected by simple crossmembers. On end, the frame looks like a ladder with steps removed.

When the Model A was created, the small cross-section side rails were not strong enough, so the new frame was made with a wider cross-section and slightly stronger crossmembers. Little else changed.

For hot rodding, the Model T frames are too small and weak! It is possible to use them, if the car is to be very light

Early Ladder Frame Style (Common to most non-Fords (Semi Elliptic Sptings)

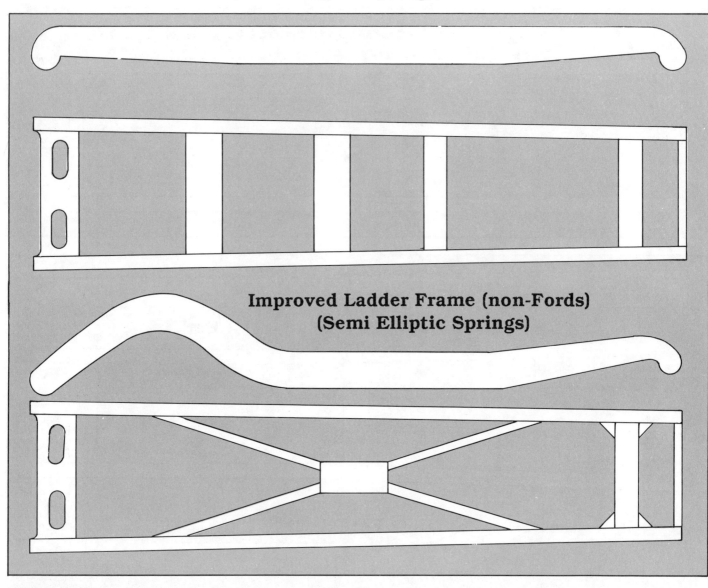

Improved Ladder Frame (non-Fords)
(Semi Elliptic Springs)

1933 And Later Ford

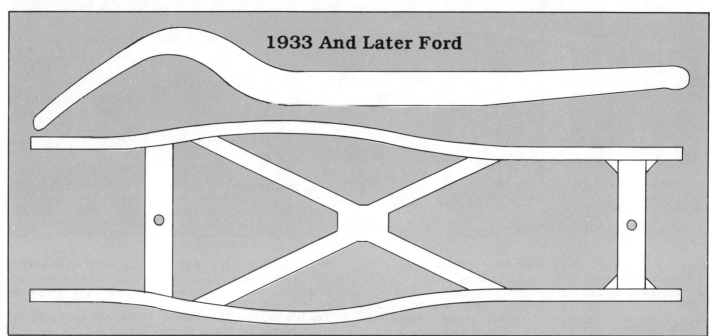

(say, under 1500 pounds) and will use a very small engine (a low horsepower and lightweight 4 cylinder). Even then, the C-shaped cross-section rails need to be boxed. In this procedure, an extra piece of metal (usually about 1/8-inch thick) is welded to the open side of the C-shape, creating a rectangular shape. This is much stronger, but since new tubing of similar dimensions is available universally, most builders will opt to make up a new tubing frame rather than box and modify a Model T frame.

The Model A frame is larger and stronger, but it must also be boxed for maximum strength with modern powertrains and contemporary load forces.

The 1932 Ford frame uses the similar ladder construction, although from the sides each rail curves upward toward front and rear ends (this allows the body to sit lower to the ground, improving center of gravity). The front and rear crossmembers are still relatively simple units, although stronger, and

the frame has a K-shaped center crossmember. In 1933, the frame was changed to include an X-shaped crossmember. Through 1948, this same basic frame design was continued, although improvements in strength continued to be made.

It is important to remember that in this basic Ford design, the body and frame were supposed to pivot about a single point at the centerline of the chassis, front to rear.

The majority of other cars used a similar ladder frame, but the springs were located at the four corners of the frame. The difference in operation was/is significant.

With the Ford idea, the body was free to roll about the centerline, restrained only by the springs and shocks. This greatly reduced any twist forces to the frame/body, so the frame could be simple and lightweight. With the other designs, where the semi-elliptic springs were used, the frames had to be much stiffer. They were stronger, and heavier, therefore such frames can usually be used on the

BELOW - This 1932 Ford frame has been boxed for extra strength and tubing crossmembers added. For maximum rigidity to twist, an X or K-shaped crossmember would be desirable to take some of the stress off the side rails. Adding a couple of hundred extra pounds to the frame with extra strength members does not reduce highway performance, improves handling.

BELOW - Frames on modern cars are very stiff, this pinched waist frame is a true box section and can be used for a swap under later model "fat fender" hot rods with some modifications, such as removing the big rear overhang and adding straight "side rails" for other bodies. In comparison, some frames swing outboard behind engine in a "perimeter" shape, but can also be modified.

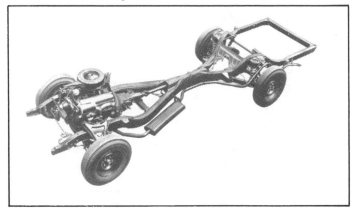

LEFT - The early ladder frame was common to most non-Fords, with semi-elleptic or similar springs mounted parallel to the frame side rails, at each corner. At first the side rails were flat (top), then they began to have kick-up's front and rear, to lower vehicle center of gravity (middle). Compare these types of frames to the 1933 and later Ford style at bottom.

BELOW - This is typical of the frames from non-Ford cars during the late 1930s and through the mid-1950s. The frames are very strong and resistant to twist forces and lend themselves readily to later model front suspensions and different rear suspension (such as coil springs). In many cases, however, it is better to rebuild stock suspensions and merely add disc front brakes.

modern rod with very little extra strength needed. As the twisting forces became more of a problem (faster and heavier cars), Ford started to address the problem, with the K-shaped crossmember in the 1932 frame. The 1948 Ford frame is far superior to the 1932 frame, in strength, but because of big design differences it is not used when building an earlier rod. Rule of thumb when building Ford rods: The Model A frame works well under A's and T's - the 1932 frame works well under A's, T's and '32s - the 1933-34 frame works best under same year bodies when there are great similarities in the car, such as 1935-36, 1937-38, 1939-40, and 1941-1948, it is possible to utilize similar frames. Expect minor variations.

Ford used the transverse (cross chassis) spring, pivoting at the centerline of the chassis. The huge majority of other builders utilized semi- or full-elliptic springs (springs run parallel to each frame side rail), mounted at the four corners of the frame. This type of suspension gives a much firmer control of the suspension members, but it also requires a frame with much greater resistance to twist. The idea is to have the spring control the suspension movement, rather than have this movement transferred into the frame in the form of twist.

Because of this type of suspension, such frames are usually much stronger than Ford units. The side rails are deeper, the crossmembers are more numerous and bigger. But, the same ladder style design is kept.

This was pretty much the way of frame design into the 1950s. With the advent of the higher horsepower engines and different body styles, the frame designs began to change. Of course, there were unusual frame designs way back into the 'teens, but mass production cars followed basic patterns. There were variations in mass designs in Europe, but not in America. The "new" cars, with improving suspensions, called up the need for much stronger frames.

Starting in the 50s, frames began to take on other shapes. The X-shaped frame appeared, wherein the side rails pinched in just behind the engine, and ahead of the rear axle. This allowed the passenger seating to be placed lower in the chassis, giving a much lower profile to the body. The perimeter frame showed up, with the side rails flaring outward to the body edge, again letting the passenger seat be lower. And the unit-body frame came into being, at first with a stub frame up front mounting to a very stiff body firewall and floor structure. With most of these frames, the rails were boxed, forming a square or rectangular cross-section. In some cases, such "tubing" frames were actually lighter in weight than the older C-section frames, and far stronger.

In hot rodding, the idea is to get as strong and as lightweight a frame as possible. This holds true for street oriented vehicles as well as race cars. The one exception is with Bonneville salt flat racers, where traction is such a problem that cars are actually built much heavier than would be expected.

One of the biggest problems for the beginning rodder is overcoming the temptation to use a "late model" frame with all its advantages under an earlier model body. For instance, a 1940 Ford frame (which already has a hydraulic brake system in the suspension) under a model T body. Yes, it can be done. Yes, it requires a ton of work. And no, it isn't worth all the work. At the same time, it is possible to put something like a 1972 Chevrolet Chevelle frame and suspension under a 1941 Ford, or a 1951 Mercury or Chevrolet. The key here is the relative size of the bodies. The Model T body is very small, and the 40 frame is large. The 1941 Ford is large, about the same dimensions as the Chevelle frame. Good rule of thumb: Pre-WW II cars, use the stock dimension frame or replacement, post-WW II cars use anything you can modify to fit! Not a hard and fast rule, but a good guide.

Building or rebuilding a vehicle frame and suspension is perhaps the worst part of creating a car. But it is much like the foundation for a house...how well the foundation is built determines how well the house is built. This is where so very many rodders fall out of love with a project, and yet it is one of the simplest parts of the entire procedure.

Most semi-elleptic rear spring systems can be used, especially on cars made from 1930 on, although the older the car the stiffer the springs will likely be (normally, they are shorter). From the mid-1930s on the rear springs are generally long enough to give a good ride, and in many cases late model rearends will fit right to the springs. If not, all that is needed is a new pad for the rearend where it sets on the spring, be sure the pad alignment hole (where it fits the spring centerbolt) is placed so the centerline of the wheel is centered in the fender opening...some springs have the centerbolt off-center.

Cars of the 1930s and through the mid-1950s will have front suspension components that may seem odd, such as this upper A-arm which combines to operate the shock absorber. These systems were quite good, and the components can usually be rebuilt by restoration services. It is usuall ythe brakes that need to be replaced, often with discs, and this can often be accomplished with nothing more than a hub/bearing change and a special disc brake caliper bracket. There are kits for some of the most popular cars, such as Chevrolet, but you can make up your own kit with careful measurements.

LEFT - Compare this 1932 Ford frame to the one on the preceeding pages, and note how strong the rear crossmember (for a Corvette rearend), as well as the hefty X-member at the middle. With independent suspension, this strong a frame is mandatory.

BELOW - The most basic hot rod frame is used for the fad-T type construction, with the siderails being simple lengths of 2x4-inch steel tubing (usually .125-inch wall thickness). At the front a "suicide" type of spring perch is used, to get the frame down, and at the rear the kickup will be around 15-inches. In this case a Jaguar rearend is being installed.

ABOVE - This 1935-1ater Ford frame has been boxed and a new X-member installed, the rearend is now suspended with coil/over shock springs, the front uses a Mustang/Pinto components independent.

ABOVE - This Chevy frame from the late 1930s is already "boxed" and uses strong front/rear crossmember construction, it will accept independent suspension components with very little extra strength required in the frame. An X-member would help.

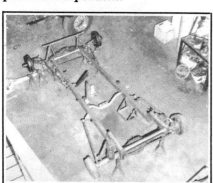

ABOVE - The fad-T frame again, this time with some extra braces involved. Because this type of frame is quite small, it often does not need an X-member, although modern practice is beginning to use the X.

This single tube frame is marginal for strength, the reason drilled plate gussets have been added to the kick-up. When a second tube is added, and angled braces installed, the tubing frame becomes the strongest of all. But making up such a frame requires considerable time and welding experience, and if at all possible, a jig should be used to eliminate warpage during welding. The really exotic "birdcage" type tubing frames can often be as much as 60 percent lighter than conventional frames, an important factor with race cars.

Finding Frames

ABOVE - Finding an old frame in this good a condition is getting harder with each passing year, although it is still possible. In rural areas, look under farm wagons, in the cities the frames are often stacked alongside buildings and forgotten. It is imperative you know exactly what you are looking for. As an example, this 1932 Ford chassis might be mistaken for a 1933 or later Ford unit, there is a distinctive lip on the bottom of each side rail that no other Ford years had. Expect to spend a lot of time doing frame repairs to these old units, it might just turn out to be less expensive in the long run to buy new frame rails.

RIGHT - frames from late model cars will not likely be found in this stripped condition, instead you can plan on buying an entire car and then taking it apart to get the chassis. In the rust belt areas, frames tend to rust, especially where the body attaches, and on enclosed rails (boxed frames) the rust can be especially bad. As a general rule, frames from the drier climates will not have any/as much rust.

The scenario for building a rod will probably follow one of three different courses. In the first, you find a good, complete vehicle from which you create a car. In the second, you contact the various mail-order suppliers and gather whatever parts you need to make a car. Third, you scrounge here and there until you have a pile of parts from which you can create something. All methods work. Some are less time consuming, some are less expensive, all are exciting.

For right now, the assumption is that you are scrounging parts, and one of the basic needs is a frame. Where to get one.

If you live in a larger city, you'll concentrate on the swap meets at first. You can get excellent leads here, but expect to pay the going rate for a frame found at the swap meet. And don't expect to find any jewels in the rough. Expect a rough in the rough. while the swap meet is one source of supply, there are many others. What you want to do is get the word out that you are looking. This starts with the bulletin boards at area speed shops and the newsletters of area car clubs. The scarcity of the item will determine the speed of response.

Don't expect to find a 1932 Ford frame behind every gas station. They are rare, and getting more so. This is the very reason the mail-order firms sell so many Deuce frames. The 1933-34 Ford frame is right behind, and the same rules apply. Model A frames are much easier to locate, and even non-Ford frames are relatively easy to find, providing you are working with a popular Chevrolet or MoPar product.

While you are spreading the word of your search, start making the rounds of your area. Finding frames is often much easier than spotting complete cars, but you have to look in places where frames go to die. Such as car repair businesses and truck yards. If you have car shops in the area that are out of business, look behind the buildings. Find the older wrecking yards in the region, and as a final check, tour the rural countryside. Frames are metal, and metal can be used by farmers and craftsmen. From all of this, you will turn up a usable frame.

As mentioned, don't expect a perfect specimen. Instead, what you will likely find is a scag that needs lots of repair. This will be especially true if you live in the Rust Belt. Even so, don't discard a rusted frame, because practically every frame can be saved if you want to spend enough time on it. What you must do is compare your estimates of time/cost doing repair versus the price of a mail-order frame.

Frames are much more available in the western states, and for the most part they have not been subject to rust decay. The problem here is getting time off to find such an item, and the solution is to correspond with the car clubs in western states. You'll find lists of these clubs published yearly by Street Rodder magazine (write them for an index) and by Old Cars Weekly (OCW is at general delivery, Iola, WI 54990).

Try to find a frame that matches the body you have, or at least will go with it. You can create a frame from just about anything, from later model pickup units to rectangular/round tubing. But this is something for the more advanced builder to attempt. It doesn't mean that frames are too difficult to create, only that they take time and extra effort. Making a scratch-built frame, however, is one of the most satisfying arts of rod building.

One of the most successful builders we know is forever on the lookout for frames. When he spots one, he tries to get it for rock bottom price, and then he takes it home to store. In his basement! Frames don't take up nearly as much room as a complete chassis. And by being patient, this builder can extend his inventory until he finds the best possible frame to start with. Then, if he wants, he can give the other units away, or sell them if the demand is high.

Buying Frames

We're not talking here about buying a frame from a farmer, we're concerned with buying frames "over the counter" from mail-order houses or rod shops.

There are several dozen frames suppliers in the country, with virtually all the Ford designs and several non-Ford items. The frames come in all shapes and degrees of completion, from bare side rails to totally welded and ready to use platforms. You get what you pay for, and in the case of frames, you are paying for work time.

If you are a good welder, or have a source, then you may want to weld up your own frame. You will hear some professionals say that you can't put a frame together without a jig table. Baloney. You can create something on the driveway if you are careful. What you are really buying with the mail-order frames is convenience. Suppose an average frame, ready to bolt the suspension to, retails for around $4000. At first, you look at this price and consider it far too high. On second thought, however, you'll find that you might get that much money, or more, into something that you create yourself. Especially if you have to go elsewhere for welding and cutting and fabrication. Only if you do most of the work yourself can you create a frame at less expense than mail-order.

A really good example of this is the Model A frame. Here is a really simple, straight-forward design that can be duplicated with channel or tubing. You can buy a bare-bones Model A frame for very little more than what the raw materials would cost retail.

The big advantage of buying the mail-order frame is that it gets you past one of the major sore spots of rod building. A very great number of hot rods are never completed by the original builder because of frustration over how long the chassis take to complete. When buying a mail-order frame, it is almost possible to paint the unit out of the box and start attaching suspension components.

Thus, the big decision with the mail-order frame/chassis is which one to purchase. Since this is such a large ticket item, most manufacturers agree that they seldom sell a unit unless the buyer has seen one. Or, the buyer has been convinced by magazine publicity. If you want to see a frame, attend one of the major rod runs. If you are at the Street Rod Nationals, chances are excellent that practically every frame builder will be there, on display. Next best thing is to visit a rod construction shop where several different frames might be available.

You can get mail-order frames/chassis in every stage of finish. Do not expect to pay economy prices for a total chassis. Prices can range from a few hundred dollars to over $10,000. You get what you pay for.

Frame Repairs

Quite often, usually more often than not, your neat-o building project has a frame that needs repairs. You can do much of this work yourself, except possibly for some complicated pulling/pushing, which might require a frame professional.

RUST: The most common problem with frames is rust. If the frame is basically good, and only has a couple of rusted areas, these can be patched, even to the extent of making a full width patch on a side rail. The key is to weld supports to the rails so that alignment doesn't change during repair. If it is just a small patch, on an upper or lower lip, there is seldom an alignment problem. When repairing a frame, try to use the same gauge metal as original.

BENDS: If the frame has been smashed, it can be repaired if the damage is not too radical. If a side rail has been pushed in, but not mangled, you can usually pull it back into position. Use the opposite rail as a reference. Let's assume that one rail has been pushed in, not severely. Run a string from center of front crossmember to center of rear crossmember. This is your base reference. Measure from the string to the good frame side, and duplicate these measurements on the bad side.

Easily said, not so easily done. If you have an acquaintance with a body shop, he will probably have a lot of pulling equipment. You just tie down the frame and start pushing/ pulling. You can do a lot of this at home, when you know the tricks.

Frame metal is not really thick, it relies on shape for strength. Which means you can move it around rather easily. If you can tie the frame down to a tree or something solid in the garage, make the tie points right at either end of the pushed-in side rail. Insert a 4x4 piece of wood inside the frame channel bent section, and wrap a short piece of chain around this area. You want to pull the rail in the same direction as the force that hit it, if you can make this determination. Use an ordinary Come-A-Long to pull with,

and work slowly. You'll probably have to pull the rail out just a slight bit more than the stock measurements, since it will spring back a bit.

Obviously, by working slowly and in increments, a rather badly bent side rail can be pulled back into shape. If a rail is really bent severely, then it is often best to find a replacement rail. Cut the various rivets, and weld the new rail in place.

When making repairs, it is vital to measure continually. Measure everywhere you can find reference points. By measuring diagonally from rail to rail, you will instantly spot bent sections. Consider a frame as nothing more than a series of boxes and rectangles. If you measure each box and rectangle, on a diagonal, then you measure the entire structure on a diagonal, you can easily bring it back to square. As a rule, if you get the frame within 1/16 to 1/8-inch, you are close enough.

If the entire frame has been centerpunched, such as in a sideways collision, it is possible for the unit to have a kind of bow in it, as seen from above. Tie the two frame ends down, and push/pull on the middle and it will usually come back into shape.

Much of this major alignment work would best be left to the professional, but I mention it to show that you can do things at home, if you want to.

CRACKS: Probably the most common problem with older frames will be in the form of cracks and splits. Especially around rivet holes and at areas of stress. With Ford frames, expect cracks where the front crossmember ties into the side rails. Much of this stress was relieved after 1935, as double wall frame rails were introduced, but stress still occurs. Weld all cracks, with good arc penetration, and if you can put a gusset at these stress points, do. It will help the frame live much longer. If there are severe rips and tears to the frame, straighten everything out, and then add a fishplate to the inside of the component. Make a clean repair and it won't look really obvious. *continued on page 24*

How To Figure Final Frame Height

One of the most perplexing problems of setting up a scratchbuilt hot rod is in trying to determine finished ride height, when all there is available is a pile of parts. This is not nearly as much a problem with cars produced after 1948, because of frame/suspension limitations, but

This is not nearly as much a problem with cars produced after 1948, because of frame/suspension limitations, but there are still considerations for the later models. First, a look at the older rod chassis.

The key to setting up ride height is diameter of tire to be used. Since proportions are such a vital part of hot rod appearance, the common practice currently is to go with a front tire of 24-25 inches diameter. Rear tire diameter will range from 28-31 inches, with the 30 and 31 inch tires looking just a bit too big for most body styles. Wheel size is not a major factor at this point, although it would come into play when

trying to figure scrub line measurements.

Start figuring final chassis ride height by setting up the front and rear ends. At the front, partially assembly the components. If an independent front end is used, block the spindle in approximate location, with the spindle bolt at exactly half the wheel diameter (say 12 inches). If an independent front end is to be used, it is probably a kit, and the manufacturer should have included absolute instructions on where to put the A-arm attachment tabs on the frame. If you are making up your own independent front end, the clue is to make sure that the frame attachment points are correct with good geometry (see suspensions chapter). When you know what the attachment brackets look like, you can determine where the front of the frame will be. On the independent front end, this height is dependent on the lower A-arm angle (from frame outward to spindle).

If a Mustang or similar front end assembly is to be used, a good rule of thumb is that the crossmember will fit flush against the bottom of the frame, Ford or any other type car. This is a starting point.

With any front end, remove the springs first, and it makes all of this initial adjusting much easier.

With a Ford type solid front axle, block the axle in place until the spindle bolts are exactly half the diameter of the front tire. Block the frame up until the frame rails clear the axle by about   inches. This is approximately where the car will ride when fully loaded. With semi-elliptics, axle/frame clearance will be right on 6 inches.

At the back, block up the rear end until the axle centerline is exactly half the diameter of the tire. Block the frame up until it is approximately 5 inches from the rearend. You will see lots of rods with as little as 3 inches travel between rearend housing and frame, but you will also note that there are invariably marks on the frame and housing where the car has been bottoming out. Five inches seems to be a minimal, more is not bad. With the frame in position, measure how high the frame midpoint is from the ground. As mentioned elsewhere, it shouldn't be lower than 5 inches at this point, it will probably be closer to 7-9 inches off the ground, and even if it is 12 inches high the car can still be very low. This is with a 1932 or later Ford frame. The straight tube or Model A type frame will be much higher.

This is roughly where the car will ride. Stand back and eyeball the frame. If it has too much rake to the front, the car will look like it is running downhill too much. If the frame is level, the car will still look like it has a front rake (an illusion caused by the different size tires front/rear). If the frame is lower in the rear, you'll probably want to raise it up.

All of this is just some preliminary judgements, because you won't know exactly how much higher (or lower) the springs will let the car ride. The measurements given seem to be about normal for cars that live in areas with decent roads. If you have bad roads, especially roads with lots of dips or potholes, you'll want to add suspension travel. That means raise the frame a couple of inches over minimal. If the axle(s) are allowed to hammer on the frame, early failure is a foregone conclusion.

The problem of the springs is discussed elsewhere, just be sure and make all spring/shock absorber/suspension linkage brackets plenty heavy. Good rule of thumb here: Make all brackets from at least 3/16-inch plate and weld them solidly. Later you'll learn where to reduce bracket weight. At the last 19 Street Rod Nationals, the most commonly seen failure has been broken suspension component brackets!

A final note. When setting the chassis up be sure that any locating brackets working across the chassis (transversely), such as Panhard anti sway links, swing through neutral points just beyond average ride height. Example: With the frame set up at desired ride height, the sway bar should run slightly downhill from frame mount to front or rear axle. This is the normal riding position. When the axle moves upward under deflection, the sway bar will pass through a level position to a position running uphill from frame mount to axle. When mounted this way, the sway bar will have minimal deflection of the axle. Even Fords with transverse front and rear springs may need such a sway bar (cross steering at front, long rear shackles, etc), so such sway bar attachment points should be considered at this time.

Frame Swaps

Early on in hot rodding, the most common question was how to use a 1939 or later Ford frame under something like a 1932 or Model A Ford. For one simple reason: Hydraulic brakes. Rather than do the work necessary for the brake swap, the builder wanted to swap the entire frame.

As we've mentioned elsewhere, limit frame swaps to the fat fender cars (from about 1935 and later).

The first thing to consider on a frame swap is engine location. If the body style being used has the engine behind the front crossmember or centerline of the front wheels, a frame swap probably won't work well. Next is front sheetmetal attachment. If the front sheetmetal is held to the body at the firewall, and at the front by a radiator support that bolts to the frame, a swap is plausible. If the sheetmetal bolts to the frame rails directly, a swap will be difficult. More simply, if the entire front sheetmetal can be removed as a single unit (taking out bolts at the firewall and at the radiator support yoke) the frame swap will probably be plausible.

Next consideration is wheelbase. The new frame can be shortened or lengthened, widened or narrowed as necessary to fit. But a radical change in wheelbase will have an effect upon the new chassis front end geometry. So stay relatively close in wheelbase when selecting a replacement chassis. Wheel track (side to side) should also be considered, to keep the wheels and tires from hitting fenders or sticking out too wide.

Late model chassis will have frame kickups at the rear (over an extended area) and at the front. Earlier chassis may have a kickup at the rear, but little or none at the front. This front kickup is why so many builders modify stock frame on cars of pre-WW II vintage, and limit full chassis swaps to cars built after the war. Yes, there is an area in here of overlap, but you get the idea.

A good example of a swap would be a 1941-48 Ford/ Mercury. The most common frame used is a 1972 or so Chevelle, because it is plentiful. This is a perimeter frame, with the siderails swinging outward just behind the front wheels and then back in for the rear kickup. Builders modify this frame by cutting the stock side rail off where it swings outward, front and rear, and substituting a section of 2x4 tubing. This goes straight between front and rear. The wheelbase length is modified at the same time, as determined by the length of tubing insert. A new X-member is installed, and the frame can be set under the body. Some sheetmetal clearance work is necessary over the rear kickup, and at the front the fender splash aprons must be trimmed away to clear the suspension upper A-arms. A new mount is built for the radiator yoke.

Similar frame swaps are done with the 1949-53 Mercury, so popular with customizers. Here, however, the frame siderails are seldom cut.

Dick Dean, a long time customizer and rod builder in southern California, has come up with the practice of including the later model flooring and firewall in the swap. The floor from the older body is cut out, the body set down on the late model floor, and the new floor trimmed to fit the body. The flooring is welded in place. The old body firewall is almost entirely cut away, and the new firewall is trimmed to fit, and welded in place. This gives all the late model wiring, steering, etc, in one fell swoop. A really neat idea that is rapidly catching on. Dean has also found that the chassis from Japanese small pickups can often be fit under early cars, such as Model A Fords, with only minor changes. These late model pickup chassis frames are relatively flat, so this is something to look into for the more advanced builder.

TEX SMITH DOES IT AGAIN!

The contemporary hot rod magazines have all gone "hi-tek", which translates to "Big Buck". Tex's new HOT ROD MECHANIX magazine is about reality, about building affordable and dependable street oriented specialty cars. All years. Rods, customs, machines, restorations. And, it is about hot rod history, which no one else covers adequately. BY SUBSCRIPTION ONLY! You can't find it on the newsstand. $20 for 12 issues.

HERE'S WHAT OUR READERS SAY ABOUT HOT ROD MECHANIX

"HRMx is great...the how-to articles remind me so much of the old days."
Larry Fulsome Arizona

"Add my name to your list of supporters"
Billy Gibbons ZZ Top

"Finally, a good how-to magazine on the market."
Pryor Passarino

"My buddies insist on borrowing my collector copies of HRMx. The only solution is for you to send them their own."
Ken Anderson MN.

"Hot Rod Mechanix looks like a class act."
Don Montgomery CA.

"Have enjoyed the new HRMx more than any magazine I've read in a long time. It's like a reunion."
Ron Gallup GA.

"Great magazine! It's guys like you and you mostly who kept the street rod torch burning through the dark years."
Brent Vandervort NC.

"HRMx is like stepping back in time to when cars were fun and individual."
Tom Kleckner IN.

"Boy, you sure know how to get someone's attention. When I opened that plain brown wrapper, I thought I had gone back 20 years!"
George Dengel MT.

"HRMx will be second to none from a purely hot rod sense."
Jay Purselley Louisiana

"Smooth as a hand rubbed candy laquer job."
Jerry Titus Pres. KKOA KS.

"Just a word...the best damn hot rod book around!"
John Pickle CA.

"Rod & Custom was great, but HRMx is better!"
Walter Janzen Manatoba

"I've been looking for a long time for a magazine like yours."
Marion Ralston OH.

"Just finished vol. 1, no. 1 for the twentieth time."
Lyndall Smith TX.

"You can't go wrong with HRMx. It is without a doubt the best."
Jim & Cheryl Washington MD.

IF YOU'RE INTO SPECIAL CARS, YOU'LL LOVE HOT ROD MECHANIX

Tex Smith's HOTROD Mechanix

HOT ROD MECHANIX The How-To Magazine
$20 for 12 issues, payable in U.S. funds only
PO BOX 726 DRIGGS ID. 83422 (208) 354-8133

NAME_____ PH._____
STREET_____
CITY_____ STATE_____ ZIP_____
CHECK ENCLOSED___BILL ME LATER___
MASTERCARD___VISA___ #_____ EXP.___

Canada and all other foreign,$28 surface postage
Add $40 for 1st class air mail to foreign countries.
Payable in U.S. funds only. Allow 4-6 weeks delivery.

25

Designing a Frame

No matter how basic a frame might be, it must be square and not twisted. Here a measurement is taken diagonally across a new frame during construction, this measurement should be the same on the opposite side, within plus/minus 1/8-inch. If you ever plan on making up more than one frame, it would be time well spent to make a frame table like the one shown. The frame pieces are clamped to the table, thus eliminating warpage during the welding phase.

A vehicle frame is a platform, under which is a suspension and above which is a body. If the platform is rigid enough, independent suspension can be used, if it is strong enough it will handle umpteen horsepower, if it is designed properly it will help vehicle handling.

You can design a frame once you have basic parameters. what will be the wheelbase? What will be the wheel track? Where will the engine be located? What kind of suspension will be used? What will be the body configuration? What will be the body/powersystem weight? What will the vehicle be used for? Too often, rodders start a project without actually thinking through these questions, and having answers.

When building a more traditional older rod, something from about 1934 back, the answers will be very similar, for Ford or non-Ford rod alike. Wheelbase will be from around 100 to 112 inches. wheel track (middle of tire across chassis to middle of opposite tire) will be around 57 inches. Engine will be just behind the front crossmember. Body will be relatively small, narrow and not very high. Body and engine/trans will come in at around 1500 pounds (V8 and automatic trans). Total vehicle weight will be right around 2500 pounds. The vehicle will be primarily a street driven machine. The variable will be suspension.

If an independent suspension is to be used, at either end or all around. the frame must be made as rigid as possible, especially in regards to twist. The idea is to have the suspen-

sion absorb road irregularities, not the frame! If the more traditional semi-elliptic springs are to be used, the frame must be reasonably stiff. If the popular coil/over shock and springs are to be used, the frame must be treated somewhat like a semi-elliptic system. If the transverse Ford type springs are used, the frame can have a bit more twist resiliency, but not lots more. The key to this latter problem is the high power potential and extra weight of the engine/transmission.

So, first decide what type of body is going to be used. If it is a model T or Model A, then a perfectly flat frame can be made. Some non-Fords, such as early MoPars and Chevrolets, accept the same kind of frame, but most require a kickup over the rearend.. If a 1932 or later Ford body is to be used, the frame can have a kickup for the rearend.

The most commonly made homemade frame is for a Fad T, using a 1927 or earlier Model T Ford body. So that's what we'll design. This car will probably have a small block Chevrolet engine and automatic transmission, with a Chevy rear end of some kind and dropped beam/tube front axle. Rear springs will be coil/overs, front spring will be transverse. Wheelbase will be 100 inches (any shorter wheelbase and the car will ride very choppy, but wheelbases down to 90 inches are not uncommon).

This is a very straight forward frame to design. It will probably be made of 2x4-inch, .125-in wall thickness mild steel tubing. Nearly every steel supply outlet in the country

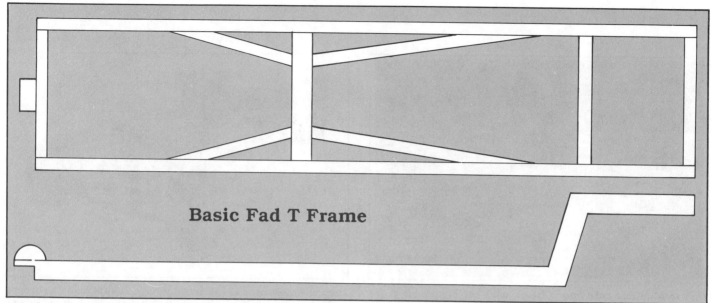

Basic Fad T Frame

This is how a basic fad-T frame would look during design stages. You will be working from several known points, including wheelbase, body dimensions, engine size, etc. Width of the *body firewall usually determines how wide frame is from there forward to the front crossmember, it can be slightly wider from the firewall back.*

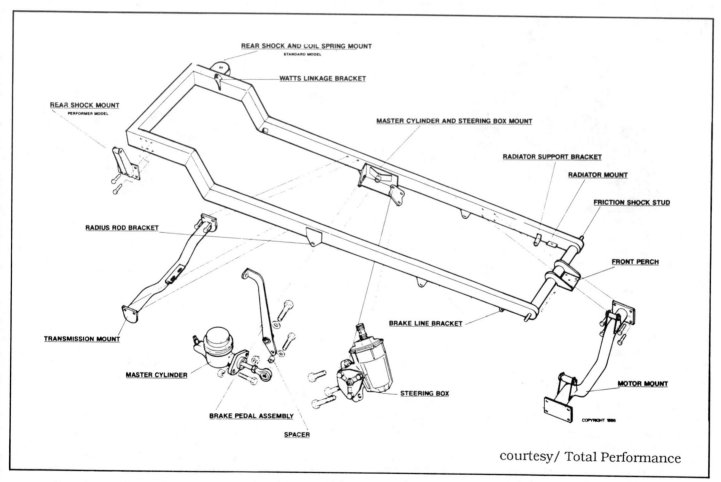

courtesy/ Total Performance

has a supply of this tubing, although 2x3-inch may be substituted. It can be slightly thinner in wall thickness, but not much! When buying this tubing, ask for surplus materials. Much less expensive if you will take scrap ends, etc.

An open channel piece of metal works very well, such as a Model A Ford (Model T is too lightweight), although this should have the open side boxed for strength. Pickup frames through the present time are often deeper C-sections, and they can be used, usually without boxing.

The simplest design will be a straight rectangle, the

average width (outside to outside) will be about 26 inches. The main rails will be straight from the front crossmember to the kickup (side view). The kickup will be approximately 15 inches high, and the frame extension (after the kickup) will be approximately 15 inches long. The same tubing will make a crossmember at the front of the rails and at the rear. An additional crossmember can be put at the top front of the kickup, and some kind of crossmember should be designed. Since this is a combination coil/over and transverse spring setup, a K-member will work, although a full X-member

This is a double tube space frame with an adjustable front "suicide" spring perch. More rod builders might want to consider both the twin tube frame and such a front spring mount.

The pro-street rage is currently in vogue, note how this frame includes a tubing X-member that attaches just ahead of where the frame has been narrowed at the rear so the extra wide tires can be used.

This Corvette rear end with cross leaf spring offers some special mounting problems in the older frames, note how the crossmember sweeps down to the centersection, special locater arms at the side are necessary.

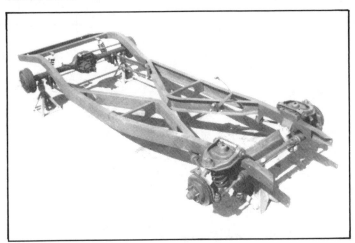

Another look at a 1935-later Ford frame built from commercially available side rails and X-member, a special Mustang independent front end uses its own channel crossmember. Rails are notched for steering.

would be best.

The coil/over shocks will attach to the frame at the kickup, the front spring will attach to a "suicide" perch, which is a strongly gusseted plate welded off the front of the crossmember. This is the basic frame, and all that will be added are various brackets for mounts. It is very simple, and can be built in a very short time. Tools needed are also basic: hacksaw, gas torch, grinder, arc welder (TIG or MIG better), measuring tape, and carpenter's level.

Make a sketch on paper of what the frame should be, and the various dimensions. If you are going to have a wheelbase less than 100 inches, you need to know exactly how long the body area is, where the back of the body is in relation to the rearend, and how long the engine is from back of block to front of fan pulley. These are the minimum measurements that are critical.

With this type of car, the radiator generally mounts best just behind the front crossmember. If a fiberglass body is used, it probably has a short turtle deck or pickup bed molded on. This deck or bed is usually centered over the rear axle. From these two locations, you can tell if you have left enough engine room.

A good rule of thumb when building an open fendered car: If the centerline of the front wheels is slightly ahead of the radiator centerline, the appearance seems to be better. Most Fad T builders have found this to be one of the most important factors in the design, which is why some time spent with pencil and paper is so valid.

Once you have the basic dimensions, you can draw a side view of the frame on the garage floor or driveway. The chalk and a straightedge work fine. You can actually outline tires and get an excellent idea of how the full-scale project will look. When you have the plan drawn correctly, cut the tubing or channel to shape and weld up the side rails. Remember, tack weld and be patient to avoid heat distortion.

With the frame rails made, you can now draw a top view of the frame if you want, which shows exactly where the crossmembers go. Once you get experience, you'll just cut and fit the crossmembers directly.

And that's really all there is to making a simple ladder frame. It gets considerably more complicated if you are going to use independent suspension, not so much at the rear as at the front. we'll save this bit of advanced engineering for a later date.

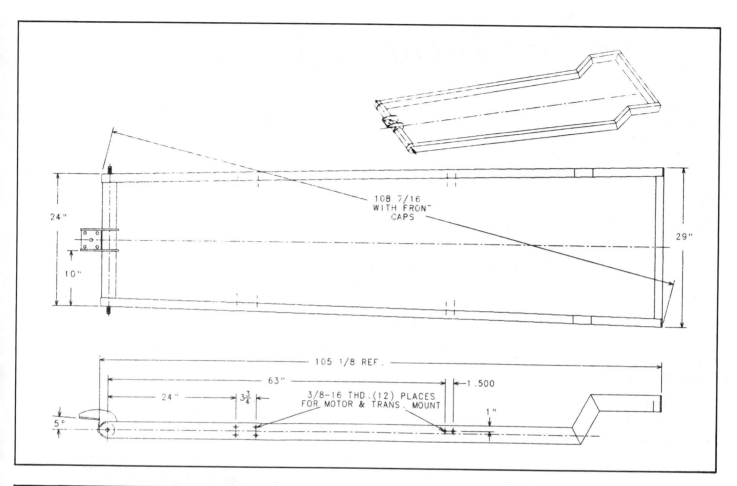

108 7/16
WITH FRONT
CAPS

24"

29"

10"

105 1/8 REF.

63"

24"

3 3/4

1.500

3/8-16 THD.(12) PLACES
FOR MOTOR & TRANS. MOUNT

5°

1"

LEFT - Really getting exotic is this square tube space frame for Model A, using Jaguar front suspension and rearend. This type of construction is much harder than a simple ladder frame, but it is just about as stiff as a frame can be, making it an ideal platform for an independent suspension.

RIGHT - A jig is essential with a space frame, note how the upper and lower tubes are supported by both vertical and angled uprights, which adds to torsional strength as well as simple compression strength. Very lightweight tubing can be used for such a frame, there has been some experiments with alloy tubing but this requires outstanding welding techniques and is not for the novice.

Frame Clips

An extremely popular form of frame modification for rods and customs is the frame clip, and it lends itself very well to pickup trucks.

Here, just the front portion of a frame such as a 1972 or so Chevelle, is attached to the rear portion of another frame. This works well with any of the pre-1955 vehicles, and pickups that use a beam front axle.

The idea is to get an independent front suspension. But suppose you have a 1941 Chevrolet that already has an independent suspension, do you need a clip? Almost all independent suspension can work very well in original form, if they are rebuilt with new bushings/bearings, etc. It is in the area of brakes where people want to make a change. Perhaps the best advice is to work at adapting late model discs to the earlier independent front end.

If the front suspension is a beam axle, the ifs will be a definite plus in comfort, and often in handling. The key is to try and find a front clip of almost the same wheel track, and from a wheelbase that is almost the same. If the front end clip is from a car with a longer wheelbase, the Ackerman principle built into the front suspension will be changed when you go to a shorter wheelbase. Where this does not hold true is on some late model cars where the steering assembly is in front of the wheel centerline. Sometimes the engineers have thrown the Ackerman principle out the window. A consideration when selecting a clip. Most builders prefer to stick with true Ackerman.

With a clip, the frame of the new unit is cut apart right at the firewall, where the side rails start to curve outboard. Measure from the front wheel centerline to this cut. Measure from the centerline of the old car frame back a similar amount, and cut off the frame. Obviously, the old frame is supported on jackstands. Set the new frame clip in tentative position. It will probably come very close to alignment.

If you are not sure how high/low the new clip should fit on the old frame, do some preliminary measuring. Find a stock car that has the frame clip you will use. Measure how high the frame is from the ground at the lower A-arm attachment points. This is a good guide. When setting the clip against the old car frame, it will probably be necessary to remove the new clip coil springs in order to get enough clearance during the setup stage. Easier is to merely set the old car frame higher on the jackstands and make adjustments in measurement.

Example: The original old car frame set 10 inches off the ground, but you jack it up to 20 inches for working clearance. The new frame clip measured 7 inches from the ground to the inner lower A-arm attachment points, so you set it at 17 inches.

Chances are you will have to make up gusset plates to attach the frame clip to the old frame. It is essential that you overengineer this attachment point. You want it strong, first, pretty second.

To save time trying to figure where to set the frame clip level, decide exactly what frame rake you want on the original frame, and set the frame at this angle (probably slightly downhill, rear to front. Again, working from a car with the frame like you clip, use a carpenter's level to determine the level of the upper A-arm. It will probably angle upward, rear to front, as a part of the anti-dive engineering built into the newer cars. When setting the clip in place, and before welding the frames together, get this stock A-arm angle.

It is possible to narrow the crossmember of such a clip, to reduce the wheel track. If you do, make absolutely certain that the relative distances between upper A-arm attachment points and lower A-arm attachment points remain constant. Don't make the front suspension attachment points closer or farther apart, relatively, than original. If you cut the crossmember to make it narrower, be sure to add a bit of extra plating for strength. You'll have to narrow the steering rods, an equal amount.

When you narrow the front end this way, you change the Ackerman again, so be aware before doing. Best to find a front end with the right wheel track to begin with.

The frame horns that stick out beyond the A-arms will probably have to be reshaped for the original car radiator yoke. And, the horns must be modified to accept the original bumper brackets. Otherwise, that's about it. Professionals can do an average clip in a day, plan on much longer. You can do the job with the engine left in place and nothing but the front sheetmetal clip removed.

Be aware of one thing. As a rule such a swap will lower the front of the vehicle. As the wheels move lower in the fender opening, they tend to relocate slightly to the rear. Drop the front about 5 inches, and the wheel centerline will move rearward almost an inch. Adjust accordingly.

Mating Frame Sections

It is often necessary to mate frame side rails. This might be caused by damaged sections, lengthening the rails, changing the curves, etc.

Most builders try to avoid a simple straight cut/weld if possible, although such a joint can be made if the section is fishplated or boxed. A simple bit of thinking will create a mating joint that gets the job done and retains maximum strength.

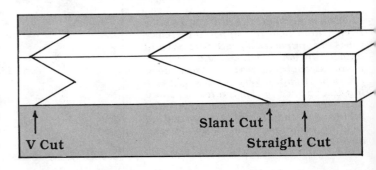

V Cut   Slant Cut   Straight Cut

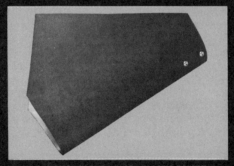

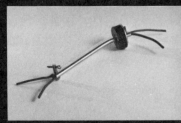

31

Frame Kickups

In hot rodding, it is desirable to have the vehicle low, but usually not for the reason most people think. While the lower the vehicle the better the seeming appearance, the real reason to get the weight and area mass lower to the ground is to get the center of gravity lower. This translates into better vehicle handling. There is, contrary to the popular cartoons, a limit as to how low a vehicle can go.

The lowest part of a vehicle should not be lower than the wheel rim. This is called the "scrub line", meaning anything lower is likely to drag on the ground should a tire go flat. We'll mention this more in the suspension section.

From a practical standpoint, the frame cannot be too low simply because there is a certain amount of ground clearance necessary. Despite all the super low California cars seen in various magazines. This distance will usually be somewhere between 5 and 9 inches as measured midpoint between front and rear wheels. As a rule on most rods, of all years, the front of the frame will be lower than the rear of the frame. That is, the frame, as checked for level at the mid point, will have a slightly forward rake. Radically lowered custom cars usually have a slightly tail-low frame stance.

In a way, this frame rake is one measure of whether the car is a hot rod or a custom.

As the original car manufacturers tried to lower the car, and the attendant center of gravity (improving handling immensely), one of the first tricks was to drop the center area of the frame in relation to either end, where the suspension mounted. Thus, from the side these frames took on the appearance of sagging in the middle. The front "kick up" was generally much less than that over the rear axle.

For the hot rod builder, this attention to frame clearance at the front and rear axle area creates the need for additional frame kick up. Such modifications may be made in a number of ways.

On non-Fords, with semi-elliptic springs at all four frame corners, the problems of kick up are more pronounced than with the Ford. As a general rule, the distance between the stock front axle and the frame is already very limited with semi-elliptic springs. The quick way with such a front suspension to a radical lowering job is to mount the axle on top of the springs rather than below. Not too difficult, just a matter of welding on different spring perces to the axle. The problem is that this roughly 5-inch lowering job places the axle almost flush with the frame! Practically no axle travel at all, and the secret to a good handling, comfortable car is adequate suspension travel.

Relocation of the spring hangars on semi-elliptic frames will lower the car, but as a general rule such lowering is limited to no more than 3 inches. Since the idea is to get the body lower (body channel is not considered here), then the answer is to kick both ends of the frame. This procedure is the same with all frames, Ford or otherwise.

When semi-elliptic springs are used, the frame kicks must be inside the front/rear spring mounts. With the early Ford, using the transverse spring, the kick can be much closer to the axle. The illustrations show how this is determined. The type of front end used with the early Ford frame will determine what kind of kick up can be used. If the stock wishbone is to be used, then the only kind of front kickup possible is at the firewall. This retains the working room between bottom of frame and top of wishbone. If the wishbone is to be split and mounted outside the frame rails, or a 4-bar radius rod setup is used, then the kickup can be close to the front crossmember, leaving enough room for tie rod clearance.

At the rear, where more suspension travel is generally needed for a comfortable ride, the frame kickup will be quite pronounced. With straight frame rails, as with tubing or something such as Model A Ford, the frame kickup will probably be as much as 15 inches. This is only a rough approximation, since each project is different, but it gives an idea of the great amount of kickup needed.

When a C-shape frame rail is kicked, it is always wise to box the inner section for added strength.

When determining exactly how much kickup will be put into a frame, it is necessary to know what ride height (vehicle loaded) will be. See the section on figuring ride height.

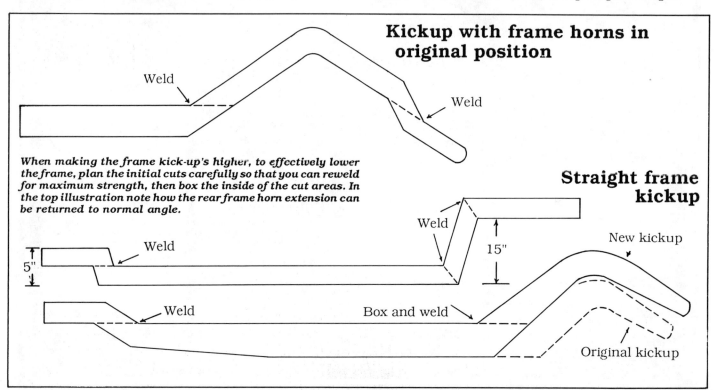

Kickup with frame horns in original position

Weld

Weld

Straight frame kickup

When making the frame kick-up's higher, to effectively lower the frame, plan the initial cuts carefully so that you can reweld for maximum strength, then box the inside of the cut areas. In the top illustration note how the rear frame horn extension can be returned to normal angle.

Weld

5"

Weld

Weld

15"

New kickup

Box and weld

Original kickup

Real
HOT ROD PARTS
come from....

Vintage Speed Equipment Headquarters for

Flathead *Ford*	Flathead '6'	Chevy & GMC '6'

Offy
Heads
Intakes
(dual, triple)
Linkage
Gen. Brackets

Offy
intakes
linkage

cast iron **Headers**

Beehive Oil Filter

cast iron **Headers**

Standard: painted body, polished lid
Deluxe: completely chromed

Stainless Steel Generator/Starter Covers

Wayne/Chevy
Rocker, Pushrod Covers

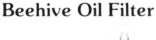

Mallory
IGNITION ®

Dual-Point Ignitions
for both
Ford & Chevy/GMC

Isky cams, kits,
Adjustable Lifters
Competition Springs

Howard's Cams
Tubular Push Rods
Competition Springs

Air Cleaners
Velocity Stacks
Stromberg '97' Kits

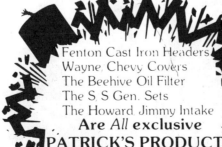

Fenton Cast Iron Headers
Wayne Chevy Covers
The Beehive Oil Filter
The S. S Gen. Sets
The Howard Jimmy Intake
Are *All* exclusive
PATRICK'S PRODUCTS

The Howard/GMC Intake
• Uses 2, 3 or 5 - '97's

Relocating Spring Perches

(Semi-Elliptic)

On most frames using semi-elliptic springs, the spring perches were attached to the frame in the quickest way possible...via cast bosses that riveted to the frame.

The semi-elliptic spring will have one spring end (almost always the front) mounted directly to a receiver perch, the other end will attach via shackles.

To lower semi-elliptic springs, it is necessary to relocate the spring perches. At the frame front, there is practically nothing to be done with the forward perch, but the rear shackle boss can be removed and a new perch made higher in the frame. Just retain enough clearance below the frame so the spring end does not bind as it swings on the shackle.

Alternative: Move the spring inboard or outboard of the frame rail. This was a very common practice on race cars of the 20s and 30s, when elliptic springs were used.

At the rear, the front perch can be relocated higher in frame, as can the rear perch. This can lower the frame toward the rearend upwards of 4 inches, usually eliminating the use of rearend lowering blocks between axle housing and spring.

When semi-elliptic rear spring kits are used in the Ford frame, look for this feature. Some kits mount the spring below the frame, some kits have the perches inset into the frame. It is possible to box the frame, then relocate the spring and perches to the inside of the frame rails. This probably means the axle housing spring perches must also be moved inboard.

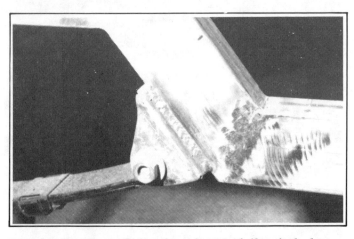

Note that on this semi-elleptic spring perch (front). the hanger has been located on the frame kick-up, gaining about 3 inches in frame height.

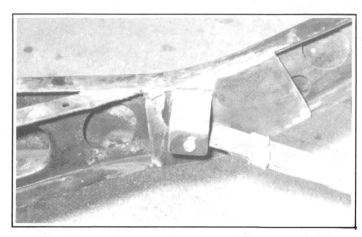

Here, the front spring perch is welded to the inside of the frame (on the boxing plate), which also lowers the frame relative to the rearend.

This is how the semi-elleptics look when relocated to the inside of a Ford frame. This might mean making new perches for the axles, but it is one way to get the frame lower. The rear shackles can also have the upper pivot raised inside the frame.

In this case, the front spring perch is welded to the top of the frame kick-up, which means that the kick-up top section must be much longer than normal to accomodate the spring length. Work it out in drawings before actually making the mounts.

34

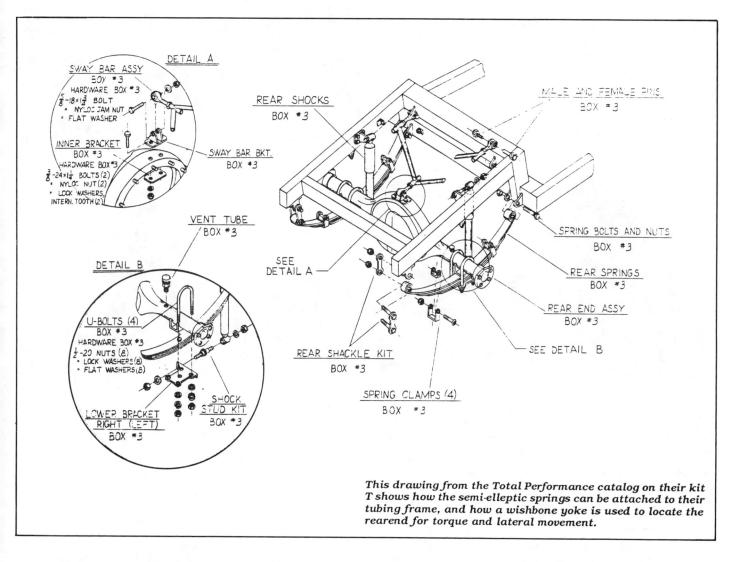

DETAIL A

SWAY BAR ASSY
BOX #3
HARDWARE BOX #3
⅜-18×1¾ BOLT
· NYLOC JAM NUT
· FLAT WASHER

INNER BRACKET
BOX #3
HARDWARE BOX #3
⅜-24×1¼ BOLTS (2)
· NYLOC NUT (2)
· LOCK WASHERS,
INTERN. TOOTH (2)

SWAY BAR BKT.
BOX #3

REAR SHOCKS
BOX #3

MALE AND FEMALE PINS
BOX #3

SPRING BOLTS AND NUTS
BOX #3

REAR SPRINGS
BOX #3

REAR END ASSY
BOX #3

SEE DETAIL B

VENT TUBE
BOX #3

SEE
DETAIL A

DETAIL B

U-BOLTS (4)
BOX #3
HARDWARE BOX #3
½-20 NUTS (8)
· LOCK WASHERS (8)
· FLAT WASHERS (8)

SHOCK
STUD KIT
BOX #3

LOWER BRACKET
RIGHT (LEFT)
BOX #3

REAR SHACKLE KIT
BOX #3

SPRING CLAMPS (4)
BOX #3

This drawing from the Total Performance catalog on their kit T shows how the semi-elleptic springs can be attached to their tubing frame, and how a wishbone yoke is used to locate the rearend for torque and lateral movement.

Modifying Front Crossmembers
(Ford)

One of the simplest ways to lower a Ford chassis is to modify the front crossmember. By flattening the crossmember, the frame rides lower, and this can be a significant change in stance/handling. Some chassis manufacturers now offer specially built, lowered crossmembers, and they work great. If you are handy, you can make the same thing with a cutting torch and arc welder.

One of the most common Ford frame tricks for 1932-1934 frames is to replace the front crossmember with a Model A crossmember. This lowers the frame approximately 1 inch. But there is really no limit to how much the crossmember can be modified, at least until the spring contacts the frame rails. The slick way to modify the crossmember is to install a new center section.

Measure across the frame rails and record the frame width exactly, at the centerline of the front crossmember. With the frame exactly level, side to side, weld two pieces of angle iron or tubing between the frame rails, one on top of the rails and the other on the bottom. These supports are only lightly tack welded in position, and they function to keep the frame at the exact width as stock.

The front crossmember is deeper at the mid-point than at either end where it attaches to the frame rails. Raise this midpoint and you lower the frame relative to the front axle. The easiest way is to make up a new center section for the crossmember. This can be with plate stock, or by cutting one edge of rectangular tubing away. As a rule of thumb, the 1932-34 front crossmembers can be lowered about 2 inches this way before notches must be cut in the frame rails for spring clearance. Later model Fords (through 1948) locate the spring ahead of the axle, and it is possible to raise the crossmember center section slightly more, depending upon model year. The front crossmembers become increasingly deep as the years progress from 1935 to 1948. However, in the later years, Ford moved the engine forward over the crossmember, which means the oil pan must fit into the crossmember, which severely limits what can be done on the later fat fender Fords.

When welding in a different crossmember center section, be sure to include front end caster angle (the amount the kingpins lean rearward at the top). This is about 5 degrees. If you're not sure, set the frame up in the desired final location (rake), and use a degree level on the crossmember. The back side of the crossmember will be slightly lower than the front

side. This puts the spring at the same cant as the axle, reducing spring bind at the perches. Assuming you will run about 5 degrees caster. Some rodders prefer to run 7-8 degrees in the Ford, while Bonneville race cars might have as much as 30 degrees. Set the crossmember angle same as the kingpin caster angle.

Once the new crossmember is welded in place (remember to tack weld several places to eliminate heat distortion), break away the angle iron/tubing that was tack welded between the rails.

TOP - When the hot rod is to be fenderless (and sometimes otherwise) it is possible to build a cantilever "suicide" type front spring perch. This must be made of heavy plate stock, and it should surround the crossmember if possible. The idea is to overbuild here, for safety sake, with good gussets a must. It is possible to make this an adjustable perch, as well,

ABOVE - While the Model A front crossmember can be used in the 1932-34 Ford frames to get about an additional 1-inch drop to the chassis, it is more common to make up a crossmember insert section from tubing or plate stock.

RIGHT - The problem with flattening the front crossmember is that now there will usually be interference between the spring and the lower edges of the frame side rails. The rails can be notched an inch or so for working clearance, but this does remove some strength.

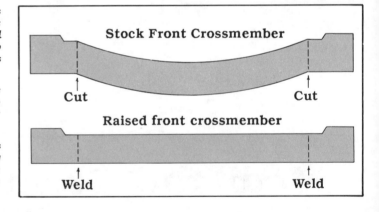

Modifying Center Crossmembers
(Ford)

There is no problem with the Model T or Model A Ford center crossmembers, because they effectively didn't really have them. The 1932 Ford uses a K- member, and if any type of transmission other than early Ford is used, this member must be removed or drastically modified. The 1933 and later Fords used an X-member, but because of the backbone of this member (where the X comes together), radical modification is also necessary with almost any non-Ford transmission swap.

The very best modification to the 1932 Ford frame is the addition of a modified X-member. Virtually all of the mail-order frames come with this X-member, although the member design will vary considerably. You can make up your own X-member rather inexpensively, simply by cutting and welding more modern pickup frame rails into the shape needed. The key to making such an X-member is in location of the mount. This,/then, shows where the transmission mount must be. Make the X-member wide enough at this point to give plenty of transmission clearance. Refer to the accompanying photographs to see how this works out.

Since the 1933 and later frames already have an X-member, it is a matter of modifying the backbone connection. It is almost always necessary to cut this backbone girdle from the X-member, not difficult since it is riveted in place. This girdle gives the frame much of its twist resistance, so keep that in mind when making up a new girdle. There are several suppliers of X-member modification kits, or you can make up your own. In some cases the closest approach of the X-members must be cut back and straight sections installed before the girdle/trans mount is made. In nearly every case, except for some standard transmissions, a small portion of the X-member must be trimmed for trans clearance.

When making up a new trans mount, it is wise to make this a bolt-in, so that the transmission can be dropped out the bottom of the chassis. The sides and top of the girdle/mount can be welded in place to regain frame rigidity.

The Model T and Model A Ford frames are very marginal in the strength category, here the Model A frame has a new commercially-available X-member added for strength.

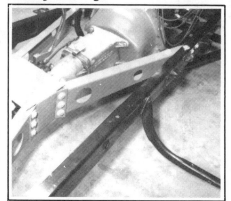

When installing a late model ohv V8 and automatic transmission in the 1933-1ater Ford frame, the center crossmember connection must be cut away for clearance. While you can make the necessary pieces at home, they are also commercially available.

RIGHT - The value of adding a strong X-member to the Ford frames cannot be overstated, because this does a tremendous job of making the entire structure much stronger. If you are making up your own X-members, you might look at late model pickup truck frames for building materials.

LEFT - Note how the special Model A frame X-member tapers to fit the rails yet is bigger at the backbone to accomodate any modern transmission. Some of these members are bolted together for easy transmission removal, some are welded solid.

This 1932 Ford frame has been boxed and a specially built X-member added to replace the original K-member. This makes the entire frame much stronger and resistent to twisting,

Modifying Rear Crossmembers
(Ford)

The Model T and Model A Ford rear crossmembers arch above the side rails, all other Ford crossmembers swing below the rails (as seen from the side). The reason is simple: The T and A springs mounted directly over the axle, and to get center section clearance between axle housing and spring, both the spring and crossmember had to include an arch. The 1932 and later crossmembers are behind the axle, because the springs are mounted behind the axle.

It is possible to lower the Model T and A frame by making a very slight kickup just ahead of where the crossmember attaches to the rails, or to move the crossmember to attach atop the rails. very few additional modifications are done to these crossmembers. The 1932 and later crossmembers can have the center section raised (similar to the raised front crossmember), but this invariably gets the frame rails too close to the axle. Very little modifying is done to the rear crossmembers, if the transverse spring is to be retained.

A special note here. The 1932 and later springs have a curve. When looking directly down from above, the ends are farther forward than the center part. The crossmember has a similar curve, so be aware of the factor should you start mixing rear crossmembers.

This curve was eventually eliminated in the early Fords, but it has proven a sore point with beginning builders.

If there is to be any kind of rearend substitution, it is necessary to block the new rearend in position, putting the

When doing any work around the rear crossmember, go ahead and take the time to box the frame. Add secondary crossmembers for mounting auxilliary items such a brake connections and locaters.

This Corvette rear-end mounts to a piece of rectangular tubing at the rear and smaller square tubing at the front.

rearend centerline directly below the frame rubber bumpers (or the hole where the bumpers once were). Make sure that the new rearend center section will clear the stock crossmember. If not, slight trimming of the crossmember bottom lip is allowable, but don't get carried away. If there is too much interference, then the crossmember must be changed. In this case, the straight crossmembers from the later Fords can be made to fit, and the later spring used.

If a quickchange center section is to be used on the rearend, the 1932 and later drop-center crossmember cannot be used because of interference. The solution is elimination of the cross spring (coils/semi-elliptic, etc) or use of a different cross spring. The Model A spring makes a good substitution. Install the Model A crossmember center section, and there is more than enough clearance. Of course, this means that the trunk flooring must also be modified.

If other types of rearends and springing systems are used, the stock Ford rear crossmember can be removed entirely.

Formula For Pro Fat Frames

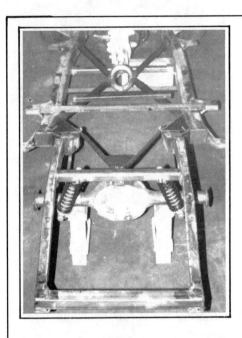  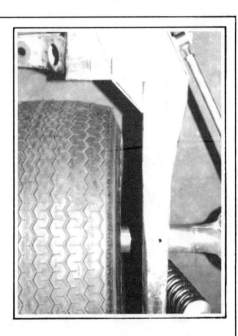

Although this particular Pro-Fat frame is for an early Plymouth, the basic building theme works for all older cars having full frames. Note that the frame now has a new tubing X-member with an oval mid-point which doubles as a driveshaft safety yoke. The transmission mount is square tubing between the frame rails.

The critical measurements are determined by tire width and clearance between outside edge of tire and fender opening. Once this has been determined, the rearend flange-to-flange measurement gives amount rearend housing must be measured. Note here that there is enough clearance between inside edge of tire and relocated frame to allow for some wheel/tire size changes to be made for racing.

Ever want to put a set of 15x12.5 beetle-crushers under a '49 Plymouth grocery-getter? For the information we went to "Squeak" Bell, one of the New Zealanders at The Kiwi Konnection at 1331 Flower Street in Bakersfield, California 93305. Squeak said the following procedure is basic for most frames. Just follow the steps, double check angles and remeasure. Squeak feels the procedure is too simple to do it any other way.

In order for the wheels to fit inside the '49 Plymouth (and you thought we were kidding) they had to be 57-inches total width with the wheels mounted on the rear axle. A '64 Galaxy 9-inch rearend was selected because of its smooth style housing. Squeak recommends '66 and earlier housings because they have oil filler plugs. 1967 and later have the plugs in the third member. When you use a '66 third member in a '67 housing there are no filler plugs. You are able to fill

the housing through an open axle end. He doesn't recommend this.

The Ford rearend was narrowed 17-inches to get the 57-inch total width with the type rim and tire that Squeak used. Of course, you will measure your own machine for total width, then set your mounted tires to your total width and measure from the mounting flange of the rim to the other. This is your axle flange-to-flange width. Remember it is wisest to leave a couple of inches between the tires and body for body sway and using larger tires or offset rims. You may also want to go bigger than what you started with. Double check and remeasure everything.

The Ford third member is offset to one side of about 2 1/2-inches so the pinion will align with the transmission. When Squeak narrowed the housing, he shifted the third member to the center. Even though the driveline no longer runs down

After following the procedures outlined in text for cutting and relocating rear portion of frame, the narrowed rearend housing can be located. Note new square tubing crossmember and frame horn crossmember are in place. Here a Ford rear end was chosen.

The type of rear springing used is a personal preference, this owner wanted coil/shocks. Pay attention to how beefy the lower shock mount is, and that it also serves as mount for lower locater bar.

Upper shock/spring mount has additional mounting holes drilled so the spring angle can be changed. Note that frame has been cut just behind body mounting pads.

the centerline that the crankshaft revolves on are parallel to each other (though they are not in alignment), you can offset a single driveline in any direction.

Next the body was modified with large fender wells (though this could be done after narrowing.) Again, Squeak allowed at least 2-inches to the inside for body sway and wheel swap. Add at least 2-inches from the tire tread, fore and aft, in the new well for racing tire growth and wheel diameter change. The fore and aft measurement is sometimes a compromise because of body mounts as in this case. There was just enough room, barely, without removing the mount. Now measure the new body well distance to figure out how far to move your rails in. Measure again to be sure.

First Squeak measures the frame for square. This is habit with any frame he works on for any reason. In this case it has to be square so that the cut will be square to the frame, when measured on the frame. To measure, it is easiest to pick a body mount hole or fender mount hole at the front that has a like hole in the opposite rail. Measure to a hole or rivet at the rear on the opposite side. Using the same reference holes measure diagonally across (figure 1). Measure with the utmost accuracy and always use the same reference points. If the two measurements are the same, it's square.
(Editors' note: Many older frames were produced to a tolerance of plus/minus 1/8-inch. Measure your frame at several diagonal points to get an idea of what the tolerance might have been.) If not, it has to be straightended. And this, my friends could be a real chore but has to be done. Double check your measurements.

It is not uncommon for stress to build up in the frame from daily driving. This condition is compounded if the car was in an accident and th frame straightened. To keep the frame from twisting hopelessly out of shape when the rails are cut, tack weld angle iron, channel, or tubing from rail to rail. A bullet-proof method to secure the rails in their same relationship before cutting is to crossbrace the rails (figure 2). When tack welding the braces in, be sure they touch where they cross each other because this point is welded. Weld braces on the rear section also.

Because a finished concrete floor is relatively level, Squeak places the frame on the floor. You may place your frame at any level but it must be secured so it can't move or shift. It is critical that it does not move from the time you start measuring until you start welding. If you can leave it secure until after you weld, it makes it bunches easier to remeasure when finished. Squeak prefers a plumb bob to layout and recheck the frame cuts, but a combination square with an on-board level will also work. To double check a line measured with a level, use a plumb bob.

The angle at which you cut the frame is not important. That the angle is identical on both rails is the secret. All you want to do is move the rear rails in but on the same angle for each side so the frame rail as a whole has not changed its shape when looking at it from the side. Also measure the exact height of the rear frame horns to the floor, they will be rewelded at this height.

After scribing the lines on the rails where they are to be cut, scribe a second set 3/16-inch apart. There will be a 3/16-inch steel plate added here and we don't want to change the length of the frame. About every half inch centerpunch your scribed lines. This is so you don't loose your line when torching off the rear section.. The rails could also be sawn or cut with an abrasive cut-off saw as long as you stay dead on line.

If you need to, especially after using a cutting torch, grind the main rail ends with a disc grinder. Check with a level or plumb bob to be sure they are square to gravity. The rear rails are just ground with care to the centerpunch line. A straight edge, whether a steel rule or a virgin section of healthy angle

The key to narrowing a frame is making the new attachment points very strong, that's the reason for the large triangle shaped gusset plates. Here the plate angle has been designed to correspond to angle of upper radius rod.

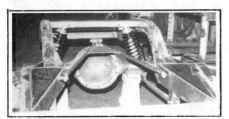

Pete & Jake's rod ends, normally destined for traditional street rod front ends, work very well for the late model as well.

Check the text for information on blind nut mounting for rod ends, necessary since the new boxing area is complete on bottom.

Big mistake that many amateur builders make on frames is using brackets from too-thin plate. If in doubt, go bigger! Rearend locaters mount to brackets welded to lower gusset plate.

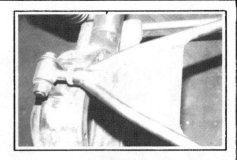

Unique reverse-triangual radius rod system for this rearend has rear mount tabs welded to top of rearend housing, adjustments on lower and upper locaters allow exact angle for driveshaft.

Try to allow enough fore-aft distance at front of frame modification so that larger diameter tires can be used at a later date, here the determining factor was a body mount pad.

iron wider than wider than your frame, is placed on both front and rear rail ends to check for high spots and to be sure the two rail face ends are on the same plane (parallel to each other). Now cross measure (figure 1) from the outside corner of the new end to a reference point at the front of the frame. These measurements should be the same.

Measure the total width of the frame and height of the rail at the cut. You will need a flat piece of 3/16-inch plate with these dimensions, with at least one long edge being straight. This edge is important as it will run from the horizontal rail surface (or body side) on each side. With the rear rail ends being the same height as the p[late, they can only fit one way, square to the plate.

Tack weld the plate in so the long edge is flush with both rail surfaces. Now you can see the plate is a perfect geometric plane through the frame. No matter how far you move the rail ends in they will butt up against the plate at the same angel as when they were attached to the rails.

If your frame has a rear crossmember (most do) remove it either by unbolting or grinding off the rivet heads (or a cutting torch if you're brave) and driving out the rivet shank with a drift punch. If the crossmember was riveted, it is better to weld it back in. If it was bolted in, rebolt it or weld it if it's permanent. Put the crossmember in position before you tack weld as it helps locate the new distance between rails. Whatever way you narrow or make a new crossmember is up to you - but it has to be exact.

You can now mount the body on the frame and use the body to align the rear rails like welding jig. The other way is to measure in how far the rails are to set and scribe the lines on the plate with a square. After tack welding or bolting the rear crossmember in the rails, check for square. Next, pull the rear section against the plate. Use a furniture bar clamp, a strap clamp or any way you can get the new section to pull up flat against the plate. It's got to be snug. Now place each rear rail on the scribed lines on the plates and make sure the

rails are squared to the top edge. Cross-measure and tack weld. Remeasure and if it's off square, square it up by moving the new section sideways at the very rear tip. Measure from the floor to the rail ends and match your previous measurement. If it isn't right, work with it until it is but it should be real close to start with. When you have the right height and it is square, remeasure and recheck the rail sides to be 90-degrees from the top edge of the plate. When it checks out, tack weld it all, top, bottom and sides and then remeasure. It's gotta be right.

Next Squeak gussets the 90-degree angle left by moving the rails, plus he boxes the gussets. The gusset on the fenderwell joint was an arbitrary size but the inner gussets was planned. As you see in the photos, the upper radius rods run parallel to the gusset. Squeak drew an imaginary line from the outside of the outside of the rearend upper radius rod bracket to the inside edge of the narrowed rails to the frame. Cardboard patterns work well in helping the gussets from 3/16-inch plate. The large gussets also make good pads for roll bars (on top) and radius rod brackets (underneath). Cut the plate out between the narrowed rails before tack welding the gussets flush with the rail surface. Recheck your angle.

The particular advantage to this radius rod system is that besides having similar geometry to a four-bar, the upper bar also acts as a rearend locater. Squeak chose a 25-inch radius rod end center-to-center. The upper and lower rearend bracket centers are on the same vertical plane as are the forward bracket centers. The radius rods are .356-inch wall seamless meld tubing. The tubing ends are drilled and tapped for 5/8-inch National fine rod ends from Pete and Jake's. The top radius rod gusset is 3/16-inch plate. All the rod end brackets are also made from 3/16-inch steel.

Measure and cut the inner gusset box from 34/16-inch plate. With the radius rod centers you chose, mark it on the box plate with it on the gusset. The rod center must be far

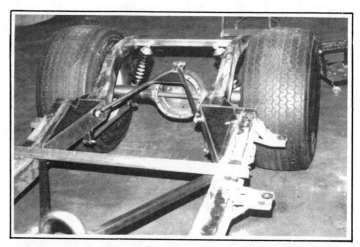

Above- This particular frame modification was done on the shop floor, proving that while nice huge and expensive frame jigs are not mandatory.

Above Right- The new triangular gusset boxed frame area may look massive, but it is not heavy, and the extra strength it gives is vital.

RIGHT - This is a highly modified Corvette frame, set up with the narrow rear frame section by Gene Reese in Dallas. Note how the area where the narrow frame extension attaches to the original frame has been beefed up considerably, which is especially important on an open car where no added structural strength is derived from the body. Keep in mind that all work on the frame must have a constant check/cross-check to make sure that the frame is square and not twisted.

enough from the edge to allow a nut to be welded to the inside. The center is the same on both plates, but the nuts must be welded on opposite sides.

Squeak first welds a 5/8-inch National fine coupling nut to the plate, then tap drills through the nut. Then a tap is run through the nut first, screw in the bolt and run the nut over it, then tighten. When the nut is welded to the plate, you have the same result as our first method. How tack weld the plate into place with the nuts inside the boxed gussets. Squeak uses 5/8-inch National fine grade 8 bolts except for the 3/4-inch on the rearend top radius rod bracket. A coupling nut is about twice as long as a standard nut and has much less chance of the bolt rocking in the nut under a load.

Squeak uses 5/8-inch National fine grade 8 bolts with an unthreaded shank the length of the rod end bushing. This is so the threads will jam tight in the plate yet allow the rod end to work. A loose bolt will snap at the point where the threads start. Drill a hole in the bolt head for a safety wire or fabricate a lock washer. Cut a piece of sheet metal about 5x1-inches long and put a 5/8-inch hole piece of sheet metal about 5/8-inch from one end. Place the bolt into the washer and tighten the bolt into the threads. Be sure the washer is in a position that the long leg is anchored to something stationary like the frame. The other ear is folded against one of the bolt head flats.

To weld the frame Squeak uses a M.I.G. (wire welder) with A.W.S. Spec. E70S-6 .035-inch wire. The wire has been triple deoxidized th´n copper coated to first clean the wire and then seal it to keep moisture out. The gas shield around the arc keeps moisture out and allows a porosity-free weld. It will give you a 70,000 pound tensil strength weld, the same as 7018 Low Hydrogen arc rod. Uncoated wire will oxidize and hold moisture and leave porous weld. Basically if the wire is copper coated, that is what you want.

Not everybody has a M.I.G. welder but an arc will work just as well except the weld is hotter. 6011 ands 6013 have the

same steel core as Low Hydrogen 7018 except the flux is different on Low Hydrogen. Low Hydrogen flux creates it's own gas shield to produce a porosity-free weld. The fumes are toxic so weld in a ventilated area. Low Hydrogen rod comes in sealed containers with a moisture content of no more than .01%. If you leave your Low Hydrogen rod exposed to the air it will absorb moisture and you won't get a good weld. The ideal machine is an A.C.-D.C. with reversible polarity. Welding D.C. reverse is best but what most guys have is an A.C. Buzz Box with straight polarity (not reversible). Expertise and dry rod will leave you with a trouble-free weld when using a Buzz Box. If your Buzz Box does not have an open circuit voltage of 73 volts minimum you don't have enough power to run A.C. 7018 which is designed for these low power machines.

Before welding, double-check and remeasure everything. It isa wisest to weld an inch or two at a time on any one seam. Then go to the other side and weld the like seam the same distance. Go back to the first rail and pick a seam that is cool. This method is time consuming, but the heat generated by the weld must be kept very low. Not so hot you can't lay your hand on it after it cools for a minute or so.

Remember when you were learning to arc a bead on an innocent steel plate? After you burned a pound of rod on the hapless victim the only amazing thing that happened was the unbelievable degree of heat warpage and distortion. The same can happen to your frame by running a long bead. After it is cold, remeasure for fun because if it isn't right, it won't be fun.

Note: When adding large rear tires to a car, you are disturbing the original design for handling as well as braking. The large rear tires may adversely effect the way the vehicle corners and rides.

Boxing

Most older car frames have a C-shaped cross-section, and rely on added strength simply by making the C-shape deeper, and sometimes from heavier material. While such a shape has considerable strength for direct loads, it does not resist twist well. Enter the hot rodder and the frame boxing technique.

Boxing is nothing more than adding a side to the .C-shape, making it into a closed O-shape, or rectangle.

You may box the entire length of a frame rail, or just sections where the strength seems to be needed most. You may remove the crossmembers, box the rails, and replace the crossmembers. Or you may box up to where the crossmember joins the frame, and continue at the other side of the crossmember.

In almost every case of earlier frame, you will want to consider boxing the front third (where the engine is), and the rear kick-up or crossmember area, where the rearend components attach. If the vehicle is to have independent suspension (at either end, or both ends), it will help give torsion rigidity to the frame if each rail is boxed the entire length.

Before starting to box a frame, inspect it very thoroughly for cracks. Repair the cracked areas, and where there is extreme damage or fatigue cracks, replace the frame section or add a fishplate to the inside. A fishplate is a length of sheet plate about 1/8 or so inches thick, welded to the inside of the frame rails, spreading well to either side of the cracks. When repairing a frame, weld the outside and the inside. The outside weld will probably be ground smooth for appearance, so the inside weld is a safety factor.

After the frame has been checked for square and straightness, attach some sort of alignment bars if the crossmember(s) are to be removed! This is vital!!! Ordinary pieces of pipe, tubing, or angle iron will do, and the primary function is to keep the frame in exact original location once the crossmember(s) has been take out. If the frame side rails are to be relocated (narrowed, widened, etc), this is not necessary.

It is far and away simpler to work around existing crossmembers when boxing a frame, than working on the crossmembers after the rails have been boxed.

The boxing material should be at least as thick as the frame rails, most rodders use from 1/16 to 1/8-inch plate. It may be attached with gas, arc, or heli/MIG arc weld. Gas welders cause far too much heat distortion, arc is fine, shielded arc is best.

The key to working on a frame without causing distortion is to weld in very short areas, almost like spot welding. Alternate sides. And constantly measure to make sure there is no distortion taking place. A frame jig and heavy duty table would be ideal, most rodders have nothing more than a garage floor. Assuming the garage floor is flat, lay some bags of sand on the frame to keep it from walking around during welding.

You can buy the boxing plate in various lengths and widths, start with a plate exactly the width you need. Lay the plate on the open side of the frame rail and trace the frame shape onto the plate. Cut the plate. Most builders use a cutting torch. Cut the plate to exactly fit the outside edges of the open frame, then grind the inner edge of this cut at an angle. This will give a groove where the plate fits against the open frame, a groove to accept the weld bead. This allows maximum weld strength when the area is ground smooth.

Position the plate against the frame and hold it in place with C-clamps. Tack weld the plate in position. Do the same to the opposite frame rail.

One caution here. Once the frame is boxed, you can't get inside to run lines or wires. Many builders drill large holes in the boxing plate for later access, this should be done before the plate is welded to the frame. Various size metal hole saws are available at the welding supply house, use patience when drilling the metal. You can use a cutting torch to make the holes, but it is a hassle trying to clean up the cut edges with grinding stones/files.

Go back and forth on the rails, adding tack welds, until everything is welded solid. No, it is not necessary to weld the plates solid for maximum strength. The tack welds probably give as much strength as you'll get, but a solid weld can be ground with a rounded corner, and it looks much better when painted.

Fit the boxing plate snugly into/against the crossmembers to get additional strength at these critical areas, especially the front crossmember.

Take your time, fit the plates well before welding, and you will get a great job without distortion. This problem of distortion is where the TIG/MIG welders come in so handy. These are "cold" welders, in that they concentrate the welding heat. The small 115-volt machines often handle up to most frames, but the 220-volt machines are far better. If you don't have an arc machine, you can cut the boxing plates and haul everything down to the local welding shop.

When an independent front suspension is being adapted to early frame rails, in this case a Mustang system using a new crossmember, the rails should be boxed well into the engine area to get maximum stiffness.

Although this frame uses semi-elleptic springs at the rear, additional frame strength can be achieved by boxing the kickup area. This would be especially vital if the area over the axle were C-d for extra axle clearance.

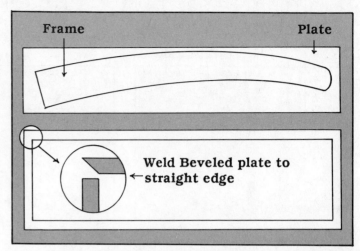

Frame   Plate

Weld Beveled plate to straight edge

Use of a welding jig is the ideal situation when boxing a frame, since there is considerable heat and warpage is likely. However, the job can be done on the floor if you go slowly, very slowly with tack welds, alternating sides. Always tack weld some kind of braces to the frame before removing original crossmembers and starting the boxing procedure.

When boxing a frame, start by tracing the frame outline onto metal plate. This plate can be thicker than the frame stock, but should never be thinner, after it is cut and ground to fit the frame contours the plate edges can be beveled. This will give a much better weld purchase area, and allow the weld edges to be ground smooth. Once the frame is boxed it is difficult to get wiring and tubing routed, so many builders drill access holes in the boxing plate. It is also difficult to reach body and suspension mounting bolts, the answer is either access holes or blind nuts welded into the frame.

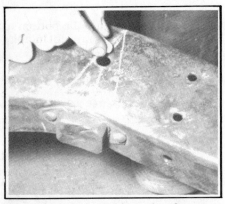

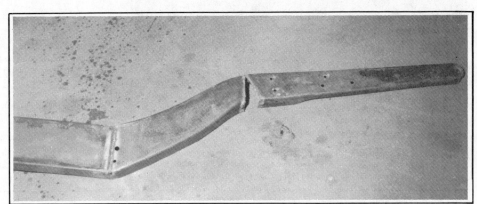

When merely notching the frame to make a kick-up, use a piece of cardboard to first determine how wide the notch must be, then cut this out with a torch.

Here the first notch has been made from the top down on the frame just where the original kick-up started. Then, to get the frame extension back in a level or near-normal position, a notch must be cut from the bottom. Work this out with drawings on the floor or on cardboard before actually cutting the frame rail.

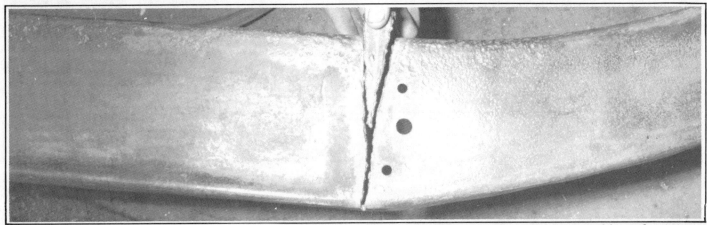

ABOVE - After cutting a notch in the frame rail, grind the area and put a bevel on the open edge so that when welding back together you get maximum weld penetration and build-up. This is critical if you are going to grind the weld for appearance.

This tubing frame has a kick-up constructed in such a manner that a single leaf semi-elleptic rear spring can be utilized. Since the end of the spring with the shackle (back) is much higher than with a normal frame kick-up.

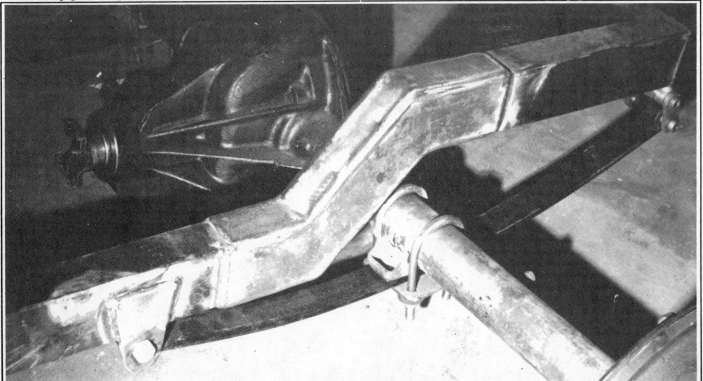

C-ing The Frame

Very popular in recent years is the old practice of C-ing a frame, which is like making a very minor kickup. This is necessary to get maximum frame lowness and still have some suspension travel. It is commonly used with solid front and rear axles, but it is sometimes seen with independent rear ends such as Corvette and Jaguar.

Essentially, C-ing is nothing more than cutting a notch, or making a hump in the frame. If a car has been lowered extremely in the rear for example, there may be only 3 inches or so rear end housing travel before the housing contacts the frame. Bad scene. Without extensive frame rework (making a kickup), it is possible to put a C-shape section in the frame.

In recent years, a number of super-low California type cars have appeared with flattened front crossmembers. This brings the transverse spring snug up against the bottom of the front frame rails. Small U-shaped sections are cut into the frame for additional spring travel.

At the frame rear, when it is C'd, the frame should also be boxed. The exception to this is a C-section that is no more than half the depth of the frame, and when this cut is within the span of the crossmember (very seldom). When any C-section is made, it should be completely enclosed if possible, otherwise the frame is extremely weak at this point.

At the front, when a transverse spring is used and the frame is notched, only a cap for the notch is required, although lots of builders go ahead and make the small boxing area inside the crossmember.

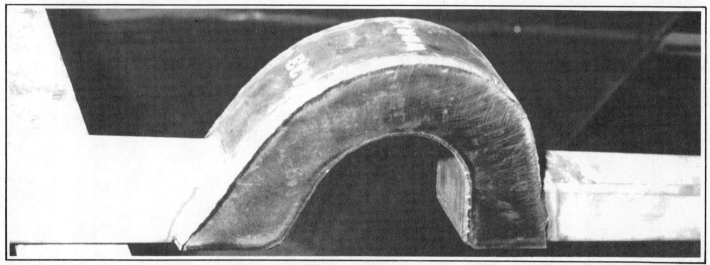

The practice of C-ing a frame is mostly done when trying to lower a custom car, but it does come into play with rod building. Here the entire C-section has been constructed of plate stock, then the C is inserted in frame tubing.

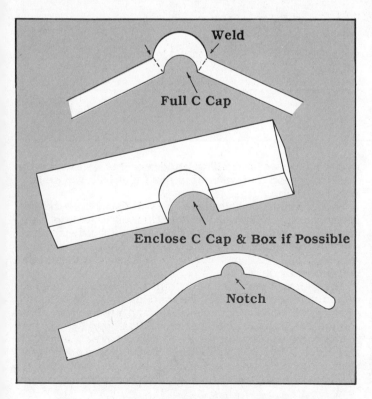

Weld

Full C Cap

Enclose C Cap & Box if Possible

Notch

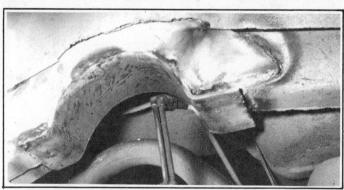

More common thype of C is cut into a 1950s frame, to give extra rearend travel clearance when the rearend is lowered. The same kind of minor C can be used at the front of semi-elleptic cars for front axle clearance

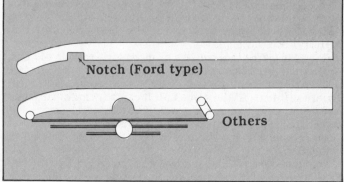

Notch (Ford type)

Others

SUSPENSIONS

The purpose of the vehicle suspension is to isolate the sprung mass (frame/body/passengers) from the shocks of the road, and vibrations. At the same time, the suspension must keep the tire in contact with the road as much as possible. If the tire is not in contact with the surface, the vehicle is not in control, and all the passenger comfort in the world is of little value.

A vehicle is free to move in a number of directions at once, all of which must be controlled. The body may roll from side to side, from front to rear, and rotate about a vertical centerline (turn). At the same time it can be going straight up and down, and it can be generating cornering forces (G-forces). So, the best vehicle suspension is going to be one that allows all of the movements under the most controlled conditions.

But we are hot rodders, and we don't really get into the far-out theory and application of suspension geometry...we work with whatever we have. All well and good, but if wc work with something good and we end up making it bad, we are in a batch of trouble.

In hot rodding, we have three types of suspensions that are used. One type is devoted almost exclusively to some forms of competition, where the front or rear (or both) axle is bolted solidly to the frame. For the street this is totally impractical, so we will limit our discussion to the solid (rigid) axle, and the independent axle.

The independent axle, both front and rear, has become very much the standard for the contemporary car, but solid axles are still favored for heavy trucks and much construction equipment. Both are good for hot rodding purposes.

The solid axle is what we see everyday in the majority of rear drive vehicles. The rearend housing is a solid unit, attached to the frame via a spring(s) and shock absorbers. Earlier cars used a solid front axle, attached to the frame with either a transverse (cross chassis) spring or semi-elliptic springs. The biggest problem with the solid axle is that of unsprung weight. All the weight of this design is flogged around by road conditions. As it moves about, it transfers lots of this energy into the springs, and ultimately into the vehicle. Remember the law...a body in motion tends to stay in motion.

If the solid axle can be made much lighter in weight, it will affect the vehicle much less. Thus the need for aluminum wheels, tubing axles, etc. The less the unsprung weight, the better control possible. If the rearend center housing and gears can be attached to the frame (becoming sprung weight), all the better. If the front solid axle can be eliminated altogether, all the better.

All of this becomes of particular interest to rodders, because one of the usual things we do when building a rod is reduce the total sprung weight. Increasing the ratio of un-sprung-to-sprung mass.

As mentioned in the Frames chapter, the Ford suspension system is the most common to rodding. Here, the solid front and rear axles are connected to cross-springs by shackles, and the springs are bolted to a centerpoint of the frame crossmembers. This system is better known as the "buggy spring" approach. The Ford body/frame is free to rock from side to side quite readily.

Elliptic springs were originally used on carriages, and the system was copied on early cars. Here, the top spring is connected at both end to the bottom spring, kind of in a squashed 0 shape. Soon the car builders did away with the full elliptic and began using only one spring. This is just like

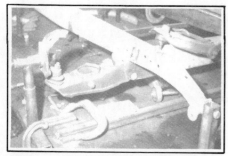

Most popular independent front end is Mustang/Pinto unit, special crossmembers can be adapted to most any frame, here it replaces semi-elleptic springs/beam axle.

Obvious progression is to make new upper/lower A-arms from tubing stock and use production spindle and coil/over shocks. Welding here must be professional, geometry perfect.

Often overlooked is the front suspension from imported trucks, which may have coil springs or torsion bars and overall sizes will work well with older American cars. The key to swapping front suspensions is to make them as near original geometry as possible.

Among the earliest IFS swaps for rods was the Jaguar (as seen on '29 A roadster pickup opposite page), here the A-arms are temporarily set in place on special crossmember.

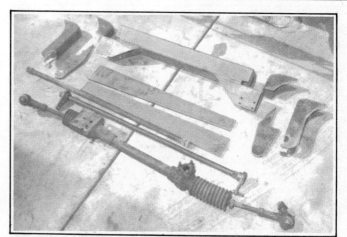

These are the parts needed to put the Jaguar front suspension on a typical early American car with some kind of ladder frame.

the cross chassis spring, except it is mounted parallel to frame rails. Some experiments were made with mounting the spring rigidly and attaching the axle to one spring end, but this never has been popular. In modern rodding, the practice of cutting a semi-elliptic spring in half, and mounting the axle to one end results in quarter-elliptic springing.

The semi-elliptic springs mount at the frame four corners, then to the axle. This gives a much wider stance to the spring, drastically reducing the freedom of body roll side to side. This is the system seen on GM and MoPar vehicles, and most other non-Fords. Ford used the transverse spring through 1948, most other companies kept the semi-elliptic front spring until the very late 1930s. The semi-elliptic rear spring is still popular. It is a simple way to get vehicle stability, passenger comfort, and rearend torque control.

The axle components can be suspended on/beneath/over a frame by several different types of springs. The common leaf spring is a simple length of tempered steel. A single leaf is too soft, by stacking ever shorter leaves atop the main leaf, the spring will increase in stiffness in direct proportion to deflection. This is the spring rate. The coil spring is a length of round steel wound in various ways. Spring rate can be increased by the shape of the wire (cross-section) and by wire thickness. The torsion bar is a length of steel rod (wire) that is twisted.

The air bag is an effective spring, as is hydraulic action. In rodding, we work primarily with the first three.

Springing works by compression. But this stores energy, and we end up with a recoil. Shock absorbers (more rightly called dampers) control this recoil. The function of a shock is not to absorb the upward movement of a wheel, but more to control the rebound. When a car without shocks hits a bump, it bobs up and down for quite a time. The shock eliminates this rebound. Our job, as good rod builders, is to select the available components and put them together on a car so that we get the best results. Not just acceptable result, but the best. A much harder job than it would seem.

Experience has shown that the average hot rod, whether a 1927 Model T or a 1978 Camaro, is not driven to anywhere near the maximum potential of the suspension. Exceptions are in drag racing, where the anti-squat forces at the rear end have been thoroughly studied and conquered. But the other elements of cornering and braking are only marginally approached. As examples, consider some of the red hot American production cars that are fine tuned (chassis-wise) for road racing. They can perform seeming miracles compared to the stockers. But the basics have been there all along, the professionals just make a touch here and a tug there to get maximum output.

Interestingly, of all the modern chassis items that really improve the performance of an older design, the radial tire is probably the most apparent. Doing nothing more than installing a set of radials seems to do wonders with an older style chassis.

This section of our book is designed to be full of short pieces of specifics, so that's what we'll get into immediately.

There are any number of relatively modern independent front ends that can be adapted to older frames, but some (as here) are rather bulky.

Here is a not-so-common switch, putting a Ford front cross-member and four-bar tubing axle under an older MoPar which used semi-elleptic springs.

When possible, it works well to bolt a suspension swap to the frame rails, making later change and modifications easier.

Welding the suspension components to the frame is fine if the builder is absolutely sure everything will work as planned

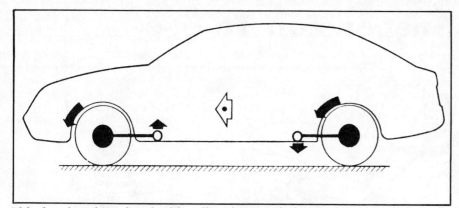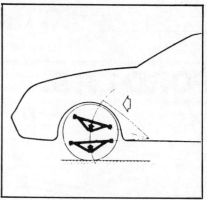

This drawing shows how braking dive characteristics can be counterbalanced with leading and trailing arm operating off the front and rearends. By angling the upper A-arm mounts, front end can get the same effect. Very important when putting an IFS under an older chassis. Copy angle from the original donor car.

The Jaguar rearend became so popular under hot rods during the 1970s that junkyard prices soared, there are different widths available. Part of the advantage of the Jag system is that the brake rotors are inboard, thus reducing the un-sprung weight significantly and improving both ride and handling.

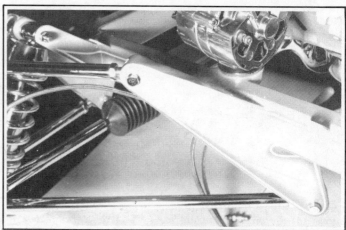

This homemade show car IFS uses a long lower rear A-arm member, race car technology often does not work well on street.

RIGHT - One of the advantages of the Jaguar IFS on older cars is the short upper A-arm, removing the need for a bulge in the fender to clear inner pivot points, or a homemade upper arm, which would place roll center below ground level.

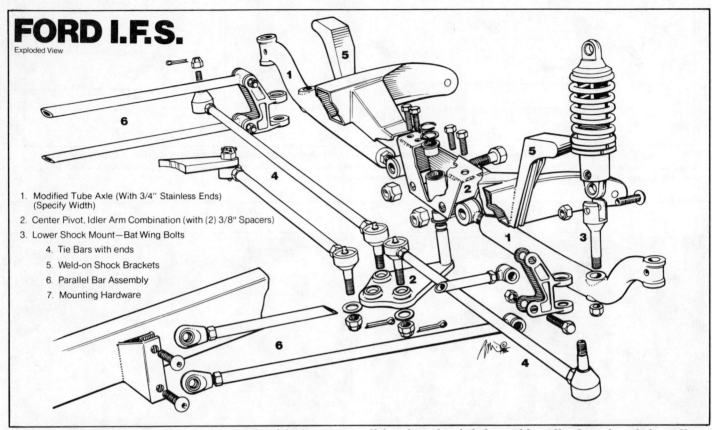

FORD I.F.S.
Exploded View

1. Modified Tube Axle (With 3/4" Stainless Ends) (Specify Width)
2. Center Pivot, Idler Arm Combination (with (2) 3/8" Spacers)
3. Lower Shock Mount—Bat Wing Bolts
    4. Tie Bars with ends
    5. Weld-on Shock Brackets
    6. Parallel Bar Assembly
    7. Mounting Hardware

Compare this radical type of beam front axle with the more traditional Ford unit below. This "Allard" style unit is really an independent front suspension that keeps traditional flavor of solid axle. But it does have an unusual appearance under extreme cornering conditions. Courtesy Street Rod Mfg., phone (303)791-1881 for more info.

A really good independent front suspension that has seen too-little use in street rodding is from the earlier Volkswagen. Dual trailing arms and torsion bars give an exceptionally smooth ride, great handling, late disc brakes can be adapted to the VW spindles.

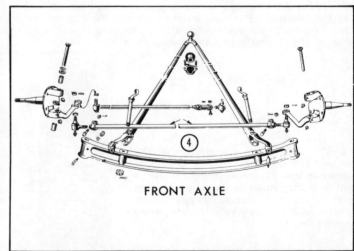

FRONT AXLE

This is the traditional Ford front end (minus spring) as used on 1935-1948 FoMoCo products. The key is that this unit pivots about center point of spring and wishbone, any alteration makes the unit much less limber. Even a dropped axle changes things enough so that bumpsteer can become a major problem for the builder.

The type of suspension you use is a matter of preference. But it will also probably be a cost decision as well. If the vehicle you have is currently equipped with an independent front end (say, a 1947 Chevy), you are best to keep that suspension. If you have a 1937 Ford with a beam axle front end, maybe that will work best for you. Still, there is a cost factor involved here that doesn't seem apparent at first.

For instance, keeping that Chevy isn't really much of a problem. About all you would have to do is rebuild it with new bushings, and adapt a set of disc brakes. You end up with a system about as good as any state of the art design. With the Ford, you could add a dropped axle, disc brakes, modified springs, and 4-bar radius rods, and you would have hot rodding state of the art. But it might cost you more than if you installed a Mustang ifs under the Ford frame. And the Mustang/Pinto front end is also hot rod state of the art.

First, a look at the stock independents that we see most often in rodding. The 1937-38 Chevrolet is a very popular car, using semi-elliptic front springs and a beam axle. To lower the car, a dropped axle is most often used, and if the springs are set up with Teflon liners, the resulting ride is quite good. Firm, but good. In 1939 Chevy tried a kind of independent front suspension called Knee Action. Don't even bother with this unit. Yes, it can be made to work, but go with a later independent system, you'll be better off. The 1940 and later Chevy ifs is good. It is an unequal length A-arm design, with the lower A-arm being longer than the top. This system was used well into the 1950s, and the basic principles haven't changed much to this day. This is a good system, and rebuilding parts are readily available through the antique parts sources.

The Chrysler Corporation cars (Plymouth, Dodge, DeSoto and Chrysler) used the semi-elliptic springs well into the 1930s, but they also went to the independent front suspension before WWII. As with General Motors, these are good units and rebuilding parts are available. The failing of the MoPar units was in brakes, but if discs are substituted, this problem is licked.

Studebaker used a kind of independent system, with a single locating arm and a transverse leaf spring. hile it is possible to make the system work, substitution with a later model ifs works even better. An example of this would be something like a 1941 Studebaker Champion. This is a small, lightweight car, so the Mustang/Pinto front end can be used very effectively.

Since the majority of rods are Ford/GM/! MoPar, we'll stick with these.

The GM and MoPar vehicles have both solid and ifs front ends to contend with. The ifs can be used, as can the solid axle. But if you have an early GM/Mopar and want to go to an independent, you can. The most common ifs swap is the Mustang/Pinto, although you can consider the Fiero, late model Mopar torsion bar, and even an unusual item such as the AMC. These are add-on's, not frame clips. With the semi-elliptic front end, using a dropped axle and disc brake conversion will cost much less than going to an ifs.

The overwhelming majority of rodders change from a solid front axle (or rearend) to an independent in the belief that this will give a superior ride, or will radically improve handling. Not necessarily so.

Experience shows that a fat fendered Ford equipped with an independent front suspension does not ride softer than one with a solid axle. And it usually doesn't handle much better. But the ifs does make a definite difference in the pitching characteristics of the Ford. For some reason, the older cement highways that are built in segments seem to have a spacing between segments that coincides very well with the earlier Ford wheelbases. With so much unsprung weight flailing around, the Ford with a solid axle will tend to pitch upward on these old cement roadways. A kind of rythym sets in that is very distracting. While the solid axle is sturdy when it comes to potholes in the road, pavement sags tend to throw the unsprung weight almost violently. In this respect, the independent front and/or rear suspension makes a marked effect on the solid axle.

When a solid front axle has the springs set up properly (see Springs), whether transverse or semi-elliptic, and some of the unsprung weight is removed (aluminum wheels, etc), and good shocking is involved, such a front suspension can rival a good independent. Improperly setup, the solid front suspension is hardly better than nothing.

Can independent suspension front and rear improve the handling of a street rod? Yes it can, but it must be fine-tuned for maximum performance after having been installed correctly. Still, the average hot rod, whether a 1931 Ford or a 1969 Camaro, will almost never be pushed into the realm of performance where this kind of ultra-handling comes into play. Hot rods are not CanAm race cars. They can be made to be that radical, but they then cease to be street oriented cars. So the final decision on which suspension to use rests squarely with the builder. The solid axle(s) work good with the older frames, when setup correctly. Independent suspensions can be substituted. Cars with independent suspensions can be updated to more modern components. It is a matter of time and money.

Finding/Buying/Using Dropped Front Axles

The dropped front axle has become synonymous with real hot rods, dating back into the 1930s, but it has been only in the last 15 or so years that a real effort has been made to produce a maximum quality dropped solid axle.

Solid axles may be of the beam type, (cross-section like an I-beam), solid type (cross-section of a rectangle), tube type (round cross-section) or combination beam-solid and tube. Most solid axles are of the beam type, with a couple of notable exceptions. Ford had a tube axle under some of its V8-60 equipped cars of the late 1930s, and some of the pickups through 1941. Early on in hot rodding, these were very popular axle swaps, and they were used on a lot of circle track race cars. Very rare today, and worth having, although they do not have an additional drop over stock height, and they can't be dropped. Chrysler corporation used a tube axle with semi-elliptic springs under its cars in the late 1930's. These

can be used with any kind of homemade front spring/radius rod system, and offer a rather unique looking axle that most modern rodders will not identify. You can use the hydraulic brake package on this axle, as well, or opt to work up some kind of late-model disc brake combination. These Mopar tube axles are much more common than the Ford tube.

One caution. Well back in the early 20s and Teens, there were a number of different tubing axles used. All of these that we know of had an Elliot-yoke attachment for the spindle. The spindle fit between the yoke ends of the axle, whereas all later axles have the yoke on the spindle so that the spindle fits over the axle end.

When identifying the Ford beam axles, the difference will be in shape and distance between the spring perch mounting holes. The Model A axle will have a constant slight curvature from end to end. The 1932 and later axles will have a semi-drop at the end, between spindle boss and spring perch mounting hole. The distance between the spring perch mounting holes changes through the years from 1935-48, depending on spring length. These axles (35 and later) have the spring mounted ahead of the axle, while 1934 and earlier axles mount the spring above the axle. Anytime you are working on a Ford front end, and you are going to be buying parts, be sure and know the distance between spring perch holes, and the width of the spindle boss (end).

Yes, it is possible to mix axles, and this is done primarily when making up a beam type axle to use in a 1934 or older Ford frame. If a 1935 and later spring-forward axle assembly were to be bolted to the 1934 and earlier frame, the axle centerline would be too far rearward. A new crossmember or spring perch can be built, bringing the axle centerline back to normal, or the assembly can be rebuilt to the older style.

Here, the spring is removed from the radius rod hangars (which are in front of the axle), and remounted above the axle using spring perch bolts from a 1934 or earlier axle. The spring should be rebuilt (see springs, this section) to fit better, and the radius rod (wishbone) will probably need to be split or replaced with 4-bars.

There are a lot of Ford axles laying around the country, and quite often you stumble across a dropped axle assembly. The Ford beam axle was first stretched/dropped in the 1930s, by rodders wanting to get the vehicle center of gravity lower. A 2 1/2 or 3-inch drop in an axle makes a radical change in the vehicle roll center and CG, this was very important to early day race car builders, especially when the wheel diameters started shrinking. But the dropped axle really didn't gain widespread fame until Ed Stewart of San Diego started making them available to friends. This is why such an axle was called a "Dago" axle in earlier rodding days. This was essentially a blacksmithing approach, since the axle ends were heated, stretched and hammered to the new shape, and tempered (sometimes). You can usually spot such an early day axle since the drop areas between spring perch and spindle boss will have an inconsistent shape, and may even show hammer blow marks.

Some early day rodders tried to improve the looks of this dropped area by filling the I-beam hollow with weld and/or plate, thus the name dropped and "filled". The axle was almost always filled if it were chrome plated. Stewart's axles are usually identified with a constant cross-section in the dropped area, a sign of better craftsmanship.

How to tell if you find a dropped axle over a semi-drop stock Ford item. You'll know, because the drop is so pronounced.

If you should find an axle that has a tube center piece and dropped beam end pieces, grab it and run for your life! you

Compare this front end to one left/below. Total Performance tube axle has tie rod ahead, but steering ends are outboard enough to bring Ackerman back into play.

have just located something rare as hen's teeth...an early day Bell axle. These will have the Bell name on them, and while they are hardly better than any other dropped axle, they do have tremendous collector's value.

If you find a dropped axle that has been bent, don't pass it by. You can have the axle bent back into shape by any competent front end specialist, and once the axle is installed in the vehicle, final alignment is possible. But, always inspect a bent axle very carefully for cracks. If you find them, get another axle!

You will probably run across a few all-tube axles at swap meets. All-tube, not partial tube. The SuperBell axle, which was introduced to street rodding just over a decade ago, has a tube center section, but the round cross-section dropped end pieces are forgings...solid. They weld to the tube center just inboard of the spring perch bolt holes. The Magnum and the Vintage Works axles are also recent aftermarket items, but they may still be too new to be at swap meets. These companies have modern forged dropped axles that are very nice pieces, you'll know them right away because of the quality.

The all-tube axle is an outgrowth of the drag racing industry. Here, a piece of thick wall tubing is bent to shape, and spindle bosses are welded to the tube ends. While these axles are usually fine for street operation, they may or may not have the exact style you are looking for. Until recently, the all-tube axle was the only hot rod industry tube axle available for the semi-elliptic springs, but now the SuperBell axle for Chevrolet is available, and this can be used under practically any semi-elliptic front end.

There are so many dropped axles now available that you are likely to find any number of different kinds/makes, at rod shop and swap meets. If you let other rodders in your area know you are looking for a dropped unit, you can almost always find a good used item and a reasonable price. Lots of dropped axles have been removed in favor of independent systems. *continued on page 54*

The dropped beam axle comes in a variety of qualities, those currently being produced are maximum quality forgings, not heated and stretched ends. Note here the tie rod ahead of axle, affecting Ackerman.

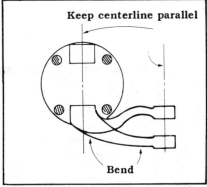

When stock Ford spindles are used on a dropped axle, the steering arms must often be bent down to allow tie rod clearance at the frame. Use plenty of heat and make sure tie rod centerline returns to parallel with kingpin centerline.

Modern dropped axles can be created in a variety of widths, this Bonneville racer uses a narrower than normal tred width. Note how far down the steering arms are to give tie rod clearance.

Buying a new dropped axle is a matter of shopping at your local speed shop or through the mail-order houses that advertise in car magazines. All of the axles that we know of, as advertised, are good, although there is one area where you might use caution.

Until a few years ago, there was only one company dropping stock axles. The workmanship was ok, but they were almost always out of alignment, so after installation it was imperative to visit the front end shop and have the axle bent into alignment. A large number of these axles got on the market, particularly for semi-elliptic front ends, and particularly for Chevy trucks of the pre-1962 era. No matter what axle you install, have it checked at the front end shop.

Which brings up a question: Should the axle be painted or plated before being checked for alignment.? Unless it is from a reputable company, is new, and the company tells you it is smack on, don't paint or plate until it has been installed and checked. Most of the new axles now being made can be installed without this problem. If it is a used axle, make certain it is aligned before paint or plating! Extra work, but necessary.

Finally, how much drop to use? Most axles will feature a drop of from 2 1/2 to 4 inches. If you are buying a new axle, the company will tell you what seems to work best for your particular situation. It is possible to get too much drop, and actually get the spring perch bolts below the wheel scrub line. This is a matter of matching the front wheel size to the amount of axle drop. On semi-elliptic dropped axles, there is some confusion about the amount of drop. Some companies making the all-tube axle will advertise a 6 inch (or more) drop. This is not the amount of drop over stock, but overall. You are interested in the amount of drop over stock. If you get too much drop on the semi-elliptic front end, you can have as little as 2 inches ground clearance...far too radical.

These big drops also pose another problem. As the drop is increased, the amount of leverage induced into the dropped end section multiplies. On the early Ford type of stretched and hammered drops, the I-beam cross-section could get so small that the axle would bend. Not much of a problem with the old Ford brakes, but when disc brakes are installed, such an axle becomes dangerous.

A final note on semi-elliptic front ends. Why not just place the stock axle above the spring, and gain upwards of 5-6 inches drop? You can, but you won't have operating room between the axle and the frame. Cut notches in the frame for clearance? Yes, but you will have to make the notches too big you loose a lot of frame strength. It has been done, but think about it carefully, and do excellent work.

Installing Dropped Axles

One of the most rewarding changes in building an older style hot rod comes from a dropped axle. It makes a marked difference in appearance, and when done right, a magic difference in handling.

One of the most frustrating jobs when building an older style hot rod is the installation of a dropped axle!

Of course, it will turn out to be a problem of parts. If you use all new parts when assembling a dropped axle, particularly the Ford spring perches(pre-35) or wishbone bolts (post-34), it is not a problem at all.

If you are going to disassemble an older Ford front end and use the original radius rods (even if these are to be modified), you will almost assuredly have a problem getting the original spring perches out. They rust in place, and they don't come out well, even with a huge hydraulic press. Remove the spring perch nut and try to hammer/press the perch bolt out. If it does not come, you may end up having to cut the bolt out with a torch. It is a messy job, and if you can get the local machine shop to do, that works best. They can drill the bolt out, usually. Do not cut the original axle , in desperation. That axle can be used on another project later, or some restorer might want it.

Buy new spring perch bolts if you ruin the originals. If you are going to use the 4-bar radius rods, you'll get all new stuff anyway. Bolt the 4-bar batwings or the old radius rod to the dropped axle,and then install the spring. Usually, the spring must be spread so that it will align with the shackles, this can be done with a hydraulic jack or Port-A-Power...use maximum caution.

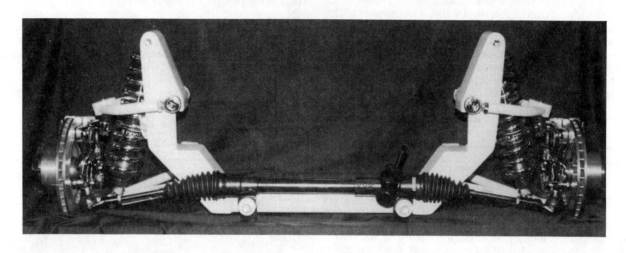

A major mistake is often made when installing spindles to the Ford axle. The kingpin kit (which is available at any speed shop or mail-order supplier) will include a round bearing about 1/2-inch thick. This bearing must go between the spindle and the bottom of the axle. It can be placed at the top of the axle boss, and an additional amount of lowering is achieved, but the reason for the bearing is to take the vehicle weight. Also, the kingpin kit will include some thin spacer shims. Use however many are necessary to eliminate up/down slop between spindle and axle. The kingpin kit will also include new bushings for the spindles, you can install these at home, but if you're not really sure how this is done, hunt up the front end shop or machine shop. A good firm push fit with the hand is just right. Too loose a bushing fit and the front end is guaranteed to shimmy.

When setting up the Ford front end, use from 5 to 8 degrees of caster. You can get a really close call on this by using a protractor or angle meter against the axle kingpin boss. As viewed straight down from above, the top of the kingpin area must be leaning backward. If you have a 4-bar radius rod setup, you can adjust this caster angle. If you have split stock radius rods, the angle is determined by how far below the frame the rod ends mount. If you use the hairpin type custom radius rod, you will have adjustments between the radius rod front section and the spring perch batwings.

Installing a dropped axle to semi-elliptic springs is simplicity itself...remove stock and replace modified. There will be a wedge between the spring and axle, to set caster with. Until alignment time this wedge won't be important.

When a dropped axle is used, particularly Ford, there are usually clearance problems with the stock spindle/tie rod. Since the spindle is now higher in relation to the frame, the tie rod is also higher. It may interfere with the stock wishbone, or hit the frame or engine. The solution is to bend the spindle steering arms and lower the tie rod. Forged spindles (most are) bend easily by using a torch. Don't try to bend any cast parts.

Heat the spindle arm right up next to the kingpin boss (do this before installing the new kingpin bushings!) and bend the arm down. Then, right next to the tie rod hole, heat the arm and bend the tie rod hole back level. The centerline of the kingpin hole and the centerline of the tie rod hole must be parallel, or you'll end up with tie rod end bind. When you are bending the steering arm, do not effectively shorten the arm length, as this will change the steering geometry.

Do not overheat the arm, or it may crack, and do be patient. The relative position of the tie rod hole must remain the same, also, as viewed from above, otherwise the Ackerman alignment is thrown off. Doing this steering arm change may seem like the most difficult part of installing a dropped axle, but it really is quite simple. Use a very large Crescent wrench on the steering arm to make the bending easy.

Radius Rods

For the sake of clarity, radius rods are used to locate the front solid axle, locater rods/bars are used for the rear axle. What you do with either is up to you, but there are some guidelines .

Remember that the original Ford suspension design has the frame/body rolling about a centerline drawn through the chassis from front to rear. The front and rear springs mount on this centerline, as do the front radius rods (wishbone) and the rearend housing locaters. In stock configuration, this is a perfectly acceptable design, although it is archaic.

In hot rodding, it is the modification of the radius rods and rear locaters that leads to problems.

If the shocks were removed from the front end, and the spring retainer U-bolts were loosened, the solid axle would move up and down at either wheel very freely. No bind to the movement whatever. Starting with circle track practice, the Ford wishbone has been split at the rear mounting point, and the radius rod ends moved out to brackets on each frame rail. Now, if you try to move the front end up and down at each wheel, there seems to be a bind at the wheel going up or down. When an I-beam axle is used, the axle actually twists as the wheel moves up and down. Just a tiny bit, but it does happen. When a tube axle is substituted, the axle will not twist, and this binding moment becomes a major problem. A problem that is not readily noticed in ordinary driving, but it is there. In an extreme case, perhaps a very steep driveway, where one wheel is driven up the driveway (on an angle) and the other wheel is on the street, the forces are enough to break something...usually the frame brackets. This same problem exists with whatever kind of radius rod is used, until things are changed to a 4-bar.

With the 4-bar setup, the caster angle of the axle never changes as the wheel goes up and down, thus there is no bind. This "frame stacking" effect is progressively less the closer to the chassis centerline the radius rods are mounted.

In circle track racing, it was an advantage to have a built-in bind on corners, a kind of race tuning that could be con-

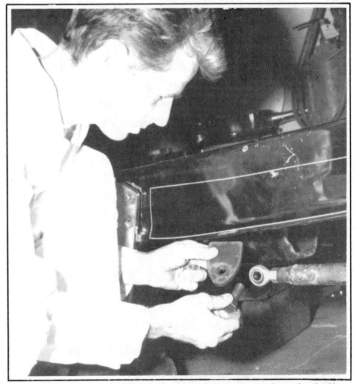

Tom McMullen, publisher of several car magazines including Street Rodder, prepares to weld on radius rod brackets to 1932 Ford frame. These brackets must be very strong and very well gusseted, use at least 1/4-inch material.

The older style "hairpin" radius rods have lost favor recently to the four-bar set-up's, but they are still practical. This one located a Jaguar rear end and needed precise front location to keep rearend alignment true. Do not skimp on the size of radius rod tubing.

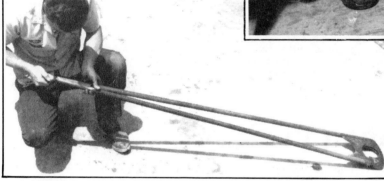

Very long radius rods came into vogue during the 1960s as a part of ongoing drag racing traction experiments. The idea was to transfer as much rearend torque force as far forward as possible on the chassis.

structed into the chassis. On the street, the objective is to get the loosest possible front end, then dampen it with shocks. This does not rule out the use of split wishbone radius rods, or custom made hairpin rods. Just be aware of what happens. As a general rule, the vehicle with a 4-bar radius rod system will normally ride slightly better than one with solid radius rods. Incidentally, the term 4-bar is really a trademark of the company that made them popular, Pete & Jake's. They didn't invent 4-bars, because rodders have been using them for many years.

When a wishbone is split, adjustable tie rod ends are welded into the wishbone tubing. These kits are available through mail-order sources, or a Ford tie rod and ends can be cut and used. The bigger truck units are best, considering the forces they encounter.

Mount the radius rod ends to frame brackets the same distance below the frame as the original central mount point (about 2 inches). Make the frame brackets out of very heavy material, with excellent gussets. If the rear of the radius rods are the same distance below the frame as the original mount point, then the axle should have stock caster. If the rear of the frame is higher than the front, this will effectively remove front wheel caster. As mentioned, 5 degrees is the common current amount of caster, and it seems to work very well with radial tires.

With the frame in approximate final rake, check the front wheel caster before making the radius rod frame brackets. Raise and lower the radius rod ends until the correct caster is found, then make the frame brackets to fit. If the frame brackets seem unduly long (something over 3 1/2 inches), the radius rods may be reshaped. The best way for this is to cut small V-notches in the radius rods about 5 inches behind the front axle, and bend to fit, then weld the notch solid. This is hardly ever needed.

A special note here: when tweaking the front axle to get caster, remember that in original configuration the front crossmember had the spring at the same angle. You may have changed this angle doing frame work. If so, you will get spring leaf tip bind. That is, the main leaf will twist just a slight amount, as will each succeeding leaf. The less bind in the spring, the better.

The hairpin type radius rod is made of heavy wall tubing, usually with clevis or ball end inserts at the forward end. When such a radius rod is used, the original attachment at the spring perch bolt has to be modified into a batwing shape. These types of rods do not work the same as 4-bar units. State of the art is the 4-bar link, or a derivative of it. But you can use the split radius rods, and perhaps you'll never know the difference in the two systems.

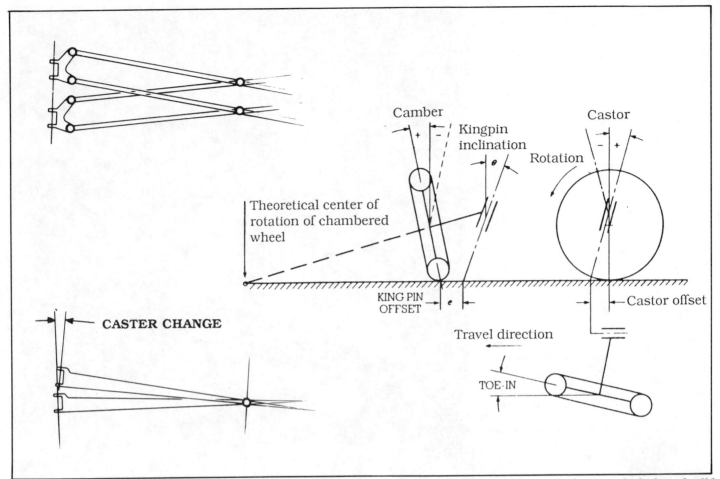

Camber

Kingpin inclination

Castor

Rotation

Theoretical center of rotation of chambered wheel

KING PIN OFFSET

e

Castor offset

Travel direction

TOE-IN

CASTER CHANGE

Jake Jacobs and Pete Chapouris pioneered modern use of the four-bar radius rod as a way to control caster deviation of solid front axle, and make use of Mustang steering easier. Caster and camber are vital elements in front end geometry that must be right on for a rod to handle properly. The drawing at bottom of page shows how Ackerman principle works, with outside wheel in turn making larger radius than inner wheel, key is having steering arms connect to tie rod ends on line drawn from center of rearend to kingpins.

The Ackerman Principle

Consider the car as it turns in a constant circle. The inside front wheel is turning a smaller radius circle than the outside front wheel. Something must be done in the front steering mechanism to allow this to happen. This something is called the Ackerman principle, and if you look at a set of spindles you see that the steering arms (on the spindles) have the tie rod end holes closer to the center of the car than the kingpin holes.

If you draw a line from the center of the kingpin to the center of the rear axle, the line should pass directly through the steering arm rod end holes. If not, the car does not have perfect Ackerman effect. But, current mass production technology is beginning to ignore this principle somewhat. Some new cars, with rack and pinion steering ahead of the front axle centerline, actually have the outer tire turning tighter than the inner wheel. Tire technology is offsetting some of this problem, and so is wheel offset, but for our purposes, stick with making a pure Ackerman effect on your rod.

If it is necessary to bend a spindle steering arm for any reason, be sure and set it so that the Ackerman check line described is obtained. Sometimes, when a Ford cross leaf spring is used on a frame with a suicide spring perch, the tie rod runs into frame interference. Rodders have cured the problem by reversing the spindles side for side. This puts the tie rod in front of the axle. And the Ackerman goes out the window, resulting in very poor turning control at higher speeds. If there were enough room, the spindles could be heated and bent outward, so that the tie rod holes would

again line up for the Ackerman check. Not really conceivable, so better to find another way and keep the tie rod behind the axle.

One method is to mount a rack and pinion steering gear directly to the solid axle. This is usually a simple matter of two sturdy brackets between R&P and the axle. This creates a problem with the steering shaft, however. As the axle travels up and down, the effective length of the steering shaft changes. Some new cars use spline sections in the steering shaft, and rodders cure the length problem this way.

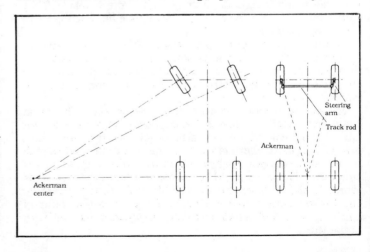

Steering arm

Track rod

Ackerman

Ackerman center

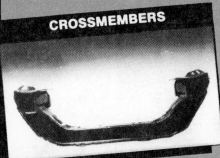

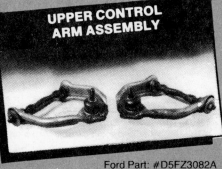

Bump Steer

Bump steer is a part of every front end suspension, but it can become a giant headache for the hot rod builder, old and new car alike. Anytime the front suspension components are altered, chances are good that bump steer will arise. Pronounced bump steer in most cases.

The problem is a simple matter of geometry, arcs of differing magnitude.

The front wheels are held in place by some system, either a solid axle or an independent system. The wheels are free to move up and down, restricted usually only by springing. The greater the movement of the wheel, the better the control. In hot rodding, we restrict this travel, sometimes absurdly so. It is not unusual to see older style rods built with no more than 3 inches of upward travel available. Five inches is a better minimum, 4 inches is most common. This is movement as measured between axle and frame, not at the wheel itself.

On a solid axle, as one wheel moves up or down, the distance from that wheel to the opposite wheel does not change. On an independent front end, the distance does change. The wheel going up and down is swinging through an arc with a base at the A-Arm attachment points. Look under cars with independent suspensions and note that the tie rod is in three pieces, with an idler arm and the pitman arm working as center points of the A-arm attachment points. Yes, the arc of the wheel is not exactly the same as the tie rod end pieces, but it is very close.

Back to the solid axle. If the car has a drag link steering, the gearbox comes outside the frame rail and a drag link connects the gearbox pitman arm to the steering arm on the spindle. Some kind of locater bar is needed to keep the solid axle in one place. On the semi-elliptic spring system, the spring itself is this locater. On the Ford system, there is a radius rod attached to the axle. In stock configuration this is called a wishbone (because it looks like one!), but many rodders cut the connection of the wishbone and remount each radius rod end closer to the frame rail(s). As seen from the side, when the wheel travels up and down, it travels through an arc (see illustration). No problem so far.

When the drag link is connected, it can swing through a slightly different arc. This causes the spindle to move from side to side slightly...bump steer. Now, accentuate the arc divergence problem by adding a dropped axle, and bump steer can increase. With this type of radius rod connection, the caster angle at the kingpin is changing, because the axle is rotating around a single point.

If a 4-bar radius rod system is used, the caster angle does not change, but there is still the requirement to get the drag link angle correct.

To determine drag link angle, draw a line between the rear pivot point of the radius rod and the rod end attachment on the spindle steering arm. The drag link must follow this same centerline. The same centerline, not an adjacent line! The more the drag link line deviates from this radius rod center-line, the worse will be bump steer. The solution is to mount the steering gearbox so that the pitman arm allows the drag link to align.

With the semi-elliptic spring, this line is the center of the spring eye (back) to the steering arm.

Cross steering can also be a problem with bump steer, sometimes moreso than with drag link steering.

Ford used cross steering on the Model T, then changed to drag link steering on the Model A through 1934 Ford, then back to the cross steering. Here, the steering gearbox places the pitman arm under the frame, working from side to side. The tie rod between spindles remains the same, but the drag link now runs across the chassis to the right spindle. Rodders are using the 1971-77 Chevy Vega gearbox as a similar item.

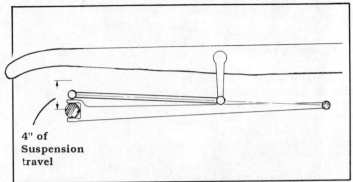

Early Ford front end, with steering drag link at pitman arm on line drawn through wishbone mount and steering arm connection at spindle. Caster deviation at A-C is minor.

4" of Suspension travel

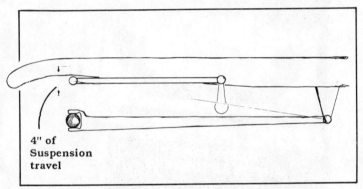

Split wishbone with Mustang or other type steering where pitman arm drag link connection is radically different. Now the change in A-C will be significant and bumpsteer assured. Thanks Pete 'N Jakes.

4" of Suspension travel

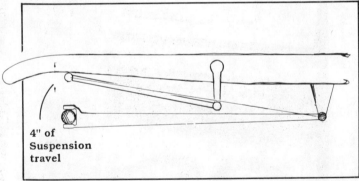

Dropped axle with original Ford steering changes the A-C difference only slightly, so bumpsteer is not quite as noticeable as with radical changes.

4" of Suspension travel

In stock position, as viewed from the vehicle front, the Ford cross steering has the steering rod mounted to the pitman arm slightly higher than the tie rod. Normal front end travel causes the tie rod to pass through the centerline of the pitman arm attachment point, or neutral, so that bump steer is minimal. Install a dropped axle, however, and all this changes. The tie rod moves up almost level with the pitman arm, so that upward movement of the axle causes severe bump steer. The solution in this case is relocation of the pitman arm attachment point, by bending the pitman arm or relocating the gearbox.

61

Another problem with cross steering is caused by the transverse spring. It connects to the axle via shackles, which allows the axle to have a lateral movement. Not much, but enough, especially on corners. If the spring (thus the entire frame) swings to one side or the other of the axle center (viewed from above), this increases or decreases the effective length of the steering rod. Instant bump steer. On some of the latest 1948 Ford products a sway bar (Panhard bar) was added to eliminate this shackle sway. Current hot rod technology includes a sway bar with cross steering. Be sure that this sway bar is parallel to the steering link, as seen from in front.

The same kind of attention to detail must be observed with cross steering on semi-elliptic front ends. In most cases, such a cross steering is much more difficult with semi-elliptics. With an independent front suspension, location of the steering link pivot points is critical. The most common problem occurs when a Mustang ifs is used. If you use the Mustang unit, or any ifs, be sure that you duplicate the stock steering mounting points exactly. This will probably mean some frame crossmember modifications...do them. As an example, if you mount the Mustang ifs rack & pinion below the 1934 Ford frame horns (for clearance), you'll get bump steer. Guaranteed! Cut arches in the frame horns and mount the R&P where it should be. This applies to the steering system on any ifs.

And it applies to a modified spindle on an otherwise stock ifs. If the spindle is modified to lower the vehicle, and the steering connection point is moved upwards, the entire steering system needs to move upwards a like amount. The key here is the steering arm tie rod attachment point. If it remains unchanged, the steering remains unchanged. Unless you radically drop the front end, then you might have to do some steering adjustments.

Scrub Line

One of the more important checks in any vehicle safety test would be that of scrub line. That is, any part of the chassis/body hanging below the wheels diameter. Unfortunately, a very large percentage of hot rod builders violate this basic safety tenet, with both early and late model vehicles.

The reason for not needing anything hanging lower than a wheel lip is obvious. Given a flat tire, the offending part(s) can cause serious problems. One example would be a steering pitman arm too low. It digs into the pavement and the car can go out of control instantly. A bracket or such grinding against the pavement sends up sparks and a fire results.

While it is true that a flat tire seldom lets the wheel rest on the road surface, good building sense says never take chances. To check for scrub line violations, have a buddy hold the end of a long string, you hold the other. Start by running the string between the two front wheel bottom edges. Then, move the string diagonally from one front wheel to the opposite rear wheel. If there seems to be something hanging too low, it is worth a further check, and repair if necessary.

Springing Systems

Separating a vehicle axle system from the frame will be some form of springing system, which may be a leaf type, coil type, torsion bar, hydraulic, or air. In hot rodding the first three are the most common, but air and hydraulic will certainly become predominant in rodding as factory units finally make it to the boneyards.

The leaf spring is most common, and modifications/repairs are the same for both semi-elliptic and transverse types. An old spring will need to be rebuilt before using. Squeeze the spring in a vise adjacent to the centerbolt, remove the centerbolt, and open the vise. For Ford springs, a rule of thumb is to remove every other leaf, counting the main leaf as number one. This will give a much softer spring rate, and it is a starting point only. You will have to use the car to find out exactly where the spring rate should be. This is with an engine weight about that of a small block Chevrolet, or a flathead Ford V8. Obviously, a Chrysler Hemi engine will require most of the original spring.

Brush and grind each spring leaf until it has all rust removed. The end of each leaf, where it contacts the leaf below, should be rounded so the leaf does not dig into the next leaf. Place strips of something like Teflon between each leaf, and bolt the spring back together. Alignment clamps toward the end of the spring will help keep the leaves running true. The vehicle can get a kind of free lowering job of about 1-inch if the main leaf has the eyes reversed. The best advice here is to have a spring shop rearch the main leaf so that the eyes are on top or make up a new main leaf. There are other ways to do this at home, all difficult and not nearly worth the small amount of cost the spring shop will charge.

Semi-elliptic springs usually don't need more than a couple of the shorter leaves removed (sometimes not even that), but they do need to be cleaned and have the leaf ends tapered. Use Teflon on these springs as well. The main leaf also may have the eyes reversed, but keep axle/frame clearance firmly in mind before doing this.

Semi-elliptic springs as used at the rear of a rod can pose some real problems. For the most part, trying to find something to use produces springs that are far too long for the early car chassis. If the car is a non-Ford, the stock springs can almost always be used. These springs will be narrower and shorter than the modern semi-elliptic, thus they will be

LEAF SPRING TYPES

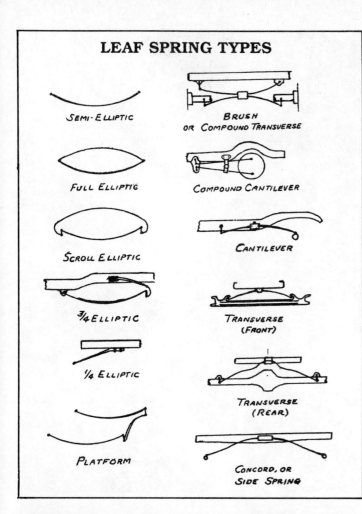

SEMI-ELLIPTIC

BRUSH OR COMPOUND TRANSVERSE

FULL ELLIPTIC

COMPOUND CANTILEVER

SCROLL ELLIPTIC

CANTILEVER

3/4 ELLIPTIC

TRANSVERSE (FRONT)

1/4 ELLIPTIC

TRANSVERSE (REAR)

PLATFORM

CONCORD, OR SIDE SPRING

Torsion bars are the most simple of springs, and they can be adapted to rods very easily, the most common types run parallel to each frame rail and connect to the axle by a lever arm. Arm must have shackles for free movement, rear end of bar can be made adjustable to control frame height.

The torsion bar and the coil spring are the same type of spring, but in different configurations. Coil springs of many varieties are used on rods, local spring companies can wind springs with different rates for special applications.

This Jaguar front end uses a parallel torsion bar beneath the frame rail connecting to front arm of lower A-arm, ride softness is determined by bar diameter, length, and length of lever (A-arm in this case). Springs need to be as soft as possible, shocks stiff.

Continued on page 66

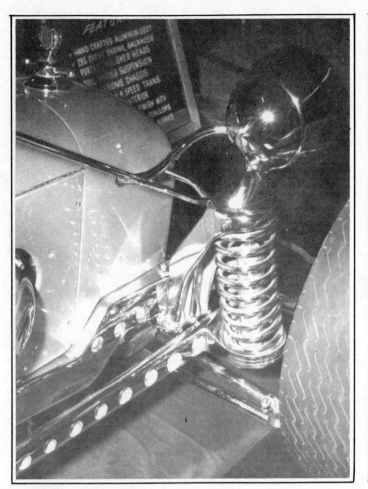

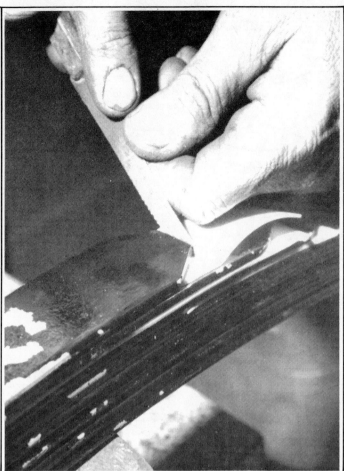

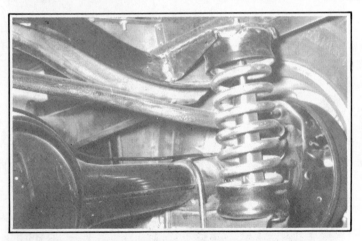

We show a variety of spring types and mountings here, just to give ideas of how coil spring and coil/shocks can be used. We throw in the leaf spring just to get your attention. Here, a Teflon sheet stock has been placed between the spring leaves and is being trimmed, this reduces friction between spring leaves and makes a dramatic improvement in ride, making the leaf spring almost as good as the coil or torsion bar. Properly set up, all these spring systems are good, set up wrong and they are all bad to varying degrees.

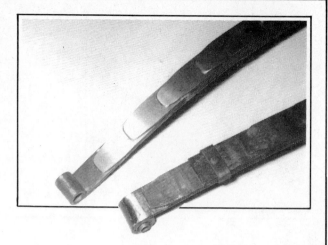

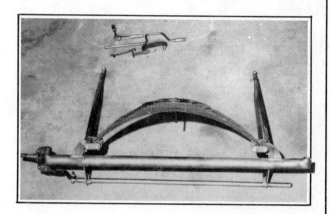

This coil spring system was photographed years ago and would probably never be seen on a modern hot rod, the two leaf springs at upper right show a reversed main leaf eye (top) versus the regular eye. Reversing the eye gets a full 1-inch chassis drop. Straight tube axle at right was very popular in drag racing during the 60s, not seen much anymore.

Quarter elleptic springs can be used on front or rear, note that they attach to axle without shackles. An upper locater bar must be used to control axle wind-up, this is a good system where space is at a premium but the springs must be strong, spring acts as one part of the suspension locating members.

This is a method of eliminating front spring twist bind, by making the shackle bolt on the axle movable. There is a commercially available hanger that does the same thing for early Ford front springs, here the idea was used on a sports car, the idea is to reduce as much bind in the front suspension travel as possible.

The absurd in front leaf springs has a dramatically arched Model A unit to hold front of drag roadster higher for maximum weight transfer during acceleration.

This is a typically traditional solid front axle with transverse spring and angled tube shocks, good layout.

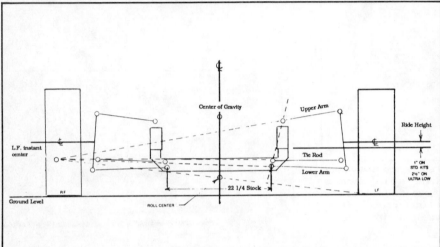

There are a great number of different factors involved in front end geometry, and a change in one usually results in a change in the others. Factory engineers have figured most of the problems, hot rodders can · make good things bad.

Model A rear spring on hangers behind Ford rearend, necessary if a crossleaf spring must be used with quick-change rearend.

stiffer. You want to make them as soft as possible and still hold the frame/body high enough.

If you are making up your own semi-elliptic rear spring system, for a Ford as an example, you need to find a short spring. The Chevrolet pickup front spring of the late 40s and early 50s will work, as will the front spring from later model Dodge pickups, or late model Dodge Dart rear springs, Note the centerbolt location when these springs are mounted.

The semi-elliptic spring for rearends will normally have a short front section and a long rear portion. The short (stiffer) front piece helps control torque wrap-up of the rear axle, while the longer rear section gives a soft ride.

The coil spring works exactly the same way as the leaf spring, it is just in a different shape. While coil springs can be made to work on a solid front axle, appearance never seems quite right. The exception is the coil/shock design, where the spring wraps the shock absorber. Coil spring rate is dictated by coil wire diameter, total coil diameter, wire cross-section, and coils-per-inch. Through trial and error, coil/over manufacturers have come up with coil rates for the most common types of hot rods, if you are working with something uncommon, you'll have to go through the same trial and error.

Weights of cars determine spring rates. A 1932 Ford roadster, minus fenders and running a small block Chevrolet, will have a total weight of approximately 2200 pounds. A coupe with fenders will come in a couple of hundred pounds heavier. The weight of these cars will be distributed almost equally, 50% front-50% rear. Most early rods will come in between 2500-3000 pounds, cars of the 50s and later will come in right around 3200 pounds. Cars produced after 1937

will have a weight distribution closer to 60% front-40% rear. This weight distribution has a bearing on spring rate as well as braking.

The torsion bar is a kind of straight coil spring, or a leaf spring that twists. In fact, some of the earlier Volkswagen torsion bars were simple stacks of flat spring stock that twisted in use. Torsion bar length and diameter, as well as actuating arm, determines rate.

A common problem in rodding is trying to match an existing coil spring to an older car. GM rearends of recent years have used coil springs, but these are much to strong for a Model A sedan. Since the Model A should weigh in at around 2500 pounds, and 50 percent of the weight is on the rear end, then each coil for the Model A should handle 625 pounds. Find a car with a very similar corner-weight requirement and the coil spring wire diameter will be close. The length will probably be way off.

Rod builders make the common mistake of cutting coil springs to fit a particular area, without regard to spring rate. Usually, the cut down coil is too strong.

If a junkyard spring cannot be found, spring shops can wind a coil spring to fit. Unfortunately, they will also be working mostly on a trial/error basis, so you may have to go through a couple of springs to get exactly what you need.

Torsion bars can be modified by changing: actuating bar length, bar length, or bar diameter. If the bar diameter must be cut down, have a machine shop do it in small increments until you get what you need. Again, best advice when selecting a torsion bar is to find one on a vehicle with similar weight characteristics to the car being built. Suggestion: Look hard

For springing, the closer the spring is to the end of the axle the better, this was not a bad approach on a show car several years ago.

Here, a 1935 and later Ford front end with spring ahead of the axle has been placed in a 1933-34 Ford frame, spring hanger is tube ahead of original crossmember.

Seldom seen in rodding is a fenderless rod with semi-elleptic front springs, but it was common practice with old-time race cars.

This spring mounted at axle midpoint will have minimal effect on either wheel/tire, car stability will be suspect.

RIGHT - The coil/over shock and spring combination surfaced during the 1960s on race cars, these on a Jaguar rearend are now seen on just about every type of car, from race to street. Springs can be "stacked" by adjustments on shock bodies, and all kinds of different spring rates are available. The big advantage is in space and weight savings.

We showed this spring elsewhere as a part of the frame chapter, this overall shows how a single leaf semi-elleptic spring can be used. Locater bars will be advised with single leaf spring

at the torsion bars under some Japanese import pickups. They bolt to the back of the lower A-arm, and it takes very little imagination to see how they could be made to work with either independent or solid front ends (or rear ends). The entire ifs from these trucks could very well be adapted to earlier cars.

There is one kind of elliptic spring that sometimes is used in rodding, usually as a space consideration. It is most normally found at the rear, but it can be used at the front. The quarter-elliptic is simply a single semi-elliptic spring cut in half just behind the centerbolt. The big end of the spring is bolted to the frame rails (parallel) and the small end is bolted to the axle. Common mistake is to make this spring too short, resulting in a very firm ride. Early in American car production the quarter-elliptic was used at the front, and recently Dave Gale created some "hidden" front springs for his 1932 roadster by using quarters, mounted inside the front frame rails.

There is a growing tendency among the more sophisticated rod builders to try and hide as much suspension components as possible, starting with the springs. This has led to the use of cantilever A-arm designs, with the coil/springs mounted inside the frame rails (usually hidden by a grille shell or race car nose piece). This is not a new or unique idea, since it has been used by road racing cars for many years. Here, the inside of the A-arm extends beyond the mounting point at the frame and connects to the spring/shock. It can be a very effective system, but it does take a lot of planning.

One interesting offshoot of such a system is that either hydraulic or air suspension can also be used. Since the hydraulic designs are still rather uncommon, the air units offer the most promise to the exotic rod builder. These can be found on some of the older import cars, and some massive units are on trucks. You would probably have to work with a manufacturer to create a homebuilt air suspension system, but it does work, and quite well.

With any kind of spring, the idea is to connect the spring as close to the axle end as feasible. This way the slightest movement at the wheel immediately interacts with the spring. You want the spring action to be smooth, and to become increasingly stiff as the wheel moves upward from static condition.

The new generation of leaf springs (and probably the coil and torsion spring as well) will be made of some kind of non-metal, like the "plastic" spring in the Corvette. It would seem entirely feasible with current technology to make a multi-leaf plastic spring that would work very well in the older rods. The Corvette single leaf spring might even be adapted to the semi-elliptic design.

Shackles

Leaf springs and some torsion bar levers use shackles between spring and axle. This is to compensate for divergent arcs during wheel movement. The shackle looks very innocent, but it is a critical part of the entire suspension system.

The most common shackle is the Ford type. Original Ford units used a simple pair of steel shackle plates that located on square shafts which were rubber-encased inside spring eye and perch. These were press-fit shackle bolts, and they were poor at best. At least in comparison to modern units. You can still get the original Ford style shackles and bolts.

Trying to remove worn out Ford shackle bolts can be frustrating. Usually, the center bolt will just fall out, and often the rubber will be bad. If you can knock the rubber out, it burns easily enough with the torch. It is the outer housing that causes the problems, since this was a tight press fit to begin with, and it is probably rusted in place. Once the centerbolt and rubber are removed, it is usually possible to drive the remaining case out with a drift punch. If this doesn't work, insert a hacksaw blade inside the case and saw a line through the case. This will relieve the tension and then the case can be driven out easily. Don't get in a hurry and use the cutting torch, unless you are a master with the "heat wrench". If you are going to re-install the early Ford type shackle bolts, place the bolts in the freezer for a half-hour. Just before you are ready to install them, heat the spring eye and the perch.

Just enough to get them warm. They will expand, and the cold bolts will have contracted. Use a socket to drive the case, do not hammer on the threaded bolt.

The best shackles are those now available from mail-order houses, designed specifically for hot rods. These are shackle plates with the plate on one side welded to the bolts. The bushings for spring eye and perch are of synthetic material.

This is a very "slick" material, reducing friction to near zero, which is what you want in the front end. The old Ford type shackle bolts were designed to actually have a twist resistance. They were snubbers of a sort.

The same synthetic material is available for bushings in semi-elliptic springs/shackles, and should be used if the original shackle bolt was a rubber resistance type.

The shorter the shackle, the better. Years ago it was popular to use long shackles on Ford springs to lower the car, and on semi-elliptics, to raise the car (rearend). The longer the shackle, the greater the sway possible between chassis and suspension.

Shock Absorbers

The English call them Dampers, which is probably a better name. The function of a shock is to absorb upward movement, and dampen downward movement. The earliest shocks were simple friction devices, the current "airplane" type shocks are far from simple, and extremely effective.

The shock is a hydraulic unit. When force is applied (in either direction), fluid moves through orifices, or restrictors, to control rate of linkage movement. By adding a gas inside the sealed chambers, the movements can be controlled even better.

As mentioned earlier, the idea is to have a very limber springing system, with very little snubbing action at any of the suspension connections points. This is to allow the tires to stay in contact with the road surface as much as possible. Obviously, however, such a soft suspension will also allow the tires to be off the road a great deal as well. Enter the shock absorber.

By springing softly, or at least making the springing action smooth, you can now add stiffer shocks. For the hot rod, a set of adjustable shocks may even be in order. Off road racers will have 4 or more shocks at each wheel! The idea is to let the unsprung mass move, but you want to eliminate as much

The idea is to spring the vehicle softly, so that the wheels can move up and down readily without transmitting lots of force to the chassis, then use stiff shocks. This tube shock works going up or down.

The lever piston shock was common on a lot of American cars in the 20s and 30s, it is still used on many foreign imports, and it works very well on rods. Most are adjustable, and easily adapted to the older frame and suspension.

force transfer to the chassis as possible. This force can be upward, when the tire hits a bump, and downward as all the mass rebounds from the bump.

On most rods, the rear shocks will be much longer than the front units. Shorter front shocks were common on earlier Mopar vehicles, which gives you an idea of where to direct the parts man. The double loop mounting system is most common to the older rods, newer cars may use a combination loop and stud, or two studs.

When mounting shocks, place them at an angle, the top inboard of the bottom. This adds a bit of chassis sway control, and it applies to semi-elliptics as well as transverse springs. Yes, the semi-elliptic spring resists side sway by its very nature of design, but angling the shocks is more of a roll control than anything. Whatever, it works.

When you are setting up the chassis initially, and you have the front/rear axles in neutral position and the frame where it should be, the shocks mounting points can be determined. Find the mid-point of shock travel, then compress it slightly. This will give more rebound length than compression length. The suspension member should bottom out before the shock compresses completely. It is a trial and error situation, at best, but you can do most of the guesstimating with a tape measure before ever buying the shocks.

Use new shocks, don't rely on junkyard items. Whether you buy the super zoomie high performance shocks, the gas filled shocks, or the econo models is up to you. The better the shock, the better the vehicle handling, assuming you've set everything up properly.

The most common mistake is to use shock brackets that are too lightweight. Make the brackets at the frame and at the axle beefy! Mount the lower part of the shock as near the end of the axle as practical, since you want the maximum amount of wheel travel transferred directly to the shock.

Steering

Hot rod steering systems boil down to just two basic types: Worm and sector or rack and pinion. Of the two, the worm and sector is common on cars up until the 1970s, then the rack and pinion took over. Both work fine, but either must been in good working order, and either must be positioned carefully and mounted solidly.

The stock steering gearboxes for older cars must generally be replaced by better boxes. This is not always true, but it is always a consideration. The early Ford gearboxes were intended for narrow tires and wheels without offset. The Model A gearbox is marginal at best, even when in perfect condition. The 1932-34 gearboxes are hardly better. Starting in 1935, when Ford went to the cross steering system, the gearboxes improved, but even here the earlier "fat fender" boxes should be replaced with the 1946-48 gearboxes when possible. Steering for the GM and Mopar products follows a general theme quite similar to Ford, although these gearboxes were somewhat better in the early years.

For Ford, any of the drag link designs of pre-1935 can probably be replaced by much better boxes. The Ford pickups produced from the late 1940s through the late 1950s had drag link steering boxes that are almost bolt-in for the earlier Ford frames. The big difference is that these gearbox mounting flanges will not be at the same angle as the early Ford frames, so shims must be used between gearbox flange and frame. The pitman arms may need to be heated and reshaped for clearance, as well. Some of these pickup gearboxes have the steering shaft above the sector shaft, which means there may be clearance problems between the gearbox and a V8 exhaust header. Other gearboxes have the steering shaft below the sector, giving much more room. Both of these boxes are good, with ratios of about 20-1, both mount through the frame ala the original early boxes, and they are easily rebuilt.

There are lots of other drag link type gearboxes that you might find, but not all of them are modern design. But the Econoline (Ford) van and the Dodge van/pickup gearboxes of the last two decades are good places to start. The key is to make sure that the pitman arm goes in the correct direction. With some of these late model drag link boxes, the pitman arm moves the wrong way, meaning that the pitman arm would need to be mounted pointing up to get correct steering direction. And, some boxes are just too big to work on the earlier cars.

Some modern cross steering gearboxes can be turned on their side and mounted above/below the early Ford frame. The most common is the Mustang type, which mounts below the frame and the pitman arm points up. Others to consider would be Volkswagen and Volvo. Corvair boxes can be modified to work.

For drag link steering in the non-Ford chassis (those with semi-elliptic springs), the same Ford pickup gearbox works well, and zealous rodders wanting to stick with the same brand, often use a Chevy pickup steering box from the 1950s. The cross steering favorite for the lighter weight cars is Vega,

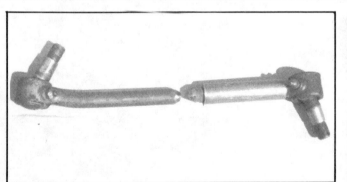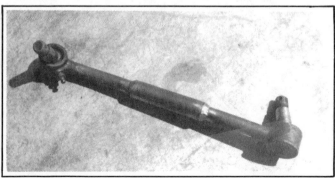

If it becomes absolutely imperative to cut a steering link, get professional welding. Here a drag link is cut and shortened, each end is beveled and welded, then the heavy-wall tubing is slipped over the weld and pinned/welded in place. You can never make steering cmmponents too strong.

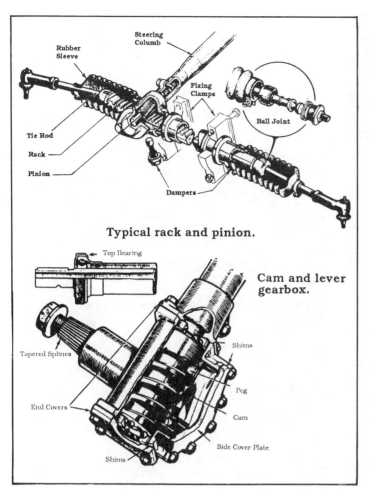

Typical rack and pinion.

Cam and lever gearbox.

and for heavier cars the GM Saginaw is the favorite (the bigger gearbox from intermediate size cars).

There are mail-order kits to mount these most popular gearboxes, or you can make up your own mounts. The key is to be sure the steering linkages are aligned as mentioned elsewhere.

If you are willing to do a bit of backyard engineering, you may want to look into the gearboxes in the import cars. Some of them are exactly the right size for a rod, especially the power boxes. What you are looking for is a box with small outer dimensions but strong enough for the weight and horsepower of your car. Very often overlooked is the role that horsepower will have on the steering gear. Increased power means increased loads will make it to the gearbox, during acceleration/deceleration/turning.

Power steering is not an absolute must for earlier rods, but as the cars get bigger and heavier, the power system begins to look better. The majority of rodders dismiss the power box because of the size of the pump. There are a lot of very small power pumps now showing up on new cars, and most of these use a remote reservoir.

With the gearbox steering, it is sometimes desirable to modify the pitman arm. The shorter the arm, the less movement of the front wheels, and vice versa. The shorter the arm, the less power must be applied to the steering wheel. The diameter of the steering wheel has an effect on the amount of effort needed to turn the gearbox. It all works together. Rule of thumb: The more turns lock-to-lock of the steering wheel, the slower the steering (the easier the steering). Power steering will usually have a longer pitman arm, or a faster gear ratio, than manual gearboxes. If you want to speed up the steering, the quickest way is to change length of the pitman arm.

If it is absolutely essential to cut and weld a pitman arm (remember that many pitman arms interchange, so you may be able to get the correct length at the junkyard), have it done

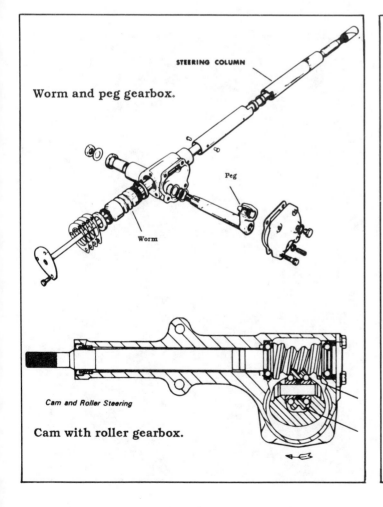

Worm and peg gearbox.

Cam and Roller Steering

Cam with roller gearbox.

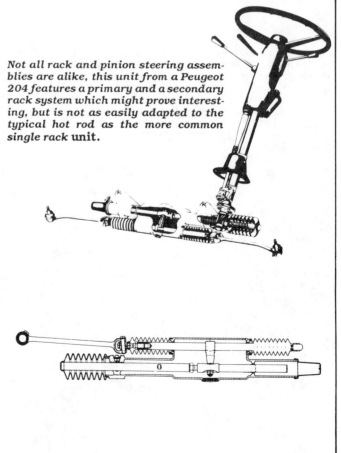

Not all rack and pinion steering assemblies are alike, this unit from a Peugeot 204 features a primary and a secondary rack system which might prove interesting, but is not as easily adapted to the typical hot rod as the more common single rack unit.

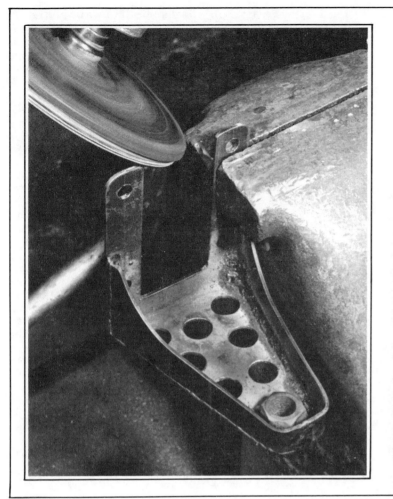

Spindle steering arms can be fabricated from sheet stock, but be sure everything is welded good and the gussets are strong, race cars do not have steering components chromed because they need to be magnifluxed often. There are various types of late model side steering gearboxes available, from the Ford Econoline vans to the Dodge vans and pickups. Sometimes the drag link side steering is much preferred over the cross chassis steering.

The drag link steering below is the simplest for most early Ford rods using solid axles, steering arms are available from most all street rod equipment suppliers. At the right is a unique approach, wherein the drag link steering gearbox is located beneath the T body, runs forward to an idler arm that works through the frame rail, then forward by a drag link to the front wheel.

by a professional. The arm is cut, then the pieces are beveled so that a very deep weld is made, in layers. Even then, you might want to have the welds X-ray'd for flaws. Another rule of thumb: Never weld on steering parts if you can help it.

The rack and pinion steering is not new, but it has only been used on American cars for the last few years. The r&p is a good system for rods, because it eliminates the clearance problems of a gearbox, but it must be mounted correctly. The idea is to mount the rack so that the rod ends move in concert with the suspension A-arms, otherwise bump steer will occur. Remove the suspension springs and move the wheel up and down as you try different rack mount positions. You'll quickly find the point where the least bump steer occurs.

Yes, it is possible to use different length arms on the rack, but remember that rack mounting position is the first consideration, then arm length can be changed. This would only happen when using a wheel track width different than what the rack & pinion assembly was original used on.

The power rack & pinion is a very good potential for the heavier rod, or for someone with arm or shoulder infirmities. It takes up only fractionally more room than the standard r&p, and it has very minimal feedback through the steering shaft.

Rack and pinion systems are designed to mount ahead of or behind the front axle centerline. If the original system mounts the rack ahead of the axle, as with the Mustang/ Pinto, you can do the same. Just remember that the Ackerman principle may not be available.

The rack and pinion can be used with a solid front axle, but the box must be mounted solidly to the axle. This way the tie rod length does not change as the wheels move up and down, causing severe bump steer. A sliding sleeve must be incorporated in the steering shaft, to compensate for different shaft lengths during wheel travel.

A rack and pinion can be mounted behind the traditional solid axle where the traditional tie rod is also used. This would be similar to the cross steering gearbox installation. The left end of the rack would not be used, and a longer rod would be used on the right end. Pivot point of the right end rod would be located similar to the cross steering linkage, to minimize bump steer. This is not as good as the conventional gearbox, however.

It is also possible to mount the rack and pinion parallel with the frame rail, running a tie rod forward to the left wheel, similar to traditional drag link steering. This has been done quite a bit, and it does seem to work. Again, the tie rod pivot point must coincide with the radius rod mounting point, otherwise b :mp steer is probable.

When hooking up the steering, either gearbox or r&p, be sure to center the steering. This is vital, since the systems are designed to add "weight" to the steering feel as you go either side of central. Set up the box in neutral position, then make the linkage fit. For tie rod ends, be sure that the majority of the rod end threaded section is inside the tubing, and that there is a jamb nut or clamp on the threaded area. A dab of thread Loc-Tite doesn't hurt. If the car is used for racing, safety wiring is even in order. Use cotter pins everywhere, for more safety.

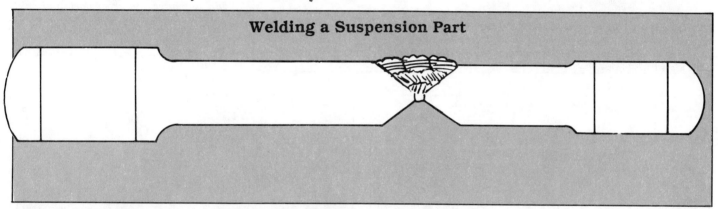

Welding a Suspension Part

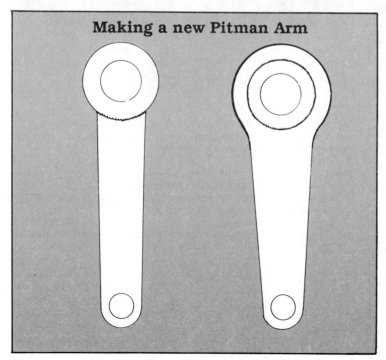

Making a new Pitman Arm

These drawings show how a pitman arm is cut and beveled prior to welding, in order to get maximum strength. Again, only a professional should make these welds. There are tremendous forces transmitted to the steering gear during ordinary road use of a vehicle, cars built for off-road use generally beef up the steering gear to a tremendous degree. When making new pitman arms, as at the left, from thick steel plate, it is possible to insert a stock arm splined top section. Either weld the splined piece to top of new arm (not recommended), or make it an insert, which is the strongest.

This is a good drag link steering mounting, with the gearbox tight against the frame and the drag link connection at the pitman arm in line with the radius rod rear location. A steering of this type will not have the cross-spring shackle induced bumpsteer that cross steering has, many contemporary rodders have gone to cross steering as a way to hide more of the suspension in the high-tech "clean" look.

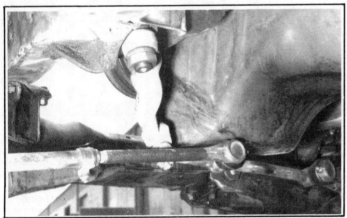

ABOVE LEFT - On the modern car with independent front suspension, the pitman arm connects to a cross link that will be segmented to eliminate bumpsteer.

ABOVE - This early rod chassis has a cross steering gearbox tucked onto the frame rail, the current popular cross steering box will be the Vega or the slightly larger Saginaw GM type from mid-size cars.

LEFT - This homemade independent front suspension uses an idler arm for the tie rods, which eliminate bumpsteer.

This car has a dropped front axle and a drag link gearbox mounted beneath the car body flooboards. Note how the drag link centerline passes through the wishbone mount centerline, and even though the drag link is at a severe angle, there is virtually no bumpsteer.

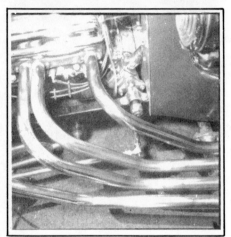

TOP - Ford pickup gearboxes from the late 40s and 50s adapt very well to early Ford frames. Some of the gearboxes have the steering shaft at the top of the box, which causes interference with exhaust manifolds on ohv V8 engines, others like this one have the steering shaft below the sector for more clearance.

ABOVE - If you have access to some of the older cars, you might find excellent drag link steering gearboxes that will adapt to your needs.

RIGHT - The steering arms at the spindles cause a lot of problem for some builders, if in doubt just check how the commercially available steering arms are made, and it may even be best to buy these arms.

Pahnard (Sway Bars)

Cars equipped with transverse springs and shackles, or coil springs, probably need a sway bar(s). This is especially true if a cross-steering is used.

When the transverse spring connects to the spring perches via shackles, the frame/body is free to sway back and forth over the axle slightly. This effect translates into some strange handling characteristics, and bump steer (with cross steering). The sway bar ties the frame directly to the axle, eliminating the sway.

The best sway bar is the longest possible, to reduce the arc divergence problem. Most late model cars have sway bars if coil springs are used, some American rearends have a form of sway control built into the locater bars, which angle between rearend and frame mount.

The sway bar should be mounted so that as the suspension member (axle) works up and down through the normal travel distance, the sway bar passes through level at the travel distance halfway point. If this doesn't happen, the sway bar will induce chassis shift and/or bump steer. Sway bars as found on 1948 or so Fords will have tie rod ends, the modern sway bar will probably have a rubber bushed end. Street rod equipment suppliers are making them with a synthetic insert.

A variation on the Panhard bar is the Wats link. Here, there is a pivot member attached to the axle. At the top of the pivot is a short rod running to one side, at the bottom point a rod runs to the opposite side. Same effect of keeping the side motion within acceptable limits. At the vehicle front, be sure the sway bar is parallel, as seen from the front, with the steering cross link.

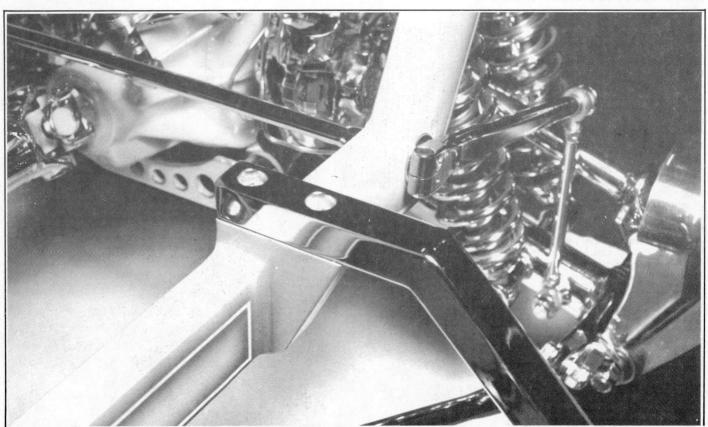

This is not a sway bar that limits axle sideways motion, but helps wheel travel control. These types of bars are used to improve vehicle handling.

Home Alignment

Once you have the suspension installed, all would seem well and good. It is...almost! Now, you must make the wheels roll true, and do what they should in a turn.

Leave the final wheel alignment to the professional shop. However, there is a bit of alignment that you can do at home to get things at least in the ball park. Since most projects are a long time from first movement to final driveaway, this initial alignment will help things considerably.

A note here: If you have an independent rear end, it is vital that this unit be aligned by the professional. Such systems have a lot to do with how the vehicle will handle, and they are not simply set with the wheels parallel to the chassis and vertical to the ground.

Rear end alignment is supposed to be right on the money if you have measured carefully when attaching all the mounting brackets. Quite often it is. But to find out, measure diagonally from the leading edge of the rear end housing at the outer brake backing plate flange, to some known point on the opposite frame rail, well forward. If the frame has measured square, then this will give exact true to the rear end. Measure across the chassis from the rear end housing flange to make absolutely sure the rear end is centered under the frame. If the rear end must be moved, now is the time to do it.

Front end alignment is similar. The axle at the spindle should measure identical on a diagonal to a frame point. Adjustment at the radius rod mount(s) or the A-arm mounts will bring this into "square". Now, lay the kingpin inclination backward until there is about 5 degrees caster in the spindle.

The wishbone/4-bar setup can be adjusted, and shims are available to be placed between A-arm mounts and the A-arm itself. Since there are a number of different adjustments in the A-arm system, ask the front end professional for adjustment points with your particular system.

Wheel camber, or the amount the wheel leans in at the bottom versus the top, is not important at this time, although a sighting down the wheel line from in front should show the bottom in slightly from the top.

If you have decent caster, and the camber is usable, then the only other factor is toe-in/toe-out. Measure across the wheels from one side to the other, using a tire sidewall or tread mid-point as reference. Generally speaking, at this early stage something like 3/8-inch toe-in will work. That is, the measurement across the front of the tires will be closer together by 3/8-inch than measuring the same place at the rear of the tires. If you do not have a toe-in or toe-out factor in the front end, you'll feel a lot of shimmy in the steering.

Trying to measure the rear of the tires is a problem (as is the fronts if there is sheet metal in the way), a quick solution is to tape plumb bob weights to the center of the tire, front and rear, then measure from these (near the floor).

Sometimes no amount of toe-in work seems to remove shimmy from a front end, especially one using a solid front axle. Try up to 1/2 -inch toe-out. This often cures the problem. Of course, shimmy can also be caused by excessive play in the kingpin bushings, or excess play in the tie rod ends. Also check the steering gearbox for wear.

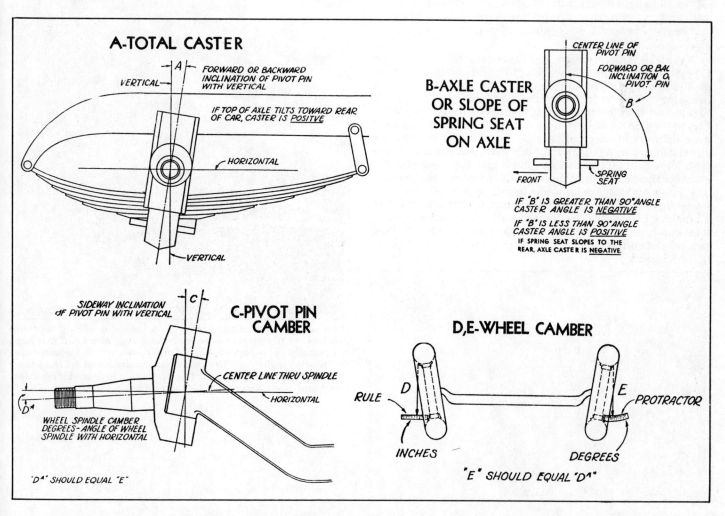

Steering Shafts

Some kind of modification to the steering shaft is very common in hot rodding. This is also no place to take chances. Any welding should be by a professional, and the weld/pinned system is even better.

Normally, it is a matter of shortening the steering shaft. Some shafts have a splined end, others have a flat on one side. If it is a flat, simply cut the shaft to length and file on a new flat. If the shaft is splined, cut the shaft to length by taking a section out above the spline, taper the shaft ends, and weld. Over this a sleeve is placed, and pinned in place. Double protection. Most modern steering boxes use just a short shaft at the box, then connect to the steering shaft with either an isolation biscuit or a universal joint.

The isolation biscuit is flexible and will allow for some shaft misalignment. If there is considerable alignment problem, use a U-joint, but be sure the joint is strong enough. Use a joint from a steering system if possible, or something from a mail-order house that has been designed for steering. If two universal joints are necessary (try to avoid this), the short intermediate shaft may need to be located with a pillow block bearing. This is available at most bearing supply stores or farm stores.

The type of steering shaft used is a personal matter, although most rodders like to get as small a shaft mast jacket as possible. Most American cars use a large mast jacket assembly, the exceptions being some of the small economy models and some vans/pickups. Some mast jackets also come without the ignition key as a part of the mast jacket. There are mail-order custom mast jackets available, or you can make up your own. The problem will be in identifying the zillion wires that seem to be part of every modern steering jacket. Eliminate every wire that you don't need.

The steering shaft shifting mechanixm can be retained or removed, as needed, and the mast jacket can be cut to length. It should reach through the flooring, and not much beyond.

U-Joints

When it is not possible to make a nearly straight shot from steering wheel to steering gearbox, some kind of alignment device must be used. This will be in the form of flexible coupling (which is not a universal joint, and should not be used as one!) for very slight misalignment, or a special steering shaft U-joint.

Not all U-joints are alike, yet this is one place where the experienced rod builder is as likely to make a serious mistake as the neophyte. The key to a steering universal joint is breaking torque in foot/pounds. Yes, universal joints will break, and the steering shaft is a very danger ous place for this to happen. A U-joint from a tractor, or something used on a lightweight race car may be too weak for the heavier street driven car. A fairly good guide to U-joint strength starts with joint diameter in inches. The bigger the diameter, the stronger the joint should be. This isn't a guarantee, so make absolutely certain you know the breaking point of a joint. As an example, a 1-inch diameter (1/2-inch socket set drive) has a breaking point of 261 foot pounds. a 1 1/2-inch diameter U-joint can have between 406 and 1034 foot pounds breaking points, depending upon construction quality and type of material used.

Here are two unusual attempts to locate a strong steering gearbox. In the photo above, note how the frame rail has been drastically cut away, making it much weaker and susceptable to failure. At the left, the gearbox was mounted on the frame ahead of the axle centerline (as with some late model pickups/vans) and two universal joints used in the steering shaft.

The steering shaft can be twisted in two, as well. A 3/4-inch shaft of low carbon steer will shear at about 340 foot pounds of torque, which is more than what a typical man can apply with A 14-inch steering wheel. But cut the shaft size to 5/8-inch and the strength is cut by almost half! most men can't ist such a shaft in half. The average production car uses a shaft plenty big enough to overcome this problem, so when building a rod keep this shaft size and U-joint size in mind. Also consider whether or not the U-joint has needle bearings. Such a joint is lubricated, and can be covered with a boot. Other joints may not be lubricated, and should definitely be lubed very often, and also covered with a boot. Very few rodders are using the boots.

When two universal joints are used on a steering shaft, the forks of the yokes nearest each other should be aligned. Do not put the U-joints out of phase. There should be no bind in the steering shaft rotation. The angle of any single U-joint should never exceed 30 degrees. If you have an angle sharper than this, use two joints.

Don't take a chance with any portion of the steering system. For universal joints, contact the mail-order houses advertising joints and get their recommendations (keeping breaking torque in mind).

Rearends

The rearend selected for your particular hot rod project should be capable of handling the engine power, and it should be reasonably easy/simple to install. The more complex the rearend componentry becomes, the more susceptible it is to problems and failure. The rearend should be common enough so that parts will be available in years to come, which may rule out using something that is already 30 or 40 years old.

Whether you use a solid or independent rear suspension is a matter of personal choice, but there are some guidelines for selection. The reason for using an independent rear end is to lower unsprung weight, change vehicle roll center, and (too often), look cool. The reason for using a solid rearend is cost, simplicity, and availability.

The solid rearend is absolutely practical, but only insofar as the unit selected and the method of suspension. For most rodders, the rearend to use is a matter of cost. The Ford 9-inch rear is certainly the most popular with the performance oriented crowd, but it is not easy to find and it is getting more expensive. A big Mopar unit is the least popular, least expensive, and most available. Somewhere in between are the Chevy units that so many builders are using.

If you are going to build a car that has lots of horsepower, and may see occasional drag racing use, you want to start with a big rearend. Something like the big Ford or Chrysler unit, or the big Chevy rear. If you can find a rearend that will work, and has the same wheel bolt pattern as the front hubs, that is a plus. But it is no big deal to drill the rearend hub flanges for any bolt pattern.

If you are sure the car is not going to see heavy race use, then you can go with a lighter rearend, or you can make suspension mounts that will make it easy to install the bigger rearend at a later date.

When selecting a rearend, try and find one that will position the wheels/tires under the fenders. Car styling is a matter of proportion and balance, and nothing so ruins the appearance of a car as do huge tires sticking way out from the fender line. This is why builders of the Pro-Street type car go to such great pains to tuck all the tire under the wheel wells. Therefore, haul out the tape measure before buying a rearend.

Measure the distance between the outside edges of the frame rails at the rear, where the tires will fit. You will need to leave enough working room between the inside wall of the tire and the frame/wheel well. Remember that the car will tend to roll and shift slightly sideways on corners, so if you figure a minimum of 2 inches, and 3 inches is better, clearance you will be in the ball park. Some builders work with only 1 1/2-inches, but this assumes a very low roll factor to the chassis. The tires will have some sidewall bulge,

This is a Jaguar rear end in the original factory housing. Some rodders include the Jag and Corvette housing in the earlier frame, most make up their own mounts.

This rearend is an open drive unit from a late model, has spring perches for early Ford cross leaf and radius rod perches added.

This semi-elleptic sprung rear end has a hefty tubing torque control bar added to eliminate rearend wind-up on acceleration.

LEFT - The Jag and Corvette independent rearends require locater bars, these bars are best made adjustable unless commercial units are used (which have been pre-set by the manufacturer). This is especially critical with the Corvette unit, which must have alignment adjustments as critical as a front end.

RIGHT - Building the frame for an independent rear suspension calls for more design considerations than for conventional rearends.

This Jaguar rearend has been installed beneath a late model pickup truck.

This is a Corvette rearend under an older frame, using as much original equipment as possible.

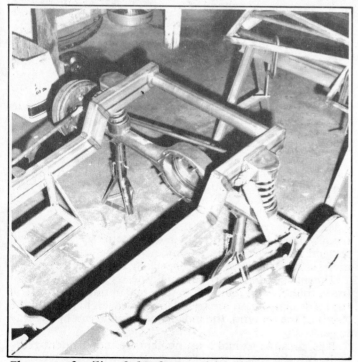

The more familiar fad-T frame with coil springs atop the rearend housing, hairpin radius rods, and a sway bar.

especially if radials are used, so this must be figured in. Be sure and give plenty of room between the tire outer wall and the fender lip.

When you have the frame width, figure in the extra width needed for tire clearance by noting how much offset the intended wheel will have. This is how much the wheel overhangs the rearend flange.

Usually, rearend width is noted as flange-to-flange, the flanges being the surface the backing plates are bolted to. As a general rule, early cars can use a rearend with a flange-to-flange measurement of around 52 inches. Rearends for large American cars will usually run from 57 inches out to over 60 inches. The Chevy II rearend has the narrow measurement, as do the smaller Ford and Mopar products, but these rearends also tend to be smaller in the ring/pinion gear area. So what you end up looking for are the small car rearends that were used behind higher performance engines. Or you realize that such a rearend is not the ultimate racing unit, and drive accordingly.

The smaller later model cars will also require the narrow rearends, or larger units that have been cut down to size.

The large rearends can have the axles and housings shortened to any width. Most any machine shop can do this job, although there may be problems with splining the axles. The large ring/pinion rear ends will also have larger diameter axle shafts. If the shaft necks down in diameter just inboard of the splines, it cannot be resplined easily. If the rearend has the third member housing offset to one side, often the shorter shaft can be used on a shortened off-side housing. But the shaft length is the limiting factor as to how much such a rearend can be narrowed.

There are mail-order machine shops that can narrow and modify rearends, and the cost is not huge. This may be the way to go, especially if you are going to do a lot of welding on the axle housing for new spring hangers or locater bars.

When you weld on the housing tubes, the heat causes distortion. Often this distortion is enough to pull the housing out of alignment. Rule of thumb: If you have to force the axle back into the housing, it is out of alignment. If it is not straightened, the bent housing will cause certain axle bearing failure.

You can buy spring hanger kits to use an open-drive rearend under a 1948 or earlier Ford with transverse spring. When this is done, you must also use rear end locater bars to counteract torque windup of the housing. If the rearend is to

When rearends are welded on, the housing will often warp out of alignment. If the axles must be forced back into place, the axle tube is warped and should be sent to a rearend specialist for repairs/straightening. Failure to do this is a sure way to accelerate bearing failure.

This homemade independent rearend uses unequal length arms, the locating arms are tubing with Heim ends, when using such ends there will be a variety to select from, some with grease fittings.

be located with semi-elliptic springs, these locater bars are not necessary, but if drag racing is anticipated, short torque bars may still be needed. If the rearend is located under coil springs, locater bars are necessary.

If you are building an older Ford rod, and anticipate using the stock or stock type rearend, be prepared to change twisted off axles often. These rearends are not very strong, even behind a hopped up flathead Ford engine they tend to break. They are ok until you get on the throttle too hard.

When mounting the open drive rearend, adjust the housing so that the pinion shaft flange is at the exact same angle as the transmission output shaft. This will get the universal joints in phase. Use shims under semi-elliptic springs, or get the angle right and then make the mount welds.

If there is any indication at all that any of the rearend seals have been leaking, replace them before installing the completed unit. And make sure the housing breather tube is unobstructed.

Some late model rearends come with rather beefy locating arms, either 3 or 4, and often one or two of these arms lead forward at an angle (for controlling sidesway). These rearends are used with coil springs. It is possible to use these locating arms, especially under any of the fat fender rods or late

models, but be sure the locating mounts at the frame are in the same position as on the original chassis.

Unless semi-elliptic springs are use ,the rear end must be located with a sway bar to eliminate sideways movement.

The two most common types of independent rear ends used by rodders are the Corvette and the Jaguar. Neither is the perfect width, although the "Vette is closer for older cars than is the big Jag car.

Kits are available for mounting these rearends to many older chassis, rodders who use them under the newer cars usually have to fabricate their own mounts. It must be remembered that these rearends must be adjusted by a professional front end shop, especially the Corvette unit.

The independent rearend usually needs slightly more axle travel than a solid rearend, to take maximum advantage of the irs design. If you are trying to get a car right down in the weeds at the rearend, the independent might not be the way to go.

It is possible to make up homemade independent rearends, but the cost is usually more than what a Corvette or Jaguar would be. Other independent rearends are available, some are terribly expensive (Mercedes) and some are too small for the average American V8 (the Japanese imports).

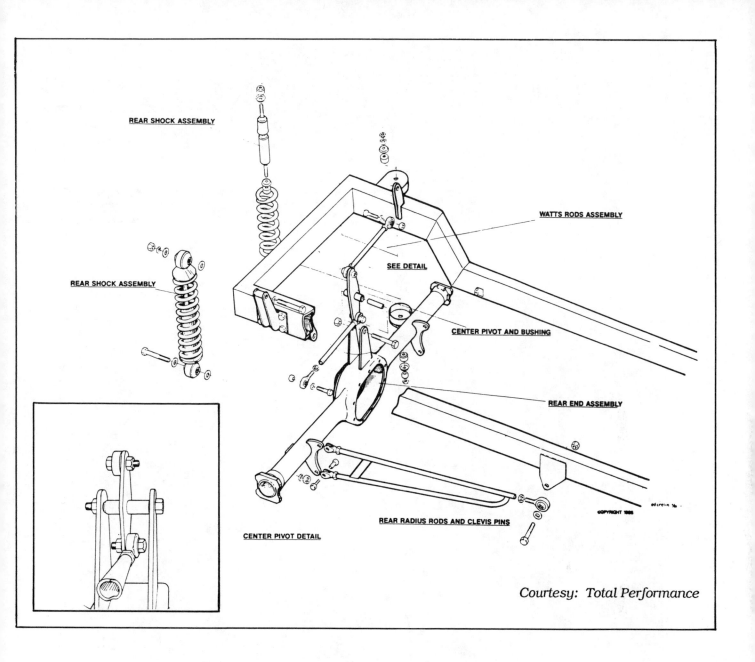

REAR SHOCK ASSEMBLY

WATTS RODS ASSEMBLY

SEE DETAIL

REAR SHOCK ASSEMBLY

CENTER PIVOT AND BUSHING

REAR END ASSEMBLY

COPYRIGHT 1985

REAR RADIUS RODS AND CLEVIS PINS

CENTER PIVOT DETAIL

Courtesy: Total Performance

Making Driveshafts

Almost always you will need to make up a driveshaft, but before you head for the machine shop, do some measuring. There is a huge selection of driveshaft lengths available, and surprisingly, there is a great deal of universal joint interchangeability. For example, the Volvo universal is a standard Chevrolet item.

You know the type of rearend you have, and you know the type of transmission. Measure the distance from the rear of the trans output shaft to the centerline of the rearend pinion yoke. This will get you to within 3 or 4 inches of the shaft length you need. Now shop the junkyards. Ask what universal joint might interchange with the shaft and your rearend. Sometimes it is a drop-in. If you are lucky, you'll find a shaft that fits.

If you must have a shaft made, plan on it costing from $60-$150 dollars. Most communities have machine shops that

will do driveshafts. Find a shaft that has a yoke to fit the transmission. Slide the yoke up to about where it has been running (the signs on the yoke are unmistakable), or roughly half the length of the splines before the yoke bottoms out. Now, measure the distance from the center of the yoke U-joint to the center of the pinion shaft yoke. This is the distance the the machine shop will need.

They will cut and fit the tube (or install a new tube) with a yoke that will fit the rearend. Have the shaft balanced while you are at it.

You do not cut a driveshaft in two and butt weld the pieces to the length you need! This might be ok for a dune buggy, but it doesn't cut it on a street car.

If you are building a car with lots of horsepower, be sure and use the bigger universal joints, and use a larger diameter driveshaft tube.

CHAPTER 4

WHEELS & TIRES

An automobile is nothing but a platform to which is attached a form of power and a number of wheels/tires. Such a simple explanation for such a complex piece of machinery.

The wheels used on a hot rod seem to be the very signature by which the owner wants to be known. They can be flashy to the point of eye strain, or sublimely subtle. The variety of wheels available is so great that most rodders actually have a problem deciding upon the units they want. Much of this decision rests on cost.

The so-call "mag" wheel is not really magnesium at all. Racing cars use magnesium alloy wheels because they are so lightweight. However, they aren't suitable for street use, since they are also subject to fierce fires. Nor are they known for longevity under normal driving conditions (curb damage, etc). "Mag" wheels are really aluminum wheels that just happen to be patterned after the racing car design.

There is some interesting research being done into graphite composite wheels, but for the moment the only wheels available are aluminum (magnesium if you are truly brave!), aluminum/steel combination, steel disc, and wire spoke.

The interesting thing about aluminum wheels, at least those made in America, come from only an handful of aluminum foundries. The wheel manufacturer/marketer will contract with the foundry to make up a specific design blank, then this blank will be taken to a machine shop where the final machining turns a rough casting or forging into the finished product.

Some aluminum wheels are really castings, others are true forgings, with the difference being that an aluminum forging is far and away superior in strength. It will also be a wheel that is far and away more expensive. It is not uncommon to find wheels that now cost $1000 or more each! These are really specialty items, and they appear more on the show rods than on the road runners.

The more common aluminum wheels will also have a wide

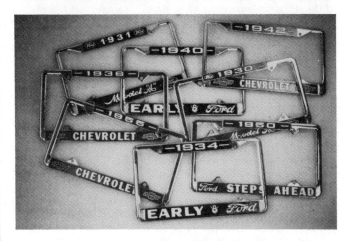
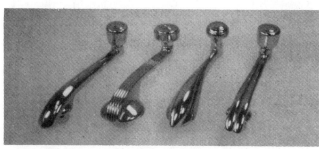
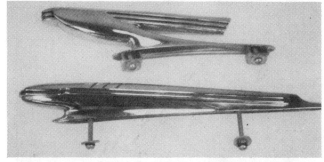

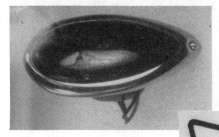

Hot rod wheels can be just about anything, so long as they are personal. Most alloy wheels are cast by a handful of foundaries and then machined to specifications by various brand names. While this rod with spoke alloy wheels may look wild, the absence of front brakes makes it a marginal street driver, as would the drag racing slicks on wide alloy wheels at the rear.

range of price, depending upon what is "hot" at the moment. A visit to any hot rod trade show will uncover a vast number of wheel merchants, and each marketer will have a full line of wheels aimed at a wide spread of buyers.

Aluminum wheels will be available in a variety of widths, what you select will be a personal preference. Some aluminum wheels have multiple wheel bolt patterns for the most popular applications, others have slotted bolt holes and must have special lug bolts. All aluminum wheels need periodic inspection and maintenance.

A sharp nick in the rim of an alloy wheel can grow into a disastrous crack, so grind or file such nicks smooth, with rounded corners. Do not remove too much material and thus create a weak spot. If there is a suspicion of cracks, use a special metal penetrant dye check. Do not use any alloy wheel that is cracked.

Most production aluminum wheels include shiny machined surfaces and rough cast surfaces. The wheels may be painted, if not they should be kept clean so that any cracks that may appear will be spotted. Cracks are not common, however.

Do not overtighten an aluminum wheel, since this easily cracks the hub section, and be sure to use the lug nuts designed for that specific wheel! Do not use the tapered base lug nuts intended for the steel or spoke wheel. Most aluminum wheel lug bolts include a thick washer, to prevent wheel galling.

A very common mistake by rodders is to select an aluminum wheel that is too wide, one that has too much offset to the outside. The "deep" look is nice, but it will often play havoc with wheel bearings (front and rear) and usually has a negative effect upon vehicle handling. While an 8-inch wide rear wheel may not be too bad, that same excess offset at the front can really mess up the steering geometry. This applies to late model cars as well as early models.

Early Cadillac wire wheels were once a big favorite with rodders, before the wide variety of currently available wire wheels came on the market. The earlier wires are still good, may be bargain priced.

The early Fords have a steering geometry that places the pivot point of the kingpin directly at the centerline of the tire where the tire hits the pavement. In this configuration, the vehicle is easily controlled by the stock steering. If the wheel is offset to the outside, and the pivot point of the kingpin is then inboard of the tire centerpoint, steering gets harder. Some later model cars have the steering designed for a wheel offset, the most convenient way to figure this out is to find a stock car and do some quick checks. Of course, wheel diameter also will affect this particular aspect of the steering.

Wire spoke wheels are popular, but usually not in original form. In wheel evolution, the first wheels were wood spokes, which gave way to wire spokes, then the pressed steel disc came on the scene. From a production standpoint, the pressed wheel is much cheaper to produce. From a maintenance standpoint, the steel wheel is better, as well. But the spoke wheel is very strong.

The wire spoke wheels seen on Fords, Chevys, and Mopars of the very late 20s and early 30s are generally of the welded variety. The spokes are welded to the hub and the rim. An adjustable spoke wheel is more of a custom item, and if you find some that fit your car, and are of the correct size, you better check into what you have. Wire spokes will come in a variety of diameters, from very large through the more common Ford Model A units of 21 inches down to some specialty wires of 15-inch diameter. For the most part, the 15-inch wires are rare, and highly desirable.

A wire spoke that is adjustable must have a wheel liner (rubber) to keep the spokes from working holes in inner tubes. The current crop of specialty wire wheels do not use inner tubes, since most of them are of the welded spoke design. Adjustable wire wheels will (and do) loosen. Sports car wires are notorious for loosening. Usually the owner can make maintenance adjustments at home, but if the wires are adjusted incorrectly the rim will almost always become

A torque wrench is not a bad idea when installing or tightening alloy wheels.

Wheels went through considerable design changes during the late 1920, and early 1930s, sometimes it is possible to find wild 15 inch aftermarket items that will fit modern bolt patterns. For the most part, however, these earlier wheels will be too large and too narrow.

crooked. The only solution then is to visit a wheel/tire shop with experience on such wheels. Not a neat condition. A loosely adjusted wire wheel will usually squeak, especially when cornering.

The early type wire wheel has not maintained popularity with rodders because the rim is now too narrow. Also, the most common 16-inch wheel doesn't fit readily available tires. Sometimes these wheels are modified by professionals, the spokes being cut down for a wider 15-inch or 14-inch rim.

The modern specialty wire wheel will be of the double or triple-lace variety, meaning the number of rows of spokes, as seen looking straight down on the wheel. The spoke wire size will vary, with the ultra-zoomie sports car wire being very thin. As a rule, the heavier the car the heavier the spoke wire size, and the number of spokes total.

Most spoke wheels are chromed, although they can be ordered in plain steel for later painting. Cleaning of the wire spoke wheel seems to be the biggest complaint by owners, a soft cylindrical brush makes an excellent cleaning implement. If disc brakes are used, spoke wheels tend to get dirty very fast.

The disc wheel is such a simple device that any kind of radical design change is difficult. Currently, there is a trend to use of the disc wheel again, since so many hot rods are using aluminum wheels that it is hard to have something different. Ever since the aluminum wheels became so prominent, any car with a steel disc wheel is usually given a second thought as to performance. The very, very serious hot rodders tend to build cars that seem to be ordinary passenger cars. Except for the wheels. These "sleepers" will need wheels with better than average tires, usually wider rubber. Such an ultra performance hot rod in peasant clothing may include small hubcaps, and it may not have any caps.

There is a wide variety of steel wheels available for almost every passenger car made, some wide enough so that no modifications are necessary. Some GM performance cars have wheels approaching 8-inch width, for example. For some rod builders, the problem is finding a wheel with a narrow enough rim (4-inch front rims are popular, with some designs). Chevy Rallye wheels have special design, but much of the character is lost if the chrome trim ring is not used. Mopar police car wheels are drilled with holes in the hub (better brake cooling), and the hubcaps are also drilled, giving a lean and mean appearance.

The majority of modern steel wheels have the hub welded to the rim, which means that wheel modification is pretty much something that must be left to the professional machine shop. Older riveted Wheels can be modified at home. Putting a wide Buick 15-inch rim on a set of 15-inch early Ford rims is an example. The rivets are cut loose with a chisel, and the rim is welded to the Ford hub.

Welded wheels are cut apart on a large lathe, and then welded with a MIG welder. If the rim needs to be widened, it is .possible to cut the rim apart (on the lathe), and insert a piece of metal however wide, then weld the rim together again. This is a very common practice in farm communities, and with dune buggy builders. A better way is to cut a pair of rims apart, in such a manner that only one circumference weld is necessary to get the rim width desired.

When using any wheel, be sure there is nothing on the hub face that will interfere with the wheel fitting snug. If there is something, perhaps a bolt head, drill a clearance hole in the wheel. Do not overtorque lug nuts, as this can/does warp wheels and brake drums/hubs.

Proportions

There is a very definite roll between wheel/tire size and overall vehicle proportion. The "rubber rake" has be come synonymous with hot rodding, larger tires on the back, small tires up front.

Early on in rodding, this was a carryover from circle track and lakes racers. The large rear tires were used to get both traction and gear ratio. But these were on 5 1/2 to 7-inch rims in the back, with stock 4 1/2 rims on the front. Very narrow tires. When the wide tires started to appear, they showed on rods as much as any other car. Interestingly, the wide tires never caught on for the front, but they did at the rear. In a major way. Too much so, it seems.

For early rods, those using clamshell fenders (meaning 1948 and earlier, as a general rule), it seems that the maximum rear tire diameter of 29-30 inches is about right. A width of 7-8 inches seems to work good. The wheels are usually 15-inch. In front, the tire diameter is about 24-25 inches, normally, with a 5-6 inch width. Since the tire diameter is much smaller, it is possible to use 14-inch front wheels and make the proportions even better.

On late model cars, those produced. after 1948, only a slightly larger diameter rear tire seems to look good, but it can be wide, up to 10 inches or so, and still work. The front tire can be wider, but at both ends the tire should stay within the body/fender lines. Most states have laws that tires may not extend beyond the body, but from a purely styling sense, most rodders agree that the tires should be inside the body. This may mean some fenderwell modifications in back. Usually not much, unless the Pro-Street look is being sought.

This car has a traditional look accentuated by the Ford 15-inch spokes front and back, and whitewall tires. These Ford wires are now getting high priced at the swap meets, although they can often be found on farm wagons in rural areas. The wide whites are not yet availble in radials, and radials make a tremendous difference in the way a hot rod rides and handles. Tire proportions, front to back, is a very important factor in hot rod design, for fenderless and fendered cars as well. Front tires in the 24-25 inch diameter seem most popular, rears are from 29-31 inches diameter.

Bolt Patterns

The neat thing about wheels is that they either fit...or they don't. There is interchangeability in wheels, but remember that while the bolt pattern may be the same, the lug nut taper may differ. It is a small thing, but you should be aware of this fact. Which is why the lug nuts may keep working loose on your trick set of steel wheels.

To measure the bolt pattern, measure from one stud across the wheel to the farthest away stud opposite. Normally, the distance will be anywhere from 4 to 5 inches. You may be able to find a wheel interchange chart somewhere, but since these go out of date with the introduction of each new year's cars, get practice at measuring wheels. One outstand-

ing tool for measuring bolt patterns is the Ident-A-Wheel measuring caliper (5290 S. Helena Hwy, Napa, California, 94558 for information). This tool has two tapered locaters on a sliding scale, and when the locaters are registered in the wheel holes, you simply read the scale to find what cars have similar wheel bolt patterns.

Even though the bolt patterns may be the same, the center register hole may be smaller, or larger. This is important, because this register hole fits snugly over an axle flange on some cars. Also, some axle flanges will have a pin locater that sticks through a register hole in the wheel. Solution is to drill a hole in the wheel to match.

Axle flanges can be drilled for different wheel bolt pattern providing there is enough diameter.

Stock drum will have a basic bolt pattern and can easily be drilled with a new pattern.

Use a special jig, or axle flange as a drilling guide on the drum, center hole is alignment guide.

Here is the drum with old and new bolt patterns. This can be done at home on drill press.

Now the redrilled axle flange and the newly drilled hubs can be mated with different wheels.

Use top grade bolts, or lug bolts for the axle flange, make sure wheel fits drum flush.

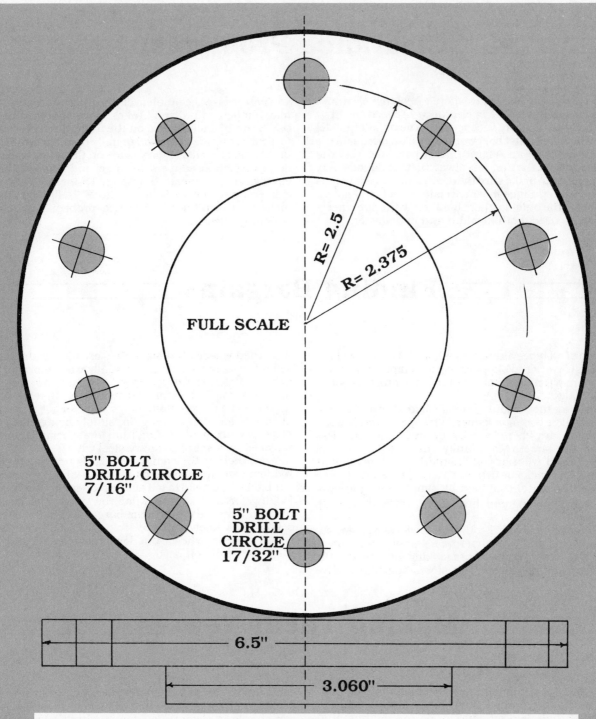

R= 2.5

R= 2.375

FULL SCALE

5" BOLT
DRILL CIRCLE
7/16"

5" BOLT
DRILL
CIRCLE
17/32"

6.5"

3.060"

Special thanks to Laurie Teichrow and the Canadian Street Rod Association for information on redrilling axles/hubs. Start by finding the center of the hub, cardboard works fine for a template. Fromtthis center, make a circle the diameter you want. Now get the straight line distance between the center of any two holes. To find the straight line distance multiply the circle diameter by the number that follows:

4 holes——0.707107
5 holes——0.587785
6 holes——0.500000
8 holes——0.382683

Suppose this is a Chevy wheel, 5 bolt pattern with a 4.75-inch bolt circle diameter. Multiply the bolt circle 4.75 X 0.587785 and you get 2.793, rounded to 2.80. Start at any point on your cardboard template and mark off a distance of 2.80, then from this point repeat the 2.80 and you should end up smack dab back at the starting point, with centerpoints for the 5 new bolt holes

Clearance Problems

There are usually two areas where wheel/tire clearance problems surface. One is clearance between the tire and body parts. This is especially true on later model cars. If the wheel well must be reworked to allow adequate tire clearance, do not leave any jagged or sharp metal edges. You can bet these will cut the tire! It is always best to do some very careful measuring to make sure the desired wheel/tire combo will clear the fender. Since most specialty wheels will have a positive offset to the outside, there is a limit to the size wheel/tire than can be used, both in width and in diameter.

There is also the problem of wheel-to-brake clearance. This may happen with drum brakes, particularly when trying to use 13 or 14-inch wheels on the front. A radical wheel offset to clear the brake drum will usually result in strange steering problems, as well as heavy loads on the outer wheel bearing. Some disc brake calipers are large, and there can be interference with the wheel. Almost all 15-inch wheels will clear calipers, not so with 14-inch wheels. Definitely not with 13-inchers. Keep these clearance problems in mind when selecting wheels.

Finding Bargains

Wheels of all types aluminum, spoke, disc are available through every rod shop and speed emporium. But there are alternative sources that may prove a boon to the budget builder.

Junkyards are the obvious source, where disc and aluminum wheels will be common fodder. Wire spoke wheels won't be as common anywhere, simply because they are less common on the street. Most junkyards will do a casual inspection of used wheels, you should be very meticulous when looking for cracks or bends. You can get a pretty good indication of disc wheel condition by simply rolling it away from you and watching the hub. Bent wheels show up quickly.

Not such a common wheel source is the local gas station. Look around back, and you often find a pair of aluminum or special wheels. Know what you are looking for, because the station owner may not know. Tire stores sometimes have discarded wheels, but since they are also in the business of selling custom wheels, they usually want more for the used items. Watch the newspaper for wheel/tire bargains, and don't overlook abandoned cars. At least, cars that don't appear to be driven. Sometimes you can get an excellent set of wheels for a super bargain, simply by agreeing to install some replacements; aluminum or special factory wheels replaced by a set of ordinary steel wheels.

And, there is the chance of picking up wheels from other rodders who are making changes (or who have some spares out back). You need to tell all the rodders in your area you are looking for wheels, and what you need. The local market bulletin board also unearths bargains. Finally, let the high school kids know you are looking. Sometimes they know where there are wheels, but don't know exactly what they are. Might be what you need.

Making Them New

While there is not much reconstruction that can happen to the wheel, other than what a professional might do, there is a lot you can do to the aluminum wheel at home. In the area of clean-up renovation. The neat thing about aluminum wheels is that they start to look really scaggy if they are not cleaned often, and this tends to drive down the cosmetic impact. Translation: They look terrible so they usually don't cost much. It is very common to find a good set of aluminum wheels for about $10 each.

Soap and water, or possibly some aniline or paint thinner, will do wonders for initial aluminum wheel clean-up. A quick cleaning of the machined surfaces with a steel wool pad will sometimes be all that is needed to make things shiny again. But if you want the wheels to look absolutely new, polish the machined surfaces. You can find buffing compounds at the parts store sometimes, or you can get complete buffing equipment through mail-order houses that advertise in the rod magazines (Eastwood has an excellent buffing kit!)

The interesting part of cleaning up a set of aluminum wheels is that it often leads to a rather lucrative business! You can buy the discarded wheels cheaply, put in several hours labor, and then get from $50 to $100 a wheel resale. Or you can charge to clean-up customer wheels. If you should get into this business, you will soon upgrade your equipment.

Don't even mess around trying to sand a steel wheel for repaint. Go ahead and strip the paint completely, either by sandblasting or with a chemical stripper. Nothing looks quite so amateurish as a wheel that has been improperly prepared for paint. When you have a wheel painted, go ahead and ask for the two-part urethane paints. They resist chips far better than regular paint, and you can get a decade from a single paint job. Yes, you can paint the wheels at home with pressurized spray cans, but they will not hold up to rocks as well. Wheels can also be powder coated for long finish life.

The Footprint

How much traction a given tire will have is a factor of how much tire is in contact with the road. This area is called the footprint, and it is one of the reasons the radial tire is so much superior to other styles. The greater the footprint, the better handling the car will have (usually).

It is in matching the tire footprints, front and rear, where so many rodders get into deep trouble. There is a reason racing sports cars have nearly the same size rubber on front as on the back. In some rare instances, the front tire(s) is even bigger than in the rear. Traction at the front is essential to proper car handling (and safety).

Perhaps the worst possible offender of tire proportion is the fad T with huge drag racing slicks on the back and motorcycle rubber in front. Everything wrong that can possibly be done wrong is in this design. First, no drag racing slick should be used on the highway...because streets get wet, and drag slicks were never, ever intended to be run on a wet surface! So, in one case it is a matter of loss of traction.

On the opposite end of the deal, the huge footprint of a drag slick on dry pavement will literally overpower the front tire adhesion, pushing the car through a turn rather than allowing the front tires to help the car through a turn. This horrendous case of understeer will lead to grief.

If the front tire footprint can't be identical to the rear, it should at least be close. A pro-street design is drag racing oriented, therefore, the end result is a case very similar to the fad-T with an incorrect tire combination. If at all possible, keep the front footprint within 20 percent of the rear. Rear tires of 29-inch diameter and an 8-inch width need front tires of at least 25-inch diameter and a 6 1/2-inch width. Even this is cutting things very tight. Running slightly different air pressures front/rear may increase the footprint proportions favorably, but this just isn't the full answer. If it is essential to have the large rear tire, then the solution may be to a slightly wider front tire.

Whatever, do some planning on front/rear tire combinations. Never mix radials with bias-ply tires, and watch the tire air pressures. Some rodders run radials with as little as 24 psi, while others opt for 35 psi. Radials definitely make the car ride better, especially on the nation's interstates that have grooves from the heavy truck traffic.

There is a current trend toward the use of "wide whites" again. These tires were very much the thing to have during the 1950s and early '60s, but they are not radial design. Wide whites in the 3 1/2 to 4-inch range are available from several tire dealers who specialize in rubber for the restoration crowd. Generally, these tires will not give the kind of mileage that the radials do, either.

P-METRIC RADIAL TIRES

P-Metric is a new tire size designation designed to identify passenger car type radial tires. The size designation is an international tire code identifier and accurately describes the Type of Tire, Tire Section Width, Tire Aspect Ratio and Type of Construction.

For example, a typical metric tire designator P215/75R15:

•**P**- Designates a passenger car type tire with related tire load ratings.

•**215**- Tire cross section width in millemiters. Increases or decreases in 10-millimeter increments to designate tire size and always ends with the numeral 5 (i.e., 205, 215, 225, or 235).

•**75**- Represents the tire aspect ratio which is the percent of tire section height to tire section width.

•**R**- Identifies radial ply construction, D- Dialgonal, B- Belted Bias.

•**15**- Rim diameter will always be shown in inches (i.e., 15". 14", or 13", which are common applications).

The tire load range in P-Metric Series Radial Tires is **not** identified with letters such as B, C, and D or with ply ratings as in the Alpha system.

P-Metric tires are offered with a Standard Load Rating or Extra Load Rating which is related to tire pressure:

Standard Load-35 psi   Extra Load-41 psi

Maximum tire pressure will be stamped on the tire sidewall in metric kilo Pascals (kPa) and pounds per square inch (PSI). In metric tire pressure, 7 kilo Pascals (kPa) are equivalent to 1 lb. per sq.in. (PSI).

The Tire maximum load capacity will also be stamped on the tire sidewall in kilograms and pounds.

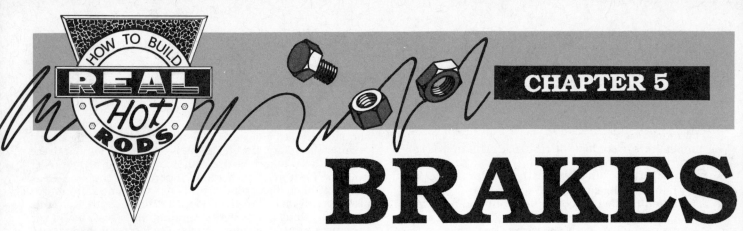

CHAPTER 5

BRAKES

The contemporary hot rod, be it an early model or some thing from the 1980s, will almost always include a combination brake system of discs (front) and drum (rear). Perhaps as many as 90 percent of all hot rods being built today have this mix. Not because this is the perfect system, or even because it is the best. It is currently what is being used by the majority of builders. This is an excellent combination, but there remains room for the more traditional all-drum system, or the improvement to four-wheel discs.

The internal expanding drum brake system is good, but it has a serious flaw. It does not get rid of heat well. Heat is the end result of any braking system. With a disc brake system the generated heat is carried away rapidly. In the drum system, the heat is trapped inside the drum. As the drum gets ever hotter, the coefficient of friction of the lining drops, and

ABOVE - Radical offset of the wheel and tire may not be the best of front end engineering, but it certainly gets this larger diameter solid rotor disc brake system in the air.
ABOVE RIGHT - This small diameter rotor is less effective than it should be, rotor is important brake factor.

Self-energizing drum brakes have leading shoe push trailing shoe into drum as brakes are applied, the adjuster (arrow) "floats" so this can happen. Usually front shoe lining is smaller than trailing shoe lining, brake fade happens when lining loses coefficient of friction.

brake fade sets in. With the disc system, by comparison, as the rotor begins to heat and expand, it gets ever closer to the surrounding caliper. Very little brake fade. Race car builders attempted to alleviate this heat problem with drum brakes by making air scoops for the backing plates, with air outlets as well. This works, but it still does not cure the problem. The result is a very large drum brake diameter and width for the high performance drum system. Very few production cars utilized such a system.

If you live in relatively flat country, the old hydraulic Ford brakes will probably be suffecient for your car in ordinary use. Even mechanical brakes would work, if they were kept in constant adjustment. Ford introduced the hydraulic brake in 1939, well after everyone had gone to hydraulics. The 1939-48 Ford brakes are minimal, and they tend to fade very rapidly under hard braking conditions. It is possible to find some Bendix brakes from Lincolns, but these are now very scarce. They are a virtual bolt-on. The Ford Econoline van spindles can be used on the pre-1949 Ford axles, which means the Econoline drum brakes can be used, a marked improvement. Some Ford pickup brakes from the 1950s can be used, by modifying the backing plates to fit the Ford spindles, another improvement. The drum and wheel cylinder make the biggest difference. It is possible to replace the old Ford drums with better units. The finned Buick drums of the 1950s and 60s can we modified to fit, using the Ford backing plates and Buick shoes. But the most dramatic difference will come from increasing the piston surface area of the wheel cylinder, when it is bigger the braking will improve.

The early Ford hydraulics are the worst of the available drum systems, with most non-Ford designs being very good. With any of the drum brakes, the idea is to keep the system in excellent condition. That means using the best brake shoe material, fitting shoe and drum as instructed in the literature for that vehicle, and inspecting the system periodically.

The good thing about drum brakes is that they have built-in power assist, by having a servo action. The leading edge of the shoe will tend to pull the rest of the shoe into ever harder

contact with the drum. But even with this kind of self-energizing effect, the drum brakes accept a power boost very well.

It is possible to do a bit of upgrading with most all the non-Ford hydraulic systems, since there was not a great deal of difference in basic engineering from the mid-1930s through the early 1950s. World War II put a hold on a lot of normal engineering changes. Since drum diameter and wheel cylinder size are major factors in drum brake performance, it is possible to often adapt the larger drums from a bigger/heavier car in a particular line to a smaller car of similar heritage. Example would be Chrysler Imperial brakes on the small MoPars. Sometimes the spindle will have changed, but it is often possible to change backing plates/shoes and then make the drum fit the smaller car hub.

The key to lining life is effective swept area, and this holds true for discs as well as drum brakes. The larger the drum or rotor diameter, the larger the brake show/pad can be. The wider the drum, the larger the shoe can be. This increases the

Brake drums should be as near factory thickness as possible, should be turned down by a professional shop before use on a hot rod. Radius and width of drum lining face are important, lining material will have a bearing on brake effeciency.

95

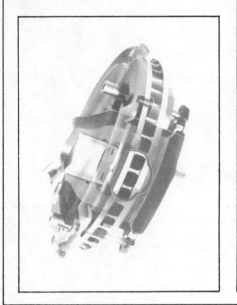

RIGHT AND BELOW - Rotors may be vented, as is the 1969 Chevrolet unit shown below, for the heavier cars, or they may be solid as the Jaguar unit at right. Vented rotors get rid of heat rapidly, by mounting the rotors adjacent to the third member unsprung weight is reduced to a minimum.

amount of brake shoe that is in contact with the drum, or swept area.

It is almost never possible to simply bolt brake shoes and drums on a vehicle (making a swap, or simply doing a rebuild) and have them mate correctly. Instead, the brake shoe should be ground to fit the drum (arched), and this you leave to the professional. If you just install a set of shoes and expect them to wear to shape, you can do more harm than good. Generally, in arcing, the center part of a shoe contacts the drum while the heel and toe are still clear.

It has been learned that the asbestos in brake lining can be hazardous to the lungs, so don't use air to blow the dirt from the brak# drum area. Use the pressurized cans with cleaning fluid that you get from any parts store.

When adjusting new shoes, move the adjustment mechanism until the shoe just touches the drum. Move the adjustment a slight bit more, and the energizing effect of the shoe should cause it to bite into the drum hard. Back off on the adjustment slightly until the wheel turns easily, without dragging. Make small adjustments at a time.

If you are using drums from the junkyard, which almost everyone will be doing, have the brake shop check them for condition. They can be out of round, worn too badly for use, or they can be bellmouthed. The open end can be bigger than the closed end. Brake drums and rotors should never be turned beyond the prescribed factory limits, so for the best results, start with drums or rotors nearest stock thickness possible.

The type of brake shoe selected is up to you. Some will give a really soft feel to the pedal, but they may also wear very fast. Others may give maximum mileage between changes, but they may be so hard that they don't stop the car very well. The parts supplier should have excellent recommendations on what to use. Obviously, if you are using a brake system designed for a 4000 pound car on a 2000 pound rod, the type of brake shoe used will be different than stock. And don't rely

This solid rotor is used on a car weighing under 2500 pounds, a car that has full fenders and weighs over 2300 pounds should use the vented rotor. Despite tradition, wire wheels do not cool the brakes significantly better than other wheels on street driven vehicles.

entirely upon cost. The shoes with the highest price may not be the best, again rely on the supplier for advice.

Bonded brake linings versus riveted? Up to you. When the shoes wear to the rivet heads, the rivets will start to score the drum, while you can wear the bonded lining clear to the metal shoe. But you don't want to let the linings go this far, you should change them when they get down to manufacturer's minimum. If you don't know this minimum thickness, ask the parts store counterman to look it up for you.

Whatever you do with drum brakes, get a reasonable match between front and rear swept areas. Since the front brakes do a bit more of the work, then can be slightly larger, but under no condition do you want the rear brakes locking up before the fronts. This will cause a killer slide of the vehicle, unpredictably.   This is why a proportioning valve is an absolute necessity with drum/disc combinations, but this valve is not the cure-all. You need to do a lot of thinking about the brake combination you are creating. Wheel radius becomes the leverage working on the brakes, thus when you use a 24-inch diameter tire in front (12-inch radius) and a 30-inch tire in back (15-inch radius), the rear tire/wheel combination has the greater leverage. Keep this in mind.

So, now you have to consider the tire diameter, as well as what happens when you engage the brakes. Suppose you have a car with 50-50 weight distribution. When you apply the brakes, you get about a 12 percent weight shift to the front brakes, changing your 50-50 distribution to about 62 percent front and 38 percent rear. But, if you go back and factor in the tire radius, you will end up with something closer to 55 percent front, 45 percent rear. Pretty close to an ideal situation.

Disc brakes come in a very wide variety of sizes, depending upon vehicle weight. This is where so many rod builders get involved with putting too much brake on their car. An example would be using the big rotors from a Lincoln or Cadillac on a Fad T roadster. While the extra potential of the big calipers is not so much a detriment, the extra weight of the rotors is. This is unsprungweight, and it defeats the idea of trying to reduce unsprung weight to the minimum.

When selecting front discs from a salvage car, try to get units that are from a car only slightly heavier than the car being built. Also consider pedal ratio and cylinder bores. The decision to use vented or unvented rotors is a matter of vehicle weight as well as air flow to the disc. If you have a full fendered car where the fenders mask the front wheels/brakes, you will want a vented rotor probably. Unless the car is very light. If you have a heavier car, from about 2300 pounds, you will probably think in terms of vented rotor.

The larger and heavier the car to be stopped, the larger the rotor diameter, as a rule. The same radius leverage principle applies as with tire radius. And, the larger the swept area of

LEFT - heat retention inside the drum brake is culprit that helps brake fade, early on racers and rodders tried drilling the backing plates full of holes to exit air. This weakens backing plate.

BELOW - Exploded view of 1966 Dodge Polara disc brake.

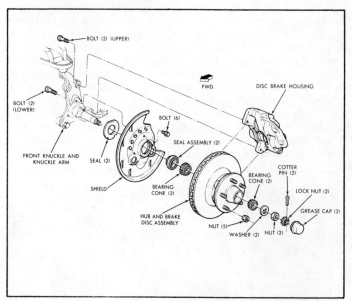

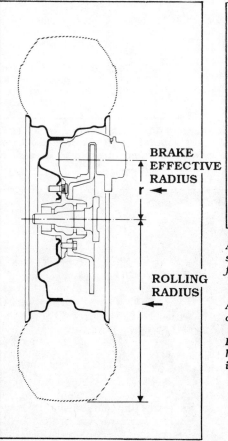

BRAKE EFFECTIVE RADIUS
r

ROLLING RADIUS

ABOVE - When adapting 1939-1ater Ford hydraulic brakes to the earlier Ford spindles/axles, it may be necessary to modify the backing plates, here notch is cut for hingpin boss clearance.

ABOVE RIGHT - Early Ford hydraulics use a stepped wheel cylinder, use new cylinders unless rebuilt units are perfect. Ford hydraulics are marginal at best.

LEFT - Both the wheel/tire rolling radius and the disc brake rotor effective radius have a direct bearing on how well the brakes work, since these leverages are involved in the braking principle.

the disc brake pad. Some of the older disc systems use round disc pucks, most newer versions use a single crescent shaped pad. This whether the system uses dual cyulinders or a single cylinder. Some disc systems use hydraulic pistons on both sides of the rotor, most use a single cylinder. Early disc calipers required removal from the mount to install new pads, later versions allow pad replacement without removing the caliper.

When shopping for junkyard discs, get the best condition rotors possible. If the rotor is grooved, find another one. The thickest is the best, meaning it hasn't been turned down excessively during rebuild. Dasic rule of thumb on the junkyard or used caliper is to rebuild it. Install new pads, period.

On some later model cars, it is possible to do some spindle changing, going from drum brakes to discs. To get an idea if this can be done with your car, compare your stock spindle with those from similar cars of later years. For instance, an early Sixties MoPar with a similar MoPar of the 70s. If the spindle attaches to the suspension in the same manner, and is the same size, chances are it will swap. Always check the angle of the spindle bolt relative to the spindle upright (they can vary), because these angles must be identical for a swap. Also note where the tie rod connects to the spindle steering arm. The two locations must be nearly identical, or bumpsteer is almost certain.

if such a swap is not possible, then it is necessary to make up a kit (unless you can find one mail-order). It is almost always possible to adapt the rotor "hat" to an earlier hub which has the drum removed. The caliper must be positioned and a caliper bracket made of very thick steel plate, at least 1/4-inch, 3/8-inch is better. This same kind of disc adaptation is possible on the early rod spindle, although there are disc kits available for practically every kind of early spindle. One caution about discs on early axles. The disc has such good stopping power that it is possible to actually twist a beam axle. The tubing axles don't twist, and the worst beam axle offenders are those with the very narrow cross-sections.

When trying to make either a disc or drum swap to some kind of different spindle, know that it is often just a matter of changing bearings. If the centerline of the inner and outer hub bearings are roughly the same as the original hub, haul the spindle and the new hub down to the bearing supply house. Engineers don't like to reinvent the wheel every time they make something, so chances are very good there are bearings that will make this combination work. Seals as well. If the centerline of the hub is slightly less than the original hub centerline, it is possible to do some machine work on the spindle, and the new hub can be made to fit. Our Volvo discs for Ford spindles illustrate this keenly.

Early Ford spindle, bottom, compared to disc brake, caliper/rotor from late model car spindle, top.

When swapping non-Ford hubs to early Ford spindles, it is sometimes possible to use spacer rather than machine spindle.

A typical disc brake swap to 1932-1948 Ford spindles will involve work on spindle or a bearing spacer, as well as caliper bracket.

ABOVE LEFT - Disc brake kit may include all of these parts, or just a couple Don't skimp on brake quality. ABOVE CENTER - Here the disc brake kit is assembled on the spindle, with caliper bracket attached with quality bolts. ABOVE RIGHT - It is vital the rotor does not have excessive "run-out" as this will cause the caliper piston/pad to cock and wear prematurely. RIGHT - Disc brakes kits are available to fit most late model car rearends, some factory cars come with four-wheel-discs (such as the biggest Ford products).

Master Cylinders

The master cylinder you use is critical to how well the system will work. If you have a late model car, you will use the master cylinder common to the car, unless you add disc front brakes. In that case, you can use a master cylinder from the same make car, but from a later year when discs were introduced. If you must install a different master cylinder, the best thing to do is select one of the dual master cylinders, the kind that have separate brake lines for front and rear.

It is in the older rods where some confusion exists over the master cylinder. As a rule, the master cylinders common to the older cars will not work well with the more modern brakes. Mostly it will be a matter of both capacity and pressure. For example, an old Ford master cylinder just doesn't have enough capaticy to move enough fluid for Jaguar discs, and not nearly enough volume. For the typical modern brake system, the master cylinder bore should be 1 1/8-inch. Light weight cars with small calipers can get by with the 1-inch master cylinder bore.

The most commonly used master cylinder is the Ford Mustang fruit jar type. This is a single cylinder/reservoir unit. If it is used in conjunction with a Midland pressure assist unit, the master cylinder residual valve must be removed. But this is not the best master cylinder to use, it is just the most common. It is small, and readily available. For the sake of safety, it might be wise to use a dual master cylinder. There are a lot of different dual cylinders available, many of them very compact and ideal for rod building.

With the proper pedal ratio and master cylinder bore, 90 percent of all cars will have excellent line pressure, therefore a power assist unit (such as Midland) may not be needed. The pedal ratio will be somewhere between 6:1 and 6.5:1. It is vital to carefully select and install the brake components on the heavier car, and this is especially true of the master cylinder.

The key is the volume of fluid moved at a certain pressure. The pressure will be determined by the master cylinder bore times stroke. If you put discs on the front, find what the car's original master cylinder bore was (for the front brakes.)Meaning the car from which the disc brakes were taken. This will tell you roughly the size master cylinder you need.

The master cylinder selected for drum brakes all around should be as near what the brakes originally required as possible. If you are using Econoline spindles and brakes on the front, and you have matched the rear brake cylinders, then consider a master cylinder near the Econoline size.

This holds true with a power brake unit as well. With a true power brake, as opposed to a power assist, engine vacumn reduces the amount of brake pedal pressure needed to operate the master cylinder. This is a direct action on the pedal/master cylinder, rather than indirict, since the power brake fits between the pedal and the master cylinder, whereas the assist unit fits between the master cylinder and the brakes. However, and this is important, if you have a maximum performance car, you may not want to include a power system of either type, since this will be utilizing engine vacumn, one of the major principles of engine performance.

For rod building, the size of the power brake chamber in diameter is a determing factor. Most of the power brakes have a very large diameter, too big for the older engine compartments. Some of the mid/small size cars have longer, smaller diameter chamber housings (such as Dodge and Mustang/Pinto). Many experts feel that these power brake systems from the factory are much better than aftermarket boosters. If the master cylinder is mounted beneath the floorboards, there is the problem of fluid feedback on the lines, especially if the cylinder is below the height of the brakes. A master cylinder used with drum brakes always must have 10psi residual pressure in the lines at all times. A residual pressure valve is normally built into the drum brake master cylinder. Some disc systems keep about 2psi in the line (Corvette, for example), to reduce pedal slack and give a kind of "instant on" feel to the brakes.

Rod builders remove the residual valve in the master cylinder when a combination of drum and disc brake is used. If this residual valve is not removed, it will cause the disc pads to drag severely. When residual pressure is required, it is achieved through valves placed in the line between master cylinder and drum brakes. For instance, with a drum/disc combination, the master cylinder might have a residual valve with 2psi built in, then a secondary valve would be placed in the line to the drums giving 10psi. Or two valves would be used, 2psi to the discs and 10 psi to the drums. In addition to the residual valve, a drum/disc combination would also include a proportioning valve between the master cylinder and the drums.

Starting in the early 1970s, most American production cars have a block somewhere near the master cylinder (on the firewall or frame rail) that receives brake lines from the master cylinder then sends the lines on to the brakes. This block will be involved when drum/disc brakes are used, and it will usually incorporate a metering valve, proportioning valve, and residual valve (there is no proportioning valve when 4-wheel discs are involved). This unit can be used on rods of all years.

Incidentally, if the discs seem to drag and you are wondering if it is a matter of too much residual pressure, just open the bleed screw. Too much pressure is immediately apparent.

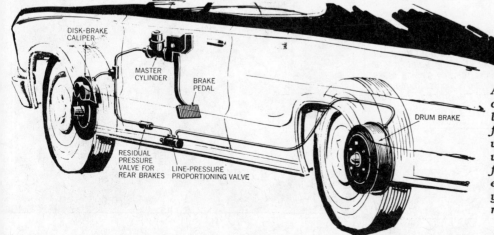

DISK-BRAKE CALIPER

MASTER CYLINDER

BRAKE PEDAL

DRUM BRAKE

RESIDUAL PRESSURE VALVE FOR REAR BRAKES

LINE-PRESSURE PROPORTIONING VALVE

A TYPICAL COMBINATION of front disks and rear drums requires a line-pressure-proportioning valve for automatic adjustment of rear wheel braking effort in relation to vehicle speed and weight transfer forward. This system has a low-cost emegency brake in the rear drums, yet offers the stability and fade resistance of discs

Original brake pedals usually work quite well if they are hooked to a new master cylinder, but be sure the actuating rod between pedal and cylinder is in a direct line. You don't want the rod intersecting the piston at an angle. And keep in mind that the "swing arc" of the pedal, that is where the rod connects to the pedal, should pass through neutral at the midpoint of its swing. If not, the actuating rod will intersect the master cylinder piston at too severe an angle, which also will effect pressure slightly.

Whether a new or used pedal is involved, it is wise to check the pivot bushing and shaft, and renovate as necessary. Early stock pedals usually had provisions for lubrication, most rod supplier pedals must be removed and lubricated periodically. You can add a grease zerk to these pedals if you wish.

Always use a brake pedal return spring so that the pedal weight doesn't keep pressure on the system. If not used, the pedal weight will be just enough to keep the piston from coming all the way back to uncover the bleed hole, which results in a residual pressure in the lines. The pedal ratio should be somewhere between 6:1 and 6.5:1, measured from the pivot point to the center of the foot pad, and from the pivot point to the center of the piston actuating rod hole. This is a straight line measurement, so the pedal arm might have any sort of engine or transmission clearance bends in it and still not effect the actual pedal ratio.

DISC INSTALLATION TIPS FROM JFZ

Rotor Installation & Run out: *We highly recommend that rotor attaching bolts be lock-wired. Rotor Run out should be adjusted upon installation to less than 0.005". Adjust by shimming between rotor and mounting face of hat or hub with decreasing thickness shims from the thickest point to the point opposite. run out should be checked periodically, but can be assumed to be acceptable if no other problems such as brake drag, pedal oscillation or piston knock-back are encountered.*

Caliper Mounting Brackets & Positioning: *If caliper mounting brackets are not available from your chassis manufacturer, they may be fabricated from mild steel. We recommend 5/16" thickness (minimum) for dual piston calipers. Be sure that the bracket is sturdy and will not deflect when the brakes are applied. A weak bracket can cause tapered lining wear, cocking of the pistons, ejection of the brake pads, fracturing of the caliper mounting ears or bracket failure. Saving a few ounces on a caliper mounting bracket may not be worth it. The mounting surfaces on the caliper mounting ears must be parallel to the rotor within 0.020" when installed. The caliper must be centered on the rotor to the extent that new pads can be easily dropped in when the caliper pistons have been fully retracted.*

Air Ducting: *When ducting is necessary, we recommend at least 3" diameter ducts, directed to the inside diameter of the rotor. Ducting is usually required for heavier cars on asphalt, such as Late Model & Modified cars. In some very severe short track instances, it is not uncommon to run a second, smaller-diameter duct directly to the caliper.*

Master Cylinder: *Always be sure to mount your master cylinders as rigidly and as high in the car as possible. When running fluid lines keep them running downward from the master cylinder. Always make sure that the master cylinder diaphragm is in place and in good condition. If you use a remote fluid reservoir be sure that you mount it as high as you can in the car. CAUTION: Be sure that the master cylinder DOES NOT have a residual pressure valve installed in it. The use of residual pressure valves is a practice which remains from drum-brake days and should be no part of a contemporary racing car equipped with JFZ disc brakes.*

PEDAL RATIO

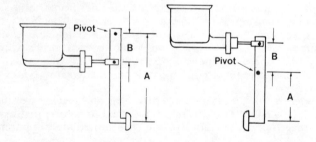

Pedal Ratio: *Pedal ratio is the distance "A" divided by the distance "B" in the illustrations above. Or simply put, the distance from the pedal pivot point to the center of the foot pad, divided by the distance from the pedal pivot point to the master cylinder actuating rod attaching point. It is a method of pushing harder on the master cylinder rod and gaining brake pressure by mechanical advantage. As the pedal ratio is increased, required pedal pressure is reduced. Also keep in mind that the stroke of the pedal will increase as the pedal ratio is increased.*

This 1932 Ford has the pedal assembly with a hydraulic master cylinder mounted to the crossmember behind pedals but no brace for the pedals. Poor design.

TROUBLE SHOOTING CHART

SYMPTOM	PROBABLE CAUSE
Brakes Drag	1. Bad master cylinder 2. Tapered lining wear caused by improper caliper mounting 3. Residual pressure valve in system 4. System hydraulically locked from lack of free play in pedal linkage 5. Weak, deflecting caliper mounting brackets 6. Caliper not mounted square to rotor 7. Excessive rotor run out

Pedal goes to the floor during a race	1. Fluid boiling caused by:
	   a. Overheating from brake drag (see brakes drag")
	   b. Old or inadequate fluid
	   c. Undersized brake system for application
	2. Master cylinder failure
	3. Leak in caliper or hydraulic lines
	4. Pedal linkage failure
	5. Excessive spindle deflection in cornering, causing caliper piston knock back

Too deep a pedal	1. Air trapped in fluid (incomplete bleeding) 2. Master cylinders too small 3. Pedal ratio too great 4. Excessive spindle deflection in cornering, causing caliper piston knock back 5. Rotors warped 6. Calipers not mounted square to rotor
Have to push too hard on pedal (car won't stop)	1. Master cylinder too large 2. Insufficient pedal ratio 3. Inadequate caliper piston area 4. Oil or grease on brake linings 5. Frozen pistons in calipers 6. Fade from improper brake lining compound for application
Oscillation feed back in pedal	1. Excessive rotor run out 2. Rotor faces not parallel 3. Cracked rotor 4. Loose or improperly mounted caliper 5. Lining build-up (welding) on rotors 6. Excessive front bearing clearance
Car pulls	1. Oil or grease on brake linings 2. Frozen pistons in calipers 3. Loose or improperly mounted caliper or rotor 4. Front end alignment

Fluids

There is an interesting debate going on about regular hydraulic fluids versus silicon fluids. Regular brake fluid will absorb water, and it will remove paint, silicon doesn't, but it has other problems. Which you use will be your own choice, but we have learned from the folks who get involved with the race car brakes that there are a couple of problems with silicon that might color our choice of a street car fluid.

Silicon is affected by atmospheric pressure, since it is very expansive. This means that a car being used at high altitudes might exhibit sponginess in the pedal feel. As the same silicon fluid heats to a high temperature, the same expansion process takes place. It also effects ethylene propelene (EPR) rubber, which is used in brake systems, causing it to expand. To its credit, silicon does not absorb water like regular fluid does, so it tends to be a popular fluid with car collectors. It is still too early to know what the long term effects of silicon will be on these stored car systems.

Race cars do not use the silicon fluid. Instead they rely on the high temperature DOT 3 fluid, and flush the system on a regular basis. This way they get rid of fluid that has become contaminated with water. It is suggested that the master cylinder have a good flexible seal between cap and bowl, which is the most effective way yet to keep water from getting absorbed into the system.

Boosters

Popular with many rod builders, especially on older cars, is the pressure booster. Usually made by Mid land, this is not a power brake system, but rather a vacumn operated booster of pressure. It is #sed to amplify the hydraulic pressure to a brake system.

If disc brakes are used with a master cylinder common to a drum brake system (such as the fruit jar Mustang unit many rodders use), the master cylinder does not have enough volume for the discs. This is a common problem when drums are used on the rear and discs on the front. The power booster is placed in the line. Such units are available from most rod shops or mail order houses, or through many brake equipment suppliers and parts houses.

Remember, this is a power assist unit. Mount the Midland unit as per unit instructions.

There are different size boosters, relative to #x line pressure, although outwardly they may look alike. Be sure and check with someone who is into brakes before installing a scrounged unit.

BOOSTER INLET — BLEEDER SCREW — VACUUM HOSE

The Midland type brake pressure booster was used on many Ford products earlier on, it is now commonly used on rods with drum/disc combinations.

Proportions and Valves

When building a hot rod, there are a lot of changes made that have a direct bearing on the brakes, but these are factors almost never considered by the builder. By the experienced builder as well as the newcomer.

Take a typical fad T for instance. It is built with a small block Chevy engine, fiberglass body, and a Ford open drive rear end from the late 50s. The front axle is a Ford Beam unit, mounting 1947 hydraulic brakes. Assume that the brakes have been rebuilt. In use, the front brakes will probably lock up before the rears. So we stand around scratching our heads, because here we have front and rear brakes of about the same dimensions.

The problem is proportions. The late model Ford had a brake system designed for something like a 60-40 ratio...60 percent of the braking was to be done by the front, 40 percent by the rear. This because the late model has more weight on the front than on the rear. Otherwise, the rear wheels would lock up under emergency conditions, and when the rears lock up before the fronts, you get a spin situation.

So look what happens when this combination is used on the fad T. The front wheels and tires are of small rolling radius, probably 12 to 13 inches (that's half the tire size of 24-26 inches). The rear tires are of 29-30 inches diameter, or a radius of nearly 15 inches. This extra leverage at the rear has the same effect as putting large diameter brake cylinders on the front of the 50s Ford, or a ratio of about 65-35.

If the rear tires are significantly larger than the fronts, there is the problem of mass inertia, making them harder to stop. Meaning more brake is needed. Mix in a fad-T weight distribution of 50-50, then add discs up front, and the problem compounds.

What is needed is more of the braking effect switched to the rear wheels. Discs help the problem, but at the rear larger brake cylinders need to be used.

Sometimes the large front cylinders from a particular model or series will bolt right in place in the rear backing plates. The front cylinders use a flat washer to seal the brake hoses, so an adapter is needed between the flared rear brake line and the front-type cylinders.

Part of the proportioning problem is trying to figure what discs to use. If you go with production car items, which are almost all of the floating type (one piston, on one side) you can only try and match vehicle weights. If you go with the rod industry aftermarket calipers, you will probably get non-floating designs that have pistons on both sides.

A good rule of thumb is that on 1934 and older cars, you can probably use 2-inch wide drum brake shoes in the rear and a smaller two-piston caliper in front. The 4-piston calipers are more common in this combination, however. For heavier cars, the 4-piston units are essential, along with vented rotors.

When drum and disc brakes are used in combination, a proportion valve must be inserted in the line between master cylinder and drum brakes, or between power booster and drum brakes. You can get the most popular Kelsey-Hayes proportioning valve from nearly every rods parts supplier, or through your local parts store. Sometimes you will even find this unit on late model Mopar products. It is easy to identify because it has a knurled adjusting knob sticking out one end. Proportioning valves are used on many production cars and trucks, so you can often pick something usable up at the local junkyard.

After the brake system is installed, it is necessary to do some real-life testing, something that too many builders skip. At 30 mph (on a clear, unobstructed surface), slam on the brakes. Do this several times, to determine if you have rear wheel lockup. The proportioning valve will have only about a 25 percent effect on the system, so remember that you have to get the system as close to right as possible even before the proportioning valve is added.

In testing, if the rear wheels lock up before the front brakes, the car will tend to spin uncontrollably and unpredictably. Obviously this problem is amplified the higher the speed.

Hydraulic Brake Lines

Hydraulic brake lines are critical items. When a late model rod is being built, the stock lines are usually retained, because there is no need for change. About the only area of concern will be the brake hoses, and if there is the slightest doubt about hose condition, put on a new one!

Older rods always need new hydraulic lines constructed and routed. This can be a problem, for the experienced builder as well as the beginner.

Only steel hydraulic line should be used. Odd as it may seem, there have been cases where the inexperienced builder has tried to use copper tubing. The only exception to steel line would be one of the synthetic type lines used for aircraft or spacecraft. You're not likely to have access to this line. The steel line you do get from the parts store (or salvaged from the junkyard) must be of the seamless type, as approved for brake systems.

If a steel line is too short, use a flare splice fitting, and as with all hydraulic fittings, do not overtighten. The tube flare can be damaged.

The line from master cylinder to the drum rear brakes will be 3/16 or 1/4-inch diameter. If disc brakes are used up front, that line will be 3/16-inch diameter. Lines bigger to the front, even up to 5/16inch size have been seen, but this seems to be a matter of the master cylinder fitting size more than anything. The 3/16-inch diameter works fine for both drum and disc.

Bending hydraulic brake line can be frustrating, unless you have a good tubing bender. Invest in one. Not a cheap tool, a good one.

The good tool will pay for itself immediately. You want a tool that allows a bend right up next to the fitting.

You also will want to own a double-flare tool. The single tube flare as used on fuel lines is not as strong as the double flare used on brake lines. Again, invest in a good tool.

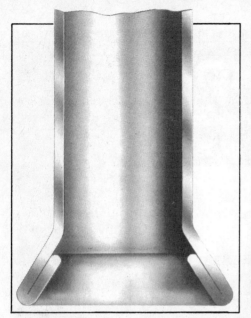

When bending tubing, be patient, and design so that you can route the line in the most direct possible way. Be sure and have the line fitting adjacent to the flare before you make a bend, sometimes the fitting won't make the bend afterwards. If you flatten a line, start again with another line.

Make all flares before making any bends, unless you have a really tight end bend that can't be done any other way. Expect to goof up a couple of flare until you have the use of the double flare tool figured out. Practice will help alleviate problems here.

Do not route the brake line immediately adjacent to a high heat source (exhaust), and keep it away from where it can be flattened (below the frame rails where a jack might go). Avoid routing the line where abrasion can take place, if you must pass through a tight hole, etc, protect the tubing with an outer layer of rubber or plastic tubing. Use line clamps often to keep the tubing from rattling against the frame, and where the tubing connects to the hose, be sure and use a support.

On at least one occasion we have known of a "phantom pedal" problem being traced directly to the brake line routing. Phantom pedal is when the brake pedal goes all the way to the floor for no apparent reason. Immediately before and after, the pedal seems to operate perfectly. In this case, the front brake tubing was routed alongside the inside frame rail, then up and over the frame and down to the hose connection. A kind of horseshoe shape on end. After tracing every possible problem, this horseshoe bend was removed and the line run directly through the frame. The phantom pedal immediately disappeared.

When routing the hydraulic lines, use only the best fittings available. If you want to go through a boxed frame, there are some special fittings available from mail-order sources. If at all possible, route the line so that any outside source damage is impossible. An example would be in the driveshaft area, where failed universal

joint could allow a flailing shaft to destroy the line (a good case for making a driveshaft safety loop, as on race cars). When routing the line, keep it flowing smoothly, with no sharp loops. Such overhead loops allow air to be trapped, and it takes almost extreme pressure to bleed such trapped air from the system.

For cosmetic purposes, the steel line can be shined with steel wool and then covered with clear paint. Or the line can be painted a color. Stainless line is available, but it is costly.

When routing the brake hoses, keep them clear of any obstacles and any sharp metal edges. Check the suspension travel from stop to stop to make sure no hose is crimped flat. Hose can be held out of harm's way with either nylon tie straps or light duty coil spring. Check the suspension for full-stop travel, both down and up, to make sure the hose is not tight at either extreme.

Always use a frame bracket where the hose connects to the rigid brake line. The spring clips that hold the hose motionless are available from most parts houses.

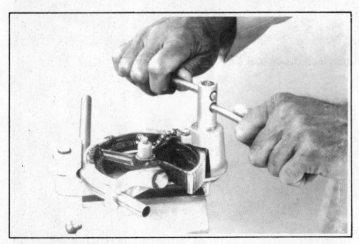

There are dozens of different tubing benders available, most are far more basic and simple than this unit. Stainless tubing will require a special bender.

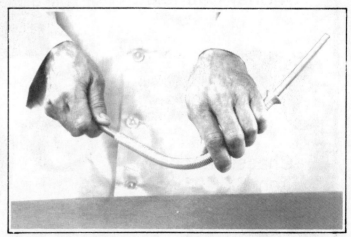

A very basic tubing bender is this coil wrap, there is some special brake tubing available that can easily be bent by hand into tight shapes.

Brake Math

The biggest single problem with working up a brake system, especially one that includes discs and drums, is in trying to figure out all the sizes. Not trial and error engineering, but working out the sizes through mathmatics.

There are two formulas to use when working out componentry for front discs and rear drums. We have a figure of .070 as a constant for discs, and .20 for drums. Here's how it works.

We'll begin with the fluid volume demands of a disc brake assembly, using the average-sized '67 Mustang/Cougar front as an example...

1. Measure the piston diameter. (1.5/8").
2. Determine the piston area from the chart (2.0739).
3. Multiply that by the number of pistons on **one side** of the rotor. (2x2.0739=4.1478).
4. Multiply that figure by the number of calipers. (4.1478x2=8.2956).
5. Multiply that number by **.070 (a constant that is used for disc brake piston stroke)**. (8.2956x.07=0.58).
6. The answer, in cubic inches, is the volume demand of the disc brakes. **(0.58 cubic inches)**.

keep that figure in mind and we'll move on to using the formula and chart for the rear drum brakes, using '57 Ford rear end as an example...

1. Measure the piston diameter. (7/8-inch).
2. Determine the area from the chart. (0.6013).
3. Multiply the area by **0.20 (a constant used for drum brake piston stoke)**. (0.6013x.20=0.12026).
4. Multiply that figure by the number of wheel cylinders. (2x0.12026=.2405).
5. The answer, in cubic inches, is the volume demand of the drum brakes. **(.2405 cubic inches)**.

Therefore, the brake system in a street rod using Mustang discs on the front and '57 Ford rear drum brakes has **a total fluid volume demand of 0.8211 cubic inches.** (0.5806 plus 0.2405 cubic inches). To operate that particular brake system you'll therefore need a master cylinder with that much capacity **(0.8211 cubic inches)** plus **30 percent more** as a safety factor.

Most master cylinder manufacturers catalog˚ the cylinder bore, and sometimes the displacement, but you can determine either figure for yourself by carefully measuring the stroke with a depth gauge. The cylinder will need dismantling to directly measure the piston diameter.

Then, multiply the area of the piston (from the chart) by the stroke to get the fluid displacement in cubic inches. However, don't forget that you'll need around 30 percent more in the master cylinder that the total required by all the wheel cylinders.

Of course it doesn't end there. In a street rod's braking system there's seating position, accessibility of foot controls, siting the master cylinder for easy fluid checking, and then the all-important part of connecting the brake-pedal linkages...these must operate effectively without any binding in the geometry, and the actuating rod must line up directly with the master cylinder's bore centerline.

And with or without power assist, you'll need to pay attention to the pedal operating ratio...if you haven't room for a booster, or a hot cam rules one out anyway, make sure you allow plenty of extra leverage on the pedal incorporate adjustment holes to change it for a more direct action if the pedal movement arc is too long.

Unfortunately, until now this is information that hasn't been readily available. Thanks to the guys down at New Zealand Hot Rod magazine for giving us this information.

PISTON AREA (area of circles)

Diameter (inches) Area	ONE INCH	TWO INCHES	THREE INCHES
1/2 . . . . 0.194	1.00 . . . . 0.7854	2.00 . . . . 3.1416	3.00 . . . . 7.0686
17/32 . . . . 0.2217	1 1/16 . . . . 0.8866	2 1/16 . . . . 3.3410	3 1/16 . . . . 7.3662
9/16 . . . . 0.2485	1 1/8 . . . . 0.9940	2 1/8 . . . . 3.5466	3 1/8 . . . . 7.6699
19/32 . . . . 0.2769	1 3/16 . . . . 1.1075	2 3/16 . . . . 3.7583	3 3/16 . . . . 7.9798
5/8 . . . . 0.3608	1 1/4 . . . . 1.2272	2 1/4 . . . . 3.9761	3 1/4 . . . . 8.2958
21/32 . . . . 0.3382	1 5/16 . . . . 1.3530	2 5/16 . . . . 4.2000	3 5/16 . . . . 8.6179
11/16 . . . . 0.3712	1 3/8 . . . . 1.4849	2 3/8 . . . . 4.4301	3 3/8 . . . . 8.9462
23/32 . . . . 0.4057	1 7/16 . . . . 1.6230	2 7/16 . . . . 4.6664	3 7/16 . . . . 9.2806
3/4 . . . . 0.4418	1 1/2 . . . . 1.7671	2 1/2 . . . . 4.9087	3 1/2 . . . . 9.6211
25/32 . . . . 0.4794	1 9/16 . . . . 1.9175	2 9/16 . . . . 5.1572	3 9/16 . . . . 9.9678
13/16 . . . . 0.5185	1 5/8 . . . . 2.0739	2 5/8 . . . . 5.4419	3 5/8 . . . . 10.321
27/32 . . . . 0.5591	1 11/16 . . . . 2.2365	2 11/16 . . . . 5.6727	3 11/16 . . . . 10.680
7/8 . . . . 0.6013	1 3/4 . . . . 2.4053	2 3/4 . . . . 5.9396	3 3/4 . . . . 11.045
29/32 . . . . 0.6450	1 13/15 . . . . 2.5802	2 13/6 . . . . 6.2126	3 13/16 . . . . 11.418
15/16 . . . . 0.6903	1 7/8 . . . . 2.7512	2 7/8 . . . . 6.4918	3 7/8 . . . . 11.793
31/32 . . . . 0.7371	1 15/16 . . . . 2.9483	2 15/16 . . . . 6.771	3 15/16 . . . . 12.177

Leverage

In addition to knowing master cylinder bores and volumes, there is the matter of line pressure, and this reverts to the amount of leverage put on the system. Ultimately, the brake pedal lengths (leverages).

A 6:1 or 6.5:1 brake pedal leverage ratio is the average on rods. That is, the length of lever from fulcrum point (pivot) to the foot pad center would be something like 12 inches if the operating arm of the pedal below the pivot is 2 inches. This is with a floor mounted pedal. But suppose you have a hanging pedal, what are the leverages there? Amazingly, according to the math people, the ratio is the same even though the fulcrum is at the end of the hanging pedal.

Therefore, if you are going to move a firewall mounted

master cylinder to a floor mount, you would use the same leverage factor. All you are doing is moving the master cylinder for convenience, and changing the direction of actuating arm travel from the pedal.

Editor's note: When preparing this brakes section, we contacted the folks at JFZ, who are widely regarded as the experts to see about race car problems. Warren Gilliland of JFZ is also a street rod builder and has helped apply company expertise to the problems of special build highway machines. We sincerely thank JFZ and Warren for helping us to make this section "right", as compared to some of the brake information that has been floating around the hobby for year, much of it erroneous.

CHAPTER 6

Engines

What to Use

The engine you select for your particular car is going to be determined by several factors. First, there is what you want to use. Then, what can you afford, what can you locate, can you afford to rebuild an engine, do you have an engine in good condition already available, etc. Of all these factors, the one that can lead you down the proverbial path is what you want. You might be all hung up on having a Ford cammer, or a Chrysler early hemi, or an Ardun Ford flathead, or a big block Chevy. Be very real at this juncture, because this is where you can spend gobs of money for very little return, if you aren't careful.

The most popular rod engine today is the small block Chevrolet V8. Not because it is overwhelmingly superior, but because it is plentiful and specialty parts are readily available. You may be better off using a small block Ford, or MoPar. Or, if you are building an unusual car, such as a 60s muscle Rambler, then you might want to go with a Rambler V8 even though parts may be more difficult to locate. If you do some long range planning, you might decide that through the next several years you are going to be working more with one type

of engine than any other. If this is the case, then you will find that during the course of time you will begin to create quite an inventory of parts for that particular engine. Thus, each time you build this particular engine you will do it for less money (and effort).

The most commonly built hot rod engines of today are the V8's and inlines produced during the 60s and 70s, especially the high performance versions created during the heyday of muscle cars in the 1960s. Parts for these engines are readily available, and look to be for the foreseeable future. Such is not always the case for the engines of the 1950s, such as the Cadillac, Oldsmobile and Y-block Ford, etc.

Building up an "antique" hot rod engine can become a labor of frustration and expense, so before you start on one of those engines (a hot Ford Model A, or a Ford flathead V8, for instance) you will want to do a considerable amount of research, get plenty of money ahead, or wait to do one until you have experience with the more common late model engines.

Do not overlook the potential of the non-V8 engines. The

inline sixes can produce more than enough horsepower, dependably, and nothing will set your buddy back so much as being dusted by a six. Some of the four cylinders can be turned into killer engines, at low expense, and they work especially well in a light car. Import engines can be excellent hot rod material. Do some thinking, and you may end up with a Datsun 6 inline for your coupe rather than a 500 cubic inch monster V8.

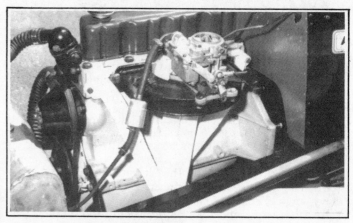

Chevy and other GM 4 and 6 cylinder engines work very well with lighter weight rods, are economical to buy and hop-up.

The author in another day, using the Oldsmobile V8 in a 1934 Ford project, strong engines that run cool.

Model A Ford engines can be reworked for interesting street and race performance, parts are getting scarce.

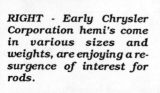

LEFT -The small block Ford is an excellent choice for nearly any rod project, fits early cars good.

RIGHT - Early Chrysler Corporation hemi's come in various sizes and weights, are enjoying a resurgence of interest for rods.

LEFT - The so-called small Chrysler engine is available up to 360 cubic inches, the 318 and 340 are most popular to build.

LEFT - The 1932-53 Ford flathead V8 engine is still popular, works better with 12-volt electrical system, modern alternator.

LEFT - The Chevrolet small block engine is the overwhelming favorite with most rodders, lots of performance equipment available and the prices are modest.

Engine Weights and Measures

We'll save you some time with a quick scan of approximate engine weights and measurements that will come into play when you are trying to decide what engine to build.

You'll note that engine weights are a lot closer to each other than you might have thought. For instance, the venerable Chrysler early Hemi is not as heavy, relative to the big block Chevrolet, as you may have thought, but note how much lighter the Buick V6 is than the Chevy small block.

We have not included the dimensions and weights of the Chevy/Mopar/Ford V6s since they are very similar to the V8s in measurements, and the weights are in ratio to the Buick engine. For the most part, the V6s will take up almost as much actual engine room as the V8s.

We do not include measurements for the exhaust manifolds, since there are so many different factory manifolds and aftermarket headers available. The oil pan sump location should not be considered as a final obstacle to use of a particular engine, since it is often possible to get a pan/oil pick-up assembly for an engine with the sump location elsewhere. You have to do some searching through the parts house listings, or visit the junkyard, in most cases, you can get this information from the hot rod racing parts suppliers who specialize in oiling systems.

In the distance **D** in our listings, this is the distance from the fan pulley face to the back of the valve cover/head or distributor...that place where firewall interference can be expected. The height B is to the top of the stock carburetor, this will change depending upon what carburetor/intake manifold you end up using.

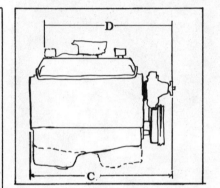

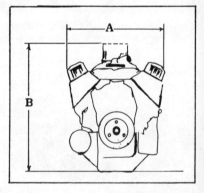

ENGINE	DISPLACEMENT	WT	A	B	C	D	STARTER	OIL SUMP
AMC 6	232/258	525	24"	26"	30"	25"	left	rear
AMC V8	304/360/401	545	21.5	28	29	21.5	left	rear
Buick V6	196/231	380	24	25.5	23	21.5	right	middle
Buick V8	350	450	23	25.5	29	21.5	right	rear
Buick V8	430/455	600	23	27	29	22	left	middle
Cadillac V8	472/500	600	23.5	29	30	28.5	right	middle
Chevy 4	153	360	16	25.5	22.5	24	right	front
Buick/Olds Pont/Chevy 6	250	415	16	25.5	30.5	24	Right	rear
Chevy V8	265-400	550	19.5	25	26.5	20.5	right	rear
Chevy V8	396-454	635	22	29.5	30.5	23.5	right	rear
Ford 6	144/250	400	17	26	29	24	right	front
Ford 6	240/300	400	13	26	30	24	right	front
Ford V8 Flathead	221/255	540	26	26	30	30	right	rear
Ford V8	260-351	460	20	25	27	22	right	front
Ford V8	332-428	625	23	30	30	28	right	front
MoPar 6	170-240	475	24	22	30	29.5	right	front
MoPar V8	273/360	555	20.5	28	29.5	23.5	left	front
MoPar V8	383/440	670	23.5	28	29	24	left	front
MoPar Hemi (late)	426	690	28.5	28	32	24	left	middle

(Note: Early Chrysler products hemi's vary in weight from a high similar to the late hemi to a low closer to the Chevy small block. Overall sizes vary as well.)

Olds V8	330-455	600	21.5	27	29	24	left	rear
Pont V8	350/400	600	22	26	28.5	20	left	rear
Pont V8	455	630	23	28.5	29.5	27	right	rear

Preparing the Block

The cylinder block is the foundation of the performance engine. it is the structural member that holds and/or encloses most of the other engine components, and can be made from many different materials; fabricated steel, cast iron, cast aluminum (with iron sleeves) or cast aluminum with a high silicone content. New technologies are creating a few other options, such as ceramics and plastic, but the majority of engine blocks are still made from cast iron.

Many feel that starting with a new block directly from the factory would be the best way to begin. However, the heating and and cooling that blocks are subjected to as a normal part of their function create dimensional changes due to different wall thicknesses and heating and cooling rates in different areas of the structure. After many of these expansion and contraction cycles, the block takes a set; i.e., while the dimensions continue to change during the heating and cooling periods, the block tends to return to its original dimensions after a cycle has been completed. A good used block, sometimes referred to as a "seasoned" block, is a better

choice than a "green" one because of its ability to maintain dimensional stability. Also, used blocks have already proven their structural integrity.

When preparing a used block there are a few cylinder wear patterns you should check for, especially if the block is in such good condition that boring may not be necessary. Cylinder warpage, indicated by a wavy wear pattern is caused primarily by cooling system problems. This wear pattern is common in inline six-cylinder engines because of the water flow, which usually initiates at the front of the block, circulates to the rear of the block, moves upward and returns through the cylinder head casting. The overall length of the block has the effect of forcing the first cylinder to run too cold and the last, or number-six, cylinder to run too hot. Maximum waviness is .001"; any amount of warpage past this will cause the piston rings to bounce and lose their seal at higher rpms.

Scores or scuffing on the cylinder walls can result in a loss of ring seal and any score you can feel should be considered to be past the maximum wear limit. Cylinder wall taper (Fig. 2), meanwhile, is due to ring wear against the wall itself. Wear tends to be more pronounced in the upper one inch of ring travel because maximum temperature and pressure within the cylinder is reached during this portion of piston and ring travel, and the ring is forced against the top of the cylinder wall with more pressure than at the bottom. The maximum wear limit for cylinder wall taper is .012", which is a circumferential measurement. This means that the lip at the top of the cylinder would be approximately .004".

If the block is in very good shape and the ridge at the top of the bore is within wear limits. removing the ridge with a reamer and finishing the cylinder wall with a geglazer would be sufficient. If the bore needs to be enlarged just a few thousandths of an inch for extra piston clearance a cylinder hone would do the job nicely, whereas if the taper in the bore has exceeded maximum tolerance the cylinder must be refinished with a boring bar and then honed to oversize.

If the cylinder is cracked but the crack does not extend to the top or bottom of the bore, the block may be salvaged by installing a sleeve. Cylinder oversizes for which pistons are readily available are .020", .030", and .040". with .030" being the most common. In some instances, other sizes such as .010", .060" and .125" are also available.

To measure these cylinder wear conditions, two instruments are common. An Ames gauge, more commonly known as a dial bore gauge, is much like a dial indicator mounted on a sled and when moved up and down within the bore will indicate changes in diameter. The dial bore gauge is useful for checking cylinder wall taper and warpage. but to determine bore size, you must use an inside micrometer, or a snap gauge and an outside micrometer. A snap gauge is a T-shaped device, and the upper portion of the T is expandable, spring loaded, and lockable in any position. Inserted into the bore, it expands at the position to be measured and is the locked to maintain the dimension before being withdrawn. The dimension may then be measured with an outside micrometer.

Before we begin our discussion of block preparation, a couple of terms that may need explanation are "deck height" and "deck clearance". Deck height is the measurement from the center of the main bearing, bore to the hood mating surface of the block. Deck clearance is the measurement from the top of the block to the top of the piston at top dead center (TDC).

The first step in engine block preparation is to strip it down completely. This means all frost plugs and oil galley plugs and don't forget the cam bearings. Inspect all parts for damage and wear patterns as often these wear patterns will reveal the conditions under which the block was operating. For instance, do the main bearings indicate that the crankshaft is bent or that the block requires line boring? Do the connecting rod bearings show signs of detonation damage? Do piston wear patterns show a misaligned or bent rod? Next, the block would be placed in a caustic solution to remove grease and accumulations of sludge and dirt as well as lime and scale build-up within the cooling system passages.

Once the block is clean, it must be inspected. Check for core shift with a sonic checker, which measures the thickness of an area by sending sound waves through it. You should check cylinder walls in any places for potential weak spots, using .150" as the minimum thickness (more if the engine is highly supercharged). Less than that, and the cylinder wall will balloon out under pressure, creating a major ring seal loss that will result in a lot of blow-by and power reduction. If you can't get a sonic checker, look for any major misalignment between machined areas and the surrounding core, such as the lifter valley in a V8 block. Ii the casting seems to be off-set from the lifter bore, there is probably a fair amount of core shift throughout the block. If sonic checking is not available, it would probably be wise to use that block for a

stock rebuild and find another block for your rodding activities.

Pressure testing and magnafluxing come next. A pressure test involves sealing all cooling system passages with plugs or rubber gasketed plates. spraying a soapy water solution over the surface of the block, and applying air pressure to the water jackets. If any cracks are present, the escaping air will cause the soapy water to bubble. Pressure testing will locate a fault whose path lies between the cooling passages and the outer surfaces of the block, but magnafluxing is necessary to find faults in "dry" areas of the block, such as the lifter valley and main cap areas. Magnafluxing involves setting up an electromagnetic field in the part to be checked and then spraying a dry iron powder on the surface. A fault creates a disruption in the magnetic field that draws the iron powder to it, showing itself as a white line.

The deck of the block, the surface to which the cylinder head bolts, is our next concern. Deck height should be equal from front to rear if it is a V8 or V6 block, the deck height should also be equal from one bank of cylinders to the other. It is not altogether uncommon for the deck height on some blocks to vary as much as .030", but variance should be no more than .005". If the deck itself is warped more than .004" over the full length, it will need to be resurfaced.

The main bearing bores should be inspected for alignment to each other and their individual concentricity. The former can be checked easily by installing the main bearings with a light coat of oil, placing the crankshaft in the block and torquing down the main bearing caps. If the crank spins freely, the alignment of the main bearing bores is satisfactory, if it doesn't, the block will need to be align-bored or align-honed.

Any time a block is align-bored or align-honed the centerline of the crankshaft is moved upward in the block. This upward movement of the crank produces a slackening effect in the timing chain, which in turn causes a change in cam timing unless corrected.

The cylinder should be rough honed with 220 grit stones to within .0005" of the desired finished size. Then, using 280, 400 or 600 grit stones, bring the bore to its finished size. A good rule of thumb when selecting honing stones is: chrome top rings-280 grit; moly top rings-280, or, more commonly, 400 grit. (The 600 grit stones can make it difficult to obtain a quality honed surface. They tend to burnish the surface, making the crosshatch pattern disappear. This causes ring seating problems and oil film problems.)

The term "crosshatch" refers to the scratches left in the bore by the honing stones. These scratches overlap one another, creating a diamond pattern. If the scratches are more vertical, more blow-by is possible. If the diamonds are flattened, excessive ring wear results. A good crosshatch has a 30- to 40-degree included angle between the marks.

Two more tips about honing, since it is so important for proper ring seal. A good speed is in the neighborhood of 350-

400 rpm. Avoid honing with old drills that employ a gear reduction system, as the gears invariably cause chatter marks.

A good flow of clean coolant should always be directed to the honing stones and cylinder walls during the honing process. As the stones break down to expose new, sharp cutting edges, the coolant flushes loose abrasive and metal particles away, and cools the work as well. Not using coolant can result in scuffing, excessive oil consumption, slow ring seating, excessive wear, and short ring life. Remember to expand the honing stones gradually, avoiding excessive pressure, as overloaded stones tend to break down too fast, resulting in a chatter in the cutting motion. Once you've brought the bore to its final size, make several passes using light pressure to eliminate any non-uniformities through "polishing".

Cleaning is an essential part of successful engine building. Lots of hot soapy water and vigorous scrubbing with a stiff, nonmetallic, bristle brush achieve the best results (liquid soap is preferable to the granular type, just in case some of it doesn't dissolve and is somehow left in the block). Scrub until the soap suds remain white, then wipe the bores with paper towels until they show no signs of dirt. I've discovered that if the bores are sprayed afterwards with CRC 5-56. Dirt seems to be drawn out of the metal even more effectively than with soap and water alone.

After cleaning, treat the block to prevent rust from forming. Use a light coat of oil or a surface protectant, such as CRC 5-56, WD-40. or General motors D.P.L.—unless you intend to paint the block, that is!

While deburring the block to smooth sharp edges, remove all the little casting "dingleberries" and small casting pockets where some of the core sand may still remain. Chase all the threaded holes in the block with a proper size tap to remove any dirt or rust build-up.

When a "serious" engine is being built, the ragged edges of all casting marks are ground away, reducing chances of small pieces of metal getting into the oiling system.

All the block surfaces are trued up to the crankshaft centerline, all bores are made perfect, then the oiling and cooling galleys are checked for any restrictions, cleaned.

Crankshaft Considerations

Before we discuss the technical aspects of crankshafts let's take a look at the relationship between stroke length and bore diameter. The terms that describe this relationship are square, undersquare, and oversquare.

In undersquare engines, the bore is smaller than the stroke, resulting in higher thermal efficiency, less heat leakage, more friction and greater piston travel per rpm than in an oversquare engine of equal displacement. On the other hand, an oversquare engine, where the bore is larger than the stroke, can use larger valves, and the piston velocity is slower per rpm, making it easier to achieve higher rpm. (now you've probably figured out that "square" means the bore and stroke dimensions are the same.) An .8 stroke-to-bore ratio is g generally good for rodding engines as it allows the engine to reach the higher rpm required and has adequate room for properly sized valves.

A crankshaft may be cast or forged or it may be machined from a solid piece of steel, commonly called a billet. Forged cranks are considered best for racing, as they are lighter and more flexible than cast, but they often require torsional vibration dampeners. Billet cranks, not quite as strong as a chromium steel forging, can be made to any desired configuration. However, unless you are experimenting with a crankshaft design or there are no forged cranks available for your engine, why spend extra bucks on a billet crank? Forged steel cranks that sometimes do not appear to be available for some engines quite often CAN be found in earlier models, truck or marine engines. They may also be available as factory performance items.

Cast cranks may be used for rodding applications if you remember that they don't like extended high rpm (over 7500 rpm), detonation, long periods of harmonic vibration, 11:1 or higher compression ratios, or bending and shock loads.

After the bearing clearances are checked, the crankshaft is torqued into place, it should spin freely by hand. All engine disassembly and reassembly can be done at home by an amateur, just follow manual specs and constantly recheck what has been done. Use care not to scratch crank bearing surfaces during assembly.

The difference between a cast crank and a forged one can be seen upon close observation. If the ridge or parting line that runs the length of the shaft on either side is quite thin with a fairly sharp ridge, it is a cast crank. If the parting line is relatively wide, 5/16" to 1/2", and flat across the top with what appears to be grinding marks, it is forged.

There isn't much crankshaft preparation a rodder can do himself because of the specialized equipment required, so take your crank to a reputable table regrinder familiar with rodding requirements. Have the shaft checked for straightness, and if it is bent more than .005", find another crank (there's no guarantee a straightened crank won't resume its former shape). Next, have it magnafluxed. If it is cracked, ask the guy who magnafluxed it for an assessment since small surface cracks and flaws often may be removed by grinding, or are just small heat checks that wouldn't affect reliability.

If the crank has progressed this far and is still satisfactory, have it reground. Ask the regrinder to put a 1/8" fillet radius where the journal surface meets the cheeks of the throws. If there is a sharp edge at this highly stressed location the crank will probably fracture here. Chamfer the oil holes with a die grinder to remove any sharp edges and allow easy oil flow onto the bearing surface. As a final step, polish the crank with 240 grit paper to remove any grinding marks, and finish with 400-600 grit.

There are some special processes that can be used for certain applications. Hard chroming makes the journals very hard so that trash will become imbedded in the bearings and not hurt the crank-useful where the motor sees a lot of teardowns or is subjected to a dirty environment. If you choose chroming, be sure to have the shaft heat-treated afterwards (called normalizing). Something to think about when considering chroming those front suspension pieces.

The oil Delivery holes in the crank can be slightly radiused with a fine stone to help oil flow onto bearing surfaces, holes must be cleaned with stainless brush during cleaning process. Do not overlook this procedure.

Indexing refers to the process of making each journal a specific number of degrees away from the next. Most cranks right from the factory are so close to being right on that unless the shaft has been abused during its service life, this process may be omitted. Even if one or more of the throws is out of index by as much as .030", correcting this would not show any measurable benefit.

Besides chroming there are a few other ways to harden crankshafts. Induction hardening, which uses electrical current, is quite expensive and rare. More common is nitriting, a good process that leaves a hardened shell about .030" thick and is also expensive. Most common in rodding is tufftriting. Tufftriting leaves a thin hard shell—about .001"—and increases journal diameter. by about .0001" to .0003".

For all-out racing, it's a good idea to cross-drill the main journals, i.e. drill through the main journal from the opposite side of the oil feed hole and intersect the oil passage.

Selecting Connecting Rods

Connecting rods are probably the most talked about yet least understood items in a performance engine. They do determine the rpm limits of the engine and are the most stressed components in a rodding powerplant, often forced to operated on the ragged edge, but they're frequently blamed for engine failures when, in fact, they are usually the victims of other problems or failures.

The most important consideration is where to put the "meat" to get the most strength and the least weight. The area where the beam blends into the big end of the rod—the shoulder area—must be meaty to prevent failure. The area around the cap and the cap retaining bolts must be substantial as well. But if the rods are so beefy and strong that they're indestructible , then they're so heavy that they overload the bearings.

Most production rods are cast from either ductile or nodular iron and usually are not suited for performance over 6000 rpm. Some companies offer special rods for heavy duty applications, which are forged from the same 1040 plain carbon steel as production rods but are designed differently, are machined more accurately and have superior surface finishing . These rods are good for budget rodders who can get by with 500-1000 rpm less than the big boys. There are also a number of factory high-performance rods. These rods have a better race track record than the factory rods, but the question arises as to whether you'd be farther ahead to buy a set of the so-called "exotic" rods.

I classify exotic as being any connecting rod that does not come from the automobile manufacturer, but is made specifically for hot rodding. The majority of exotic steel rods are machined from solid blanks of 4340 chrome-nickel-moly alloy steel, and are heat treated and polished. These rods are available in any custom size, but are relatively heavy and

rarely used in engines intended for use over 8000 rpm (they are considered the best for endurance rodding at speeds of 7000-8000 rpm.) There is another type of steel rod that is gaining favor with street rodders and that is the investment cast steel rod manufactured by Mechart, which has proven extremely reliable and is also very light—lighter, in fact, than some aluminum rods.

Aluminum rods are most popular for drag racing, where light weight is needed for 10,000-plus rpm and quick acceleration, even if the rods only last for 50 to 75 runs. A less obvious advantage has to do with the cushioning effect of aluminum rods: Supercharged engines may get into violent detonation or pre-ignition at certain times and the cushioning effect will keep the bearings from getting pounded out as easily, or even save the engine from breaking a crank.

Titanium is as light as aluminum, but it can be made as strong as chrome-nickel steel with proper alloy and heat-treating. Titanium rods, therefore. don't have to be as meaty as aluminum rods; they actually weigh 30-40% less.

To digress a moment, there are two methods employed for rod cap retention. Some steel and all aluminum rods use a cap screw that threads into the upper portion of the rod. The other method used is through-nut and bolt. Either is satisfactory.

Rod bolt breakage is the most common form of rod failure. Some experts say you can double the strength of regular production rods merely by substituting special high-strength rod bolts. On American V8 engines, high-performance rods have 7/16" diameter bolts where standard rods usually have 5/16" or 3/8" bolts. Chrysler Hemis use 1/2" bolts and 1/2" bolts are optional on Carillo rods.

It material is also important. The best rodding insurance

you can buy is the best set of rod bolts available for your engine.

Connecting rod length has been the focus of much experimentation by almost every engine builder over the last few years. Rod length is measured from the center of the wrist pin hole to the center of the rod bearing hole. The ratio of the rod's center-to-center distance, compared to the stroked of the crankshaft is known as the L/R ratio, and it's a useful relationship as it gives a common denominator when comparing engines of similar configurations rations but different bore and stroke. Changing rod lengths is one way to improve the performance of a hot rodding engine but its effect will depend on such factors as the camshaft, induction system, rpm range, combustion chamber design, etcetera.

If you purchase a set of pure racing rods, there will be little if any preparation required before installation into that killer motor you're preparing for battle. If, however, you plan on using a set of factory rods, there are a few operations that must be performed to make the rod street ready.

If at all possible start with a new set of rods. At each end of the rod there will be a square or small block of metal that is an extension of the rod itself, called the balancing pads. Choose a set of rods with the smallest possible balancing pads, so they will start out being as light as possible.

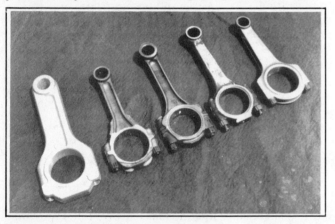

Different types of connecting rods, from a special aluminum forging at the left through various stock rods to welded and polished steel rod at right. For most street applications heavy duty factory rods work fine, but in all-out racing the special rods are required.

Magnaflux the rod, rod cap and that set of high quality rod bolts you've just purchased. Along the side of the 'I' beam, or shank, of the rod there will be a parting line left from the manufacturing process. Grind away this parting line with a longitudinal movement. (If the grinding marks go across the shank they will act as a series of tiny stress risers and the rod will surely fail.) Remove the balancing pads from each end of the rod, as this will lighten the rod substantially yet still keep it balanced. Remove all sharp edges, as they will only serve as stress risers.

Polishing the rod will remove any surface imperfections. Some engine builders polish the rod completely while others polish only the shank on the top and bottom of the 'I' beam. There is no performance difference between the two methods and the difference in reliability would be slight, if any. One of the more critical—and often overlooked—areas on a rod is the contact surface between the rod and the cap, which must be very smooth. The seat areas for the nut and bolt should be smooth and at right angles to the bolt axis.

Next the rod should be shot-peened. Mask the bolt holes, bearing bore and the piston pin bore. Using number 230 cast-steel shot, shot-peen the entire rod—the bolt head and nut seats, the machined surfaces on both sides, and corners and edges. Check the rods center-to-center distance. The generally accepted tolerance is .001"-.002" variation for a complete set of rods.

If the small end of the rod is to be bushed or honed, now is the time to have it done. Resize the rod big end, holding it to the small hole size of the factory tolerance. Afterwards, do not remove or switch rod bolts from their respective places as this will misalign the rod caps.

Install the pistons to the rods and have the rods aligned; .002"-.003" out of alignment is allowable with short-skirt pistons. Of course, if you purchased a set of those exotic rods, then you can bypass all the preceding steps except the last. If piston pin oiling is needed and there is no factory provision for such, then holes may be drilled for oil flow, with the single top hole preferred.

An often overlooked point that contributes to rod failure is the use of asymmetrical piston dome shapes that weigh differently from side to side. A small-block Chevy can have a dome of 25 grams entirely on one side of the piston which imparts as much as a 1500 lb bending load right below the pin eye. Properly designed pistons will weigh the same on each side. Most engines that start blowing oil out the breathers at high rpm are running asymmetrical pistons, and they're losing ring seal as the pistons rock due to the weight difference on each side.

Bearings

Practically all four-stroke engines today rely on bearings that are plain; i.e., they don't incorporate anti-friction devices such as rollers or balls. Rather, they comprise a steel- or bronze-backed shell with a babbitt overlay (babbitt is a mixture of tin and lead—the more tin, the harder the babbitt—with a small amount of antimony acting as a bonding agent.)

A bearing's ability to accept and hold foreign particles is known as embeddability, while its ability to accommodate small irregularities in the crankshaft journal surface and the bearing housing bore is known as conformability. The psi rating is the load rating per square inch of bearing surface.

What type of bearing should you use? Generally speaking, it's best to use a softer bearing on a racing engine that's torn down a lot because you can replace the bearings frequently, and save the expensive crank. On engines that stay together

for a longer time, use stronger bearings that will not flake or fatigue as easily. Naturally, the harder the bearing you use, the harder the crankshaft you need, so that all foreign material gets embedded in the bearing and doesn't score the crank.

More particularly, a steel-backed shell with a babbitt overlay would be suitable for light use only, as it resists scuffing, has low friction loss, features good conformability and embeddability and is rated at 2000 psi. On the other hand, a steel-backed shell with an aluminum alloy center and then babbitt overlay has little embeddability and a 6000-10,000 psi rating. This type of bearing is good only with hardened shafts and usually requires slightly more clearance.

Speaking of clearance, it's critical because oil throw-off increases as the square of the clearance; in other words,

113

has lost its shape, stretched, and can no longer secure the bearing properly; in short, the bearing has been moving around. Aluminum rods, expanding twice as much as steel, cannot depend on crush to hold the bearing in place so dowel pins are used with corresponding holes in the bearing shells to provide the necessary security.

The parting line edge of a rod or main bearing saddle as it comes from the factory is usually razor sharp, and should be touched with a stone to avoid scraping a chip off the back of a shell.

Bearings must be installed DRY. Wipe their backs and the bearing bore with lacquer thinners and install. Remember, any dirt, oil, Loctite or whatever behind the bearing is a big no-no. And never, never, NEVER sand, steel wool or Scotch-Brite bearings. All you're doing is gouging the surface and embedding garbage in it.

By all means prelube the engine before starting, and examine all bearings that are removed from the engine, failed or otherwise; they can tell you more than a toolbox full of dial indicators and micrometers. Bearing failure charts are available from most bearing manufacturers.

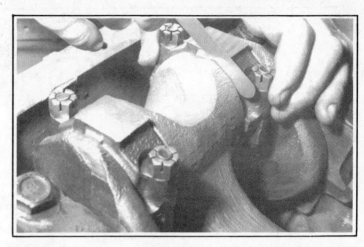

Side clearance between crank cheek and rod big end must be checked with a feeler guage, too little causes excessive heat build-up, too much will reduce pressure/film thickness at bearing surface.

Plastigage is a simple way to check bearing clearance, caps must be torqued to specs to get correct reading.

increasing clearance from .0015" to .0025" will increase oil throw-off FIVE times. Not only does this conflict with what the rings can handle, but it would also require increased oil pump capacity.

Each engine is different when it comes to clearance requirements. For example, a 426 Chrysler Hemi likes .0025" on the rods and .003" on the mains, but a 427 Ford likes as much as .0045" on the mains.

Anything less than .0025" main bearing clearance on a racing engine restricts oil flow and cooling capabilities. Rod journal clearance on the high side of the manufacturer's specification is usually adequate for most applications, while rod side clearance on the high side of the specs is also the norm.

The most frequently used and inexpensive method of checking clearance is Plastigage, which is nothing more than

an accurately sized thread of plastic substance that is placed between a journal and shaft, then squashed and measured. Green Plastigage is used for clearances of .002" to .003" and red Plastigage for clearances of .003" to .006".

Plastigage may prove inaccurate if the clearance is under .002", but these small gaps can be measured with a telescopic gauge and micrometers.

Before instaling bearings, remember that cast iron cranks have an unusual crystalline grain structure that tends to wipe the bearings if the crank isn't highly polished. Steel crank also require some polishing, although not to the same extent as cast cranks.

Check for any misalignment between the bearing oil hole and the oil galley. If the bearing covers too much of the galley hole, the back of the bearing shell might flood with oil, so if necessary, chamfer the oil galley hole just enough to line up with the bearing hole.

On cars with automatic transmissions, very little end thrust is applied to the crank, but with standard transmission, clutch release pressure reacts full force against the thrust bearing. When installing this thrust bearing (usually part of one main bearing), tap the crank in one direction then in opposite direction to center the bearing and prevent the crank from riding against just part of the face. Usually, the thrust surface will have two radial grooves (per shell) to ensure lubrication to this highly stressed area, but if not use a small round file and make them yourself.

The small locating tangs on one end of each bearing shell help keep the bearing in position but provide only about 10% of the total actual holding power. Bearing "crush" makes up the other 90%. If upon disassembly you notice that the rod bearings have gall marks on their backs, the rod bearing bore

Piston Selection

Most of the time, a person considering pistons for an engine thinks of just two things—what compression ratio will result and whether the pistons are forged or cast. But the piston selection is a lot more involved than that. For one thing, the piston also determines ring selection and position. For another, the piston is the bottom half of the combustion chamber and therefore has a profound effect on the combustion process.

There are five basic design features for any piston: (1) it must produce as little operating friction as possible; (2) it

must transfer the maximum possible heat to the cylinder walls; (3) it must be of low net weight; (4) it must provide the necessary piston pin support (in accordance to cylinder pressure loadings); and (5) it must prevent oil passage in to the combustion chamber (inasmuch as piston design can accomplish this).

All pistons today are made of aluminum alloys; different alloys are used depending on the application and the manufacturer. For street use, all aluminum alloy affords high strength at high temperatures, scuff resistance and a small expansion rate. In contrast, only high strength at high temperatures and scuff resistance are significant for racing applications. If the pistons make a slapping noise when a racing engine is cold, it is of no consequence, whereas it would be a major factor in a production engine. Also, due to the extremes in which racing engines operate, the pistons are always made of fresh or virgin aluminum, never remelted aluminum.

The majority of pistons are formed by one of three methods. Sandcasting is used on small production runs but is too expensive for large quantities. All engine manufacturers needing a cast piston for large production runs use permanent mold castings while racing pistons are generally forged. Forging (extrusion) is difficult and expensive, but the metal is more dense and uniform and the grain structure follows the shape of the piston, making a forged piston inherently stronger, and usually lighter; also, it will run slightly cooler than cast pistons.

The piston dome, which can be varied to adjust the compression ratio, isn't always a "dome"—some pistons are flat and some have a reverse dome, or dish. The ring lands, the areas where the piston's rings sit, determine the thickness and location of the rings, while the compression height is the distance from the center of the wrist pin hole to the top of the piston, not including any dome or dish. Skirt taper is the taper from top to bottom of the piston skirt (usually about .002" on stock pistons), necessary because the upper portion of the skirt runs hotter and thus expands more than the bottom of the skirt. Tapering makes the piston run much quieter. On racing pistons, a skirt barrel is used instead of a taper, to help maintain skirt clearance and aid wear life.

One might think that the piston pin would be centered (laterally) in the skirt, but it isn't, which is why even flat-top pistons have a definite front and back. Piston pin offset counteracts combustion pressures, thus reducing piston-to-wall frictional losses. Connecting rod length is a factor in the amount of offset, shorter rods having greater offset due to greater rod angularity.

Note that there is a major and minor thrust side, with piston pin offset toward the major side. (The major side is the one the crankshaft would hit first when rotating in its normal direction.) Viewed from above, pistons are slightly oval or cam-shaped. The amount of cam depends on piston design, the way the skirt is tied to the pin bosses and the operating temperature of the piston itself. Because of this cam, pistons should always be measured at the piston pin centerline across the thrust faces.

The dome you see on most racing pistons is there for one reason to raise the compression ratio for more power. But along with this advantage come a number if disadvantages, such as increased weight, valve interference problems, and a high surface area to volume ratio, which allows more heat leakage. The mixture burns slower due to dome interference and there is poor flame propagation; i.e., the flame travels outward in an awkward pattern. Finally, domed pistons are difficult to machine.

If you are planning an engine that only operates at higher rpm (above, say, 7500), it would be better to use a little less dome and give up some compression to get a better combustion chamber shape—and usually an overall power increase. If possible, select a piston with an even thickness across the top to aid in heat transfer. Top thickness on forged pistons should be not less the 5/16", although 1/4" is allowable in a small, low-stressed area on non-supercharged engines.

Obviously, the higher the compression ratio the more power, or so the tale goes. But what is often overlooked is the difference between mechanical compression ratio and the actual compression PRESSURE. If there is a late intake valve closing for instance, some of the mixture will be forced back into the intake manifold, thus changing the compression pressure but not the compression ratio. A good example of this effect is the Crower Mileage System, which uses a specially ground camshaft with the late closing intake cycle. The compression ratio is 16.5:1 but it produces only 160-170 psi compression pressure, allowing the engine to run on regular pump gasoline.

One last thing on compression. The old—and unfortunately still too common—method of gaining compression by milling the cylinder head(s) is no longer viable. Thin head surfaces flex and move around, causing blown head gaskets. Worse, the cylinder head will cave in completely. If the extra compression is needed, it is much safer to replace the pistons, although admittedly this is more expensive.

Piston pins are another area where there is a strength/weight compromise. With a stronger piston pin, you can lighten the piston more, but if the pin is too heavy, extra stresses are placed on the connecting rod and bearings. Then the rod must be made stronger and then the crank must be beefed up to handle the heavier rods...It's a vicious circle that never quits. To help solve this strength-weight problem, all quality pins are made from stainless steel alloy, heat-treated and chromed. (With stronger alloys it is possible to use a thinner wall on the pin and maintain the strength.) Most good racing pins are taper-drilled: that is, the wall section (thickness) is thinner at the end of the pin than in the center, giving a high strength-to-weight ratio. There are two types of piston pins, oscillating and full floating. Oscillating pins are secured motionless at the connecting rod (usually) and pivot or oscillate in the piston. They should never be used in a performance application because the oscillating heats up the pin boss in the piston at higher rpm and they are too difficult to disassemble, making the frequent maintenance racing engines require difficult. Full floating pins are just that; they float fully in the piston and the small end of the connecting rod. However, because they are not held in place by the con rod, something must stop them from riding against the cylinder bores. Circlips, wire locks, Truarcs and buttons accomplish this. If you stand a circlip on end and look at the edge to side, notice that one end or face is rounded and the other is squared off. Install the squared faced toward the cylinder wall,so that, if the piston ever hammers against the circlip, the squared face will dig into the piston, securing itself. Piston pins have hammered out circlips before and it si usually because the clips have been installed backwards. So pay attention, because if the clip pops out and the pin rubs against the cylinder wall, the result will be one very heavy doorstop. To prevent pounding out, piston pin-to-circlip clearance should not exceed .018-.022"; snug is even better.

Buttons are often used for pin retention on engines that require frequent teardowns, such as in drag racing. A button is nothing more than a stepped cylinder that has the small end located in the end of the piston pin, with the other end, which is radiused, riding just off the cylinder wall. Buttons are usually made of aluminum or teflon, but teflon resists cylinder wall fuel washing better than aluminum, and because of this teflon buttons have become almost standard fare in nitro methane-burning engines. On the minus side, teflon does pick up abrasives and can put small score marks on the cylinder walls, so aluminum is the better choice for all but nitro engines.

If there is no original provision for piston pin oiling, or if you just want to ensure that enough oil will reach the pin regardless, drill a small hole (about 3-32") from the back of the oil ring groove diagonally downward to the pin bore. This, alongwith the oil hole in the connecting rod will adequately lubricate any full-floating pin.

By close examination of the top of the piston you can discern many things that may well aid you in your search for more power. The top of the piston should be a grey-light brown sooty color across the complete surface after running. Any washed-out areas around the perimeter indicate oil seeping past the rings and preventing the carbon from sticking. Color on the underside of the piston dome means the piston is being subjected to excessive temperatures, causing the oil that is thrown there to burn. Bad valve guides show excessive carbon build-up as well as a splotchy effect. A clean area around the intake portion of the piston shows a certain amount of washing from the incoming fuel-air mix. Lean or lightly stained areas indicate a lack of combustion (too tight piston-to-deck clearance, etc.), and/or lack of flame front turbulence, allowing fuel to drop out of suspension (usually preceded by valve notches or sharp corners).

These are a few of the things to look for. Even if it requires a bit of head grinding to achieve good piston coloring, and thus a drop in compression, the trade-off almost always results in increased horsepower.

Just a couple of bits to finish off. Try to keep as little piston-to-wall clearance as possible, within the manufacturers specs, of course. Too much clearance results in cold scuffing, and piston rock, which cases ring seal loss. Also minimum piston-to-valve clearance should be kept at .080"-.100" for intake and .090"-.120" for exhaust. The reason that the exhaust needs more clearance is that the piston chases the exhaust valve up the cylinder, and if valve float should occur, there is more of a chance for collision with the exhaust than with the intake. Some people have run closer clearances, but this requires a very rigid valve train, smooth-acting camshaft action and a bit of luck— one over-rev with a bit of valve float and you're looking at a lot of expensive paper weights that you can give out to friends.

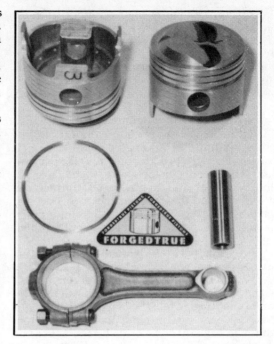

Piston Rings

You often hear racers discussing engines with seemingly limitless knowledge, but let the topic turn to piston rings and these pillars of learning give the impression that serious piston ring talk can only be spoken by a handful of individuals deep within the bowels of some multi-national corporation. Are piston rings really a black art? As Scrooge would say, humbug!

The Piston rings have three jobs to do: (1) provide sealing against the cylinder wall and against the side of the groove in the piston; (2) provide good oil control; and (3) do both these jobs with as little friction as possible.

Two basic ring types do these tasks. A compression ring is used to seal combustion and compression pressures, while an oil ring meters a certain amount of oil up to the compression rings so that they may function properly and scrap any excess oil back towards the pan. Compression rings do aid in oil control, especially in the second ring.

In a carbureted gas-burning engine, the top ring may reach 600F, while the second ring will get to 300F and the oil ring only 250F. Because of the high heat, the top ring is made of a ductile iron, which offers good impact resistance (for detonation) and will not heat-set at these higher temperatures. The second ring is made of a plain iron which can easily do the job because it sees no direct detonation and the overall temperature range is less. What's more, plain iron has less cylinder wall loading and friction. Which means less horsepower loss. Oil rings, being formed stamped expanders and two very thin rails are usually stainless steel.

With all the horsepower we are building into our engine, we must make sure that all the pressure gets to the flywheel and doesn't just blow out of the crankcase vents. The top ring is the one that is going to get the brunt of this force so let's look at it first.

The top piston ring has been getting smaller (thinner) over the years from 5/64" down to 1/16" to .043", then .031". There's even been some experimenting with .017" top rings. The rings are being made thinner to reduce their weight and

thus avoid ring flutter, which occurs at the top of piston travel when the piston changes direction violently, causing the ring to lift slightly in the piston ring groove and break its seal temporarily. Naturally, the lighter the ring, the higher the engine may be revved before ring flutter and the resulting horsepower loss occurs. For engines with a maximum 7000-8000 rpm, a 1/16" ring is the norm as it is physically stronger (this strength makes it a good choice for handling turbochargers or other high-pressure modifications).

Most top rings seal partly by spring tension against the cylinder wall and partly by twisting in the groove under pressure to seal off the groove itself. Some rings are designed to seal by combustion and compression pressure only. The .043" ring works this way with gas ports, but this is an adaptation; the "Head Land" ring and the .031" "pressure back" ring also work this way.

Top rings are usually made of a ductile iron or stainless steel. However, stainless steel rings are very stiff and so do not conform to the cylinder wall very well with normal unblown cylinder pressures. These rings are used almost exclusively in supercharged, exotic fuel-burning engines because they are about the only ring that will survive.

Passenger car to rings are usually just plain iron, but for heavy duty applications and racing there is either a chrome (chromium), moly (molybdenum), or ceram coating applied to the periphery. Chrome is very hard and dense, but its porous surface can retain a small amount of lubricant, improving parts life. Chrome rings are a good choice for dirt driving because of their excellent abrasion resistance.

There are two types of moly rings, moly-filled, and plasma sprayed. In a moly-filled ring the molten moly is poured into a machined groove on the outside of the ring. Under intense vibration or detonation this moly may actually break out. The advantages of moly are many: it has a lower coefficient of friction than chrome or cast iron, along with a greater hardness and a higher melting point. Best of all from a rodding standpoint, where time is always at a premium, moly

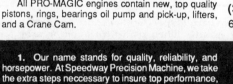

117

rings seat quickly.

On the other hand, moly rings need a clean environment, as the moly traps abrasives and will nicely rehone your cylinder walls. Not good. This means dirt roads are out.

The second ring is normally made from plain cast iron instead of a ductile iron, as noted earlier. Second rings are round in 5/64" and 1/16" sizes, with the 1/16" able to handle more rpm. The second ring does aid compression by catching any blow-by past the top ring, but its primary function is a second oil ring. If any excess oil gets by the second ring it could interrupt the seal between the top ring and the cylinder wall, fouling spark plugs and reducing the octane rating of the fuel (by oil contamination), thereby reducing detonation. Moly second rings are available and are good for long-distance racing engines to prevent wear, but are really not necessary.

The bottom ring is the oil control ring and almost always comprises three parts—two scrapers to skim oil off the cylinder walls, and an expander that provides tension to help hold the scrapers against the cylinder walls. The connecting rod throws a tremendous amount of oil on the cylinder walls (especially with larger rod side clearances) and the oil ring must remove this, leaving only a microscopically thin layer for ring seal. Oil drainback is through the holes behind the oil ring. Because of this the 3/16" rings are preferred as they do a better job of controlling oil since the drainback holes can be larger. A long rod with the pistons high in the block needs less oil control because less oil makes its way up there.

Oil rings are offered in three tensions standard, low and ultra-low. Standard tension is ideal for street and mild high-performance engines. Low tension offers more horsepower but uses a little more oil, and this is o.k. in a race engine. An ultra-low-tension ring saves even more power but will be a real loser unless some method is used to prevent oil from migrating up the cylinder walls, such as a vacuum balance system.

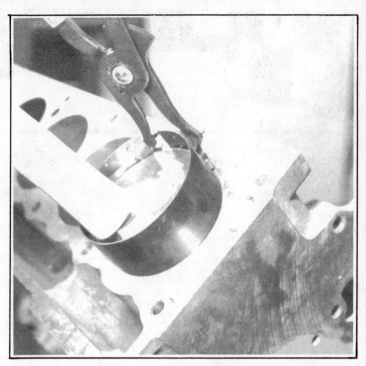

Pistons fit in cylinder bore a specific direction, tap gently on dome with hammer handle when using ring compressor for installation. Oil piston and cylinder wall liberally first.

Ring end gap should be as small as possible without the ring ends butting. If, when the rings are removed from an engine, they have shiny areas on their ends, this means the gap has closed while the engine was running and the ends have butted together. Obviously, the gap should be increased.

If gap size must be increased, use the tool that is made just for this purpose or place a file in a vice and move the ring against it from the outside diameter edge to the inside diameter edge. Do not stroke in the opposite direction as the surface which rides against the cylinder wall could be chipped or cracked. Once the desired gap is achieved, break the sharp edges with 400 grit emery cloth.

If you are just freshening up an engine, the oil ring is ok as is, the second ring should be replaced only if it is shiny across the entire face, and the top ring should be replaced if it has worn more than .002". You can check for ring face wear by measuring ring end gap. If the gap was .015" when the engine was first assembled and it now measures .018", then the difference is .003". Divide the circumference change .003", by pi to get a diameter change of .001". It is not necessary to hone the cylinders unless bad scratches or score marks are present because the rings are lapped at the factory and if the bores are smooth and round the rings will seat almost immediately.

One last point: Don't forget to match cylinder wall finish to the type of rings being used.

Often overlooked by inexperienced engine builders is the vital clearance of piston rings in the pistons grooves. Ring should also be squared in cylinder bore and end gap checked.

Engine Balancing

Now that the basic short block is ready for final assembly, the rotating and reciprocating parts must be balanced. Although there are two categories of balancing, power and mechanical, we can look after only the mechanical because the former is established at the design state (power imbalance results from gas pressure that is applied at irregular intervals and relates to firing order).

Mechanical imbalance is vibrations due to weight differences in the rotating and reciprocating assemblies within the engine. Even if you are using a stock short block, do not trust factory balancing. Factory tolerances are "right on" if the weight differences on pistons and rods are kept within four grams and they have an imbalance of no more than 14 gram-inches on rotating assemblies. Compare this with a good

balance shop's space tolerances of one-half gram and one gram-inch and it is easy to see why a properly balanced engine will be much smoother.

Precision engine balancing for a street performance engine or especially a racing powerplant is a must, because imbalance increases as the square of the rpm. So an imbalance of one ounce, say 3.5" from the axis of rotation, would create an imbalance of 1.55 pounds at 500 rpm, 55.8 pounds at 3,000 rpm, and a whopping 303 pounds at 7,000 rpm.

The reciprocating parts, pistons, rods, etc., are balanced statically, or, while they are at rest. The rotating parts—crankshaft, flywheel, etc.—are balanced dynamically, or, while they are in motion. Static balance is when the center of gravity of the rotating object lies on its axis of rotation. Dynamic balance is when a part while rotating has an absence of rocking couples.

Static and dynamic balancing of the engine will make a marked difference in the way it performs, even at lower rpm s. This is farmed out to the professional shop, sometimes requires substitution of parts to make everything balance correctly. Here a rod big end is being checked.

Lubrication

When you think lubrication, oil is the first thing that comes to mind. Motor oil has nine basic tasks to perform: 1) lubricate the engine and prevent wear; 2) minimize friction; 3) provide rust and corrosion control; 4) keep the engine clean; 5) minimize combustion chamber deposit formations; 6) cool the engine; 7) seal combustion Pressures; 8) resist foaming; and 9) permit easy starting. A term associated with oil is viscosity, which simply refers to an oil's thickness. Viscosity, by being thin, controls the ease of engine starting during cold weather, and by being thick, determines the degree of engine protection when the temperature rises towards the critical level.

It's easy enough to see oil, but you don't see all the other things that are mixed into it, such as viscosity index improvers, deterrents, dispersants, anti-oxidants and antiwear additives. In fact, the major difference between street and racing oils is in the additives. Racing oils have more anti-foam agents, higher corrosion-control abilities and a special ashless detergent-dispersant to minimize combustion chamber deposits. However, racing oils are becoming a thing of the past, as they are now labelled "performance oils."

Racing oils can be used on the street and would be highly recommended for high-performance use, but stay away from the heavy oils, such as Volvoline grade 60, Pennzoil Special Racing Oil 50 and 60, and Kendall 70 (nitro), as these are intended for a specialized application, nitro-burning drag race motors.

No discussion of oil would be complete without covering synthetics. Synthetics are not new. The Germans started working with them during World War II and they've been used in jet turbines for years. Synthetics are but one of three basic oil groups offering added protection, as well as long interval changes.

The true synthetics, such as Mobil 1, Amsoil and Chemlube, are chemically constructed lubricants. Then there are the mineral-based oils that are strengthened with a solid lubricant, such as Arco Graphite. Finally, there are the premium mineral oils with supplemental additives, like STP's 15,000-mile Oil or Shell Super X.

Synthetics have excellent temperature range capabilities, will flow at temperatures that would turn most oils solid, and will perform well up to 500F—well beyond the 300F limit of mineral oils. Synthetics also have a superior shear strength, meaning lubrication will be provided when subjected to extreme pressures. There is also a superior level of lubricity which permits a reduction in viscosity while maintaining the lubrication level equal to horsepower required to drive the oil pump, thus freeing that power for use at the rear wheels. Also, because of this improved lubricity, there is a drop in oil temperature, reduced oil consumption.

The lubrication requirements of a racing engine depend on three things; total engine output, length of time that the output is sustained and the rpm attained. Let's start with the oil pump. The volume of oil the pump must put out is determined by the various clearances within the engine. The major oil leak-away spots are the main and rod bearings and the valve lifter bores. Looser-than-stock bearing clearances are not needed in street performance engines. Some racing engines are looser to allow more oil flow for cooling purposes, but there is a trend away from this, thus reducing the amount of the "leak-away". Valve lifter-to-lifter-bore clearance should be no more than .0015" to keep the leakage as low as possible.

High volume oil pumps can be purchased for many engines but are not needed if stock clearances are used, even at 65000 rpm. But if clearances are penned up into the .002"-.003" range then a high volume pump is a good investment. Also, if a heavy-duty oil pump driveshaft (if used) is available, use it by all means. This is a particular problem on some Ford and

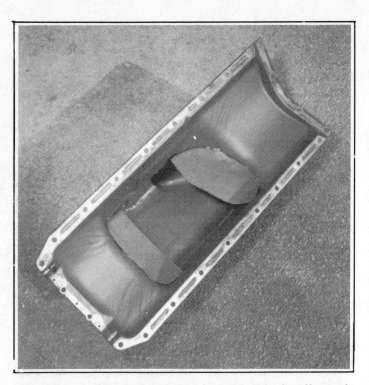

When the crankshaft is flailing around inside the oil pan, it will whip up a tremendous amount of oil spray, which robs horsepower. The simple addition of pan baffles will reduce much of this spray, and keep the oil around the oil pickup, special pans are available for different types of serious racing engines.

Chrysler V8's. Remember, a broken one can wipe out a very expensive engine in the blink of an eye.

Any oil pumps output can be drastically increased at high rpm by increasing the suction area with larger diameter lines and/or multiple pickups. If possible, dual feed the pump and ensure smooth radii throughout the internal passages. Larger pump gears will have little effect at high rpm unless the suction side is also increased in size. A good approximation of the ideal pump inlet area (like comparing apples and oranges) is that the inlet cross-sectional area, in square inches, should be twice that of the pump's volume-per-revolution, in cubic inches. All oil pumps have bypass valving or an oil pressure relief valve, which is an internal valve that returns excess oil to the suction side of the pump and is operated by pump pressure. Some pumps route excess oil to a fitting, returning it to the oil pan (make sure that this oil is not directed toward the crankshaft). Pump pressure can be increased by installing a heavy duty oil pressure relief spring or by placing shims against the stock spring. A maximum end play of .001" between the oil pump case and the gears or rotor should be observed. Excess clearances within the pump can really destroy the pump's volume and pressure.

The oil pump pick-up should be located no more than 1/4" above the oil pan floor. Higher than this, there is a chance of the pump picking up some air; lower than this, the oil pan floor may become a restriction to oil flow into the pick-up. The oil pick-up screen should be oval or rectangular in shape as round ones tend to create a vortex and draw in air.

How much oil pressure is enough? I've got the same answer for everyone: "It depends" Thin-film-lubrication theory states that maximum loads can be supported with a .0001" oil film. Practice tells us that this doesn't work. The crank journals are not smooth, round or straight and require at least .001" to rotate. The crank, while in operation, bends and twists along its entire length. Connecting rod big ends distort and temperatures increase. All these factors together determine at volume and pressure the oil system must deliver to avoid making scrap metal out of our expensive engine.

All engines are different but here are some rules of thumb to help out. First, you probably need less oil pressure than most people think. Actually only 10-15 psi is needed to force oil through most engine blocks. Smaller-diameter journals on the crankshaft require less oil pressure. As the rpm is increased, the oil pressure must also be increased. Sloppy or worn clearance leaks oil pressure as well as oil volume. An engine with good oil galley routing and crank journals on the smaller side should be adequately protected with 10 psi oil pressure per 1,000 rpm; i.e.,—7,000 r m=70 psi.

How do YOU measure oil pressure? I hope it's not with one of the guages that is fitted with a clear plastic line which has the inside diameter about the size of a fly's leg. The oil pressure line should have a minimum INSIDE DIAMETER of 1/8" to get good gauge response and help detect momentary pressure loss while braking or cornering.

When the crankshaft is spinning at a high rpm, the oil that flows down onto the crank from above, and the oil that flows out from the crank journals, tends to cling to the crank. The air turbulence around the whirling crank also draws oil up from the sump, gathering it around the crank. This oil, which wraps itself around the crank and rods, creates a frictional drag called crank windage and the tray which fits under the crank separating the crank from the sump is called the windage tray. A properly shaped and close-fitting windage tray, with louvers or screen, will stop 90% of this windage effect. Tests show average gains of 10-15 hp at 65000 rpm from typical performance V8's. There is also an item called a scraper, which sits on one side of the oil pan rail and protrudes outward towards the crankshaft, coming as close as possible to the crank without actually causing interference. As the crank is swinging upward past the scraper, the oil is actually cut or scraped from the crank. Together, a good fitting windage tray and fine-fitted scraper, fitted to the right side pan rail, will show an average gain of about 25 hp on a high-revving V8.

Get the best filters you can buy. If there's sufficient space; use extra-capacity filters (example: the standard filter for the small Chevy V8 is about 5", but some engines—in station wagons and light trucks—use a filter that's about 7" long and medium duty trucks use one about 10" long).

All street rods should monitor their oil systems with pressure and temperature gauges. You want to monitor the temperature of the oil going to the bearings after filtering and cooling, not the oil that's in the pan, and you need an oil cooler whenever the temperature rises above 275F, although it is better to keep it under 225F. One of the most commonly used coolers is the Harrison 3157807 available from General Motors.

As will all oil coolers, remote oil filters and dry sump systems, there are a few rules to avoid oil contamination and excess oil pressure loss. Use at least 1/2" inside-diameter oil lines for all exterior hoses. Never use 90° fittings as they cause too much of a pressure loss. Never use coolers or other exterior oil plumbing "out of the box;" they must be cleaned or flushed as outlined below. Fill the cooler and lines, etc., with oil before starting the engine for instant oil pressure.

If you are installing new exterior oil plumbing, or if you blow an engine, the engine itself will no doubt be cleaned, but what about all that extra plumbing? It must be cleaned as well. Empty the system completely. Flush thoroughly in both directions with solvent, then flush again with clean oil; about 3-4 quarts should do it. One fellow I know blew seven engines in a row, all because he didn't know enough to flush the oil cooler after the first engine blew, leaving debris in the cooler.

The camshaft selection will turn out to be something very specific to your particular needs, and the very best advice we can give is for you to very carefully consider all your driving needs...then talk to the cam people. Take their advice. The two areas of engine excess, usually caused by an exuberance rather than by experience, will be valve timing and carburetion. In too many cases, the builder will opt for a cam that is too wild, either on duration or lift, and a carburetor that is too large. Bigger and more is not always the way to go in these two areas.

Because these two areas are so specific in nature, we will not get into them in great detail, but will refer the reader to the manufacturers. But we will pass along some tips on installations.

When preparing the block for a rebuild, the cam bearings will have been removed and new bearings installed taking care to align the bearing oil delivery holes with those in the block. Use great care not to nick or gouge these bearings during installation, most parts stores will have a special installation tool just for cam bearings. You won't use this tool often, but when you need it, you need it!

When you buy a cam, go ahead and get the entire kit, which will include the lifters. Whether you go with solid or hydraulic lifters is your choice, but the hydraulics are so good now that most street engines are built with them. The kit will include a special installation grease...use it liberally, on the bearings

and on the cam bearing surfaces. When putting the cam into the block, work very patiently, and be very careful not to let the cam lobe edges gouge the bearings. Go slow and you'll be ok. Once in place, align the cam gear and crankshaft gear marks and install a new cam drive chain. You won't need the exotic cam gear drives unless you're going hog wild in racing. Thoroughly lubricate each lifter bore with the assembly lube, as well as each cam lobe, and install the lifters as per instructions that will come with the cam kit.

For carburetion, select a carburetor that is going to flow the correct amount of air for your particular engine. As mentioned, many rodders tend to add a too-large carburetor in the mistaken belief that bigger is better. For most big street engines, a carburetor that flows about 600 cfm will be about right. The size of the carburetor will depend upon the engine displacement, operating rpm range, valve timing (cam), exhaust design, and engine use.

It is wise to select the carburetor and intake manifold as a set. Some intake manifold manufacturers do not include the carburetor, but they will have exact recommendations on what to use, and they will ask you the specifics of your engine and the type of driving.

Install the carburetor, and adjust it, exactly as the builder recommends. Trying to make a lot of trick adjustments before the engine runs is just asking for trouble. Once the car is operable, then you can make the fine tuning necessary.

Do not overcarburate an engine. These four side-draft ,Weber carbs are set up to flow engine requirements at high rpm, most street engines can do very well with a single modern four barrel.Manifold design is very important on the performance engine.

Do not use too radical a camshaft, either. Follow grinder's recommendation for cam timing, when installing the cam be extremely careful not to scar the cam bearings, use plenty of assembly lube (which is usually supplied by the grinder). Use entire cam kit when possible.

Cylinder Heads

The cylinder head is the main catalyst to, or restriction of, horsepower production. Regardless of all other factors a goodly quantity of quality air must pass into and out of the combustion chamber. Getting a large quantity of air to and from the engine is easy, just install a couple of sewer pipes. Of course, one must allow room for the valve train, water jackets, head bolts, etc., but it seems a simple task. The problem comes with trying to obtain quality airflow. That is, the air-flow must not be too fast or too slow, and in the intake tract it must keep the fuel mixed or suspended in the air. A cylinder head designed to work well in one application may not work well, or be totally unsuitable for another application.

Because cylinder heads are so important to the production of horsepower, and because it is next to impossible to produce a really good set of highly modified heads without an air-flow bench and years of experiance, I suggest that the heads be sent out to a qualified cylinder head porter. Or, if the heads are strictly for street use, perform only basic modifications outlined in this book, especially the modifications that enhance air-flow at low valve lifts.

It is not possible in one book to describe how to port every cylinder head that any particular reader may be working on. So I will cover porting techniques in general, and give you this advice: It is very easy to turn an expensive cylinder head into a very unique doorstop by porting it wrongly. What may seem right may not necessarily be so. To do a proper job, an air-flow bench and experiance is necessary. So, if you can take a chance on scrapping a head, and a small horsepower loss (compared to a professionally prepped head) is not a major concern, then, go ahead!

When a combustion chamber is to be modified for greater airflow and to make the chamber itself more efficient, you must look at the complete combustion chamber. This means the chamber in the head, the top of the piston, and any portion of the cylinder wall exposed to air-flow and initial combustion. Any shrouding of the valve while it is open will decrease air-flow past the valve. A reduction in air-flow equals a drop in volumetric efficiency which equals a loss in power. During combustion chamber reshaping do not worry too much about removing material. Increased air-flow and/ or improved combustion will more than compensate for the slight decrease in compression ratio.

If the combustion chamber has a quench area, be sure to radius its edge, blending it gently into the chamber. This is especially important near the intake valve, as it will help airflow into the cylinder during periods of low valve lift. Also if the piston has valve reliefs formed in its dome, leave a fairly sharp edge on the reliefs near the exhaust valve. Make sure it is not sharp enough to cause preignition, but don't blend it as smooth as the intake side. This edge will act as a scoop shoving the exhaust gases towards the exhaust valve, and will also act as a dam if the exhaust gases try to flow backwards, which usually happens at low rpm with a camshaft that has a long exhaust duration period.

One procedure regarding combustion chambers, which has received much attention for decades, is the equalizing of the chambers, or CCing. The term CCing is derived from the device used to measure the volumn of the chamber. It is a burette and was originally designed to be used in scientific experiments. It is graduated in cubic centimeters or CC's. The idea behind CCing is to measure and then equalize all combustion chambers, thus all cylinders will have the same compression ratio and therefore the same power output. Unfortunatly, usually only one side of the combustion chamber gets measured, the cylinder head side, with no attention being given to the piston side of the chamber. Add to this the inequalities of air/fuel mixture delivery between the cylinders, variations in valve timing, and ignition timing from one cylinder to the next and CCing becomes a measurement of little value. Normally when CC a head it is strictly to determine the engine compression ratio and no attempt is made to equalize the chambers unless their volumns differ considerably.

Valves, whether intake or exhaust do not directly relate to an engines displacement. A valve only 'sees' air-flow. For instance, the same size intake valve would work equally well on a 350 c.i. engine at 8,000 r.p.m. or a c.i. engine at 550 rpm, as both engines at those particular rpm levels require 810 cfm flow, assumming 100# volumetric efficiency. The size of the valves should be determined by air-flow requirements and guided by experiance. Larger than stock valves must be used with care as there may be physical interferance problems or the larger valve may be so close to everything else in the chamber that there may be an air-flow problem due to shrouding. Also, at lower operating speeds, there may be a decrease in power because flow velocities may be too low.

Cylinder head porting and port matching can be done by the amateur, the key is to stay conservative. Here the port area has been marked by scribe on machinist's blue dye, rotary file used for major cuts.

Intake valve size is controlled by the amount of flow necessary to feed the engine in its operating range. Exhaust valve size is usually about .80 the size of the intake valve. The exhaust valve need not be as large as the intake valve because the waste gases in the combustion chamber are at a much greater pressure than the atmosphere and they will literally force their way past the valve. Depending on the camshaft etc., this pressure may be from 60 psi to 120 psi. This pressure forces itself against the exhaust valve trying to keep it closed. If a larger exhaust valve is used then more force will be required to open the valve, adding an extra stress to the valve train. For instance, an exhaust valve of .6 inches in diameter with an exhaust pressure of 120 psi would have a force of 241.2 lb (valve area x psi) keeping the valve closed. This is in addition to valve spring pressure! So, larger than stock valves should be avoided unless absolutely necessary for high rpm breathing or supercharged applications.

Because air-flow is the main ingredient for horsepower and the valves are placed directly in the air-flow, then it stands to reason that any change in the shape of the valve would affect air-flow, for better or worse. Valve size then is just one factor to be considered. The valves shape, surface finish, length and weight should also fall under close scrutiny. A valve weight should be as low as possible without sacrificing reliability, so as to place less strain on the already overworked valve springs. The length of the valve has to do mostly with spring selection, and will be discussed later. The surface finish on a valve is usually left as it comes from the factory, either machined or swirl polished. Swirl polished is prefered, especially on intake valves, and performance aftermarket valves usually come this way. There is an ever so slight flow increase with swirl polishing, but, more importantly, the polishing removes any stress risers which may lead to valve failure.

There are two basic valve shapes available, tulip and flat. The valve shape must be matched to the particular design of cylinder head in order to achieve maximum air-flow. Tulip shaped valves are used in hemi's and some canted valve heads, where the intake port centerline is close to the valve axis. In this case the air-flow through the port uses the radius on the tulip valve to help bend the flow out and into the chamber. On the other hand, wedge style cylinder heads have a port centerline that is nearly perpindicular to the valve axis. The air flowing through the port must pass over the head of the valve to get into the chamber. A tulip valve in this application would restrict flow and cause a power loss. The 340-360 ci Mopar engine is a wedge head design that is factory fitted with tulip valves and this engine will pick up quite a bit of power when changed over to the flat style valve. Valve guides should have bronze inserts installed. There are several styles and tradenames but all perform equally well. Standard valve to guide clearance with a cast iron guide is .0015" to .0035", whereas clearance with a bronze guide is

all performance engines use a 45 degree angle on both intake and exhaust valves and seats, because modern cam design and higher operating rpm ranges negate any low lift flow advantages of the flatter angles. #he actual angle on the seat is a true 45 degree cut but the valve is usually cut at a 44-44 1/2 degree angle. This 1/2-1 degree difference is called the interference angle and it allows the valves to 'pound' into the seat, providing a good seal.

The valves in an engine run extreamly hot and the heat in the valves is transferred to the valve seat and from there into the cooling system. The wider the seat the greater its ability to pass heat from the valve. But a very wide seat will actually seal less well than a narrower one, and it may also cause a hinderance to air-flow. Recommended valve seat widths vary, depending on application, valve material, fuel used and whether or not the engine is naturally asperated or super-charged.

At low to medium valve lifts the main restrictions to airflow into and out of an engine are the valves. By doing some careful work on the valve and valve seat total air-flow will increase dramatically. This work performed on the valve and seat is commonly referred to as a"three angle valve job". It simply refers to the number of angles ground on the valve seat. In a production engine the valve is normally finished to a 44 degree angle and the seat to a 45 degree angle. When a cylinder head is rebuilt the valve and seat are ground to these same angles. When this is done the seats become too wide, so they are usually narrowed with a top angle cut of 15 or 30 degrees. A three angle valve job places one more angle on the

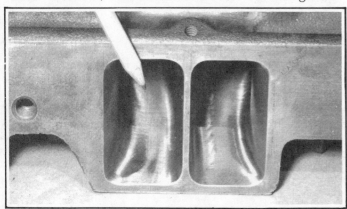

Exhaust ports can be very smooth, intake ports should have a rougher surface to keep fuel mix in suspension. Stones can be used for final finish and shaping.

Huge does not equate to better when it comes to ports, find out what porting will work best for your particular engine. Ports in lower head are only slightly larger than stock.

only .0002". This smaller clearance keeps the valve much more stable and seats the valve better (less wobble). Also, bronze guides work very well under marginal lubrication conditions. Just the ticket if you have restricted oil flow to the top end because of roller rocker arms.

Where the valve sits on the cylinder head is called the valve seat. The valve seat works in conjunction with the valve to seal the cylinder as required during engine operation. This sealing is critical for low rpm power production, but because things are happening so fast at higher rpm, valve seal has little effect in this range. Of course, a valve that has a leak of major proportions will make itself known, regardless of rpm. After a valve job is done and the head is assembled, an easy way to check for proper seal is to pour a little varsol into the combustion chamber, and using an airline, blow air up into the port. Any bubbles will indicate a leak that needs to be fixed.

The valve and valve seat are machined to a similar angle, usually 45 degrees, so the valve will seal, yet also allow for the valve vertical movement. Exhaust valves should always be finished to 45 degrees. Intake valves have also been made at 30 and 15 degree angles. These flatter angles lose some sealing ability but do flow air better at very low valve lifts. Practically

valves and another on the seat to help blend air-flow around this juncture. Usually there is a 45 degree cut on the seat, with a 30 degree top cut to blend it into the chamber, and a 60 degree bottom cut to blend it into the port. The valve is cut at its usual 44 degrees but with an added 30 degree backcut to aid air-flow. The exhaust valve also has its margin rounded to aid air-flow moving from the chamber into the port. For street use three angle valve jobs are highly over-rated. The horsepower difference between a good stock production seat and a three angle seat is not that much, but it does make for impressive talk on cruise night.

One of the most important areas to be modified when porting a cylinder head is the bowl area. The bowl is the area directly below the valve head, from the valve guide boss up to and including the lowest angle on the valve seat. Because this area is so important, as well as sensitive to air-flow, it is very easy to make a mistake unless a flow bench is used. Usually a gentle smoothing and blending of all bowl surfaces works pretty well, but, a flow bench is necessary if a change anywhere major is considered. This area is so important because it is that part of the port that aims the air-flow past the valve. One of the reasons that the bowl is so sensitive to work on is that the majority of air-flow at low valve lifts is usually in a different location than the flow at higher valve lifts. The bottom, or short side of the port, is the area of most activity at smaller valve openings and as the valve opens farther the flow shifts to the high side of the port. This happens on most engines, especially those with wedge design cylinder heads.

The area between the manifold and the bowl is called the port. The shape of this port, in cross-section, will have an influence on the air-flow through the cylinder head. Let's look at the exhaust port first. Exhaust ports on many nroduction cylinder heads are more restrictive to the engine than the intake ports. This is especially true on V8 engines where design dictates that the exhaust and its plumbing be tucked in close to the cylinder block to make room for the front suspension etc.

In most cylinder heads the major portion of the exhaust flow is across the short side radius and along the port floor, at low to medium valve lifts, with the flow changing to the port roof at maximum valve lifts. It is critical therefore that the short side radius be a gentle curve. If there is a sharp directional change in the port, flow can be improved by making the port floor flat rather than round (eg. a 'D' port). Of course modifications in the port are limited by the amount of material in the head casting.

The intake port can be shaped using much of the same rules as used when modifying an exhaust port, but with a slight differance. First, the intake flows in the opposite direction, into the cylinder, and second, an intake port handles two materials, air and fuel. It is a wet flow as compared to the dry flow in the exhaust. The problem arises from the liquid fuel (in fine mist form) being heavier than the air which is also passing through the port. If this wet flow is asked to abruptly change direction, the air bends relatively easy, but the heavier fuel wants to continue in a straight path. So, it is possible to have the proper amount of air enter a cylinder while the fuel ends up spreading itself on a port wall, and the cylinder ends up running lean. Then, the fuel finally

gets pulled off the port wall and what happens is that after one or two lean firings, the cylinder finally gets this fuel and runs rich. Obviously not the way to make power. The fuel must be kept in suspension. By keeping the flow velocity as equal as possible in all areas within the port and avoiding any sharp bends, air/ fuel separation may be eliminated almost entirely.

In each port where the valve guide protrudes slightly, there is a buildup of material called the valve guide boss. Best flow through either port is achieved by reducing the width of the valve guide boss and generally smoothing it. Some people like to shorten this part of the guide, which does improve flow slightly, but I do not recommrend it, as it reduces valve stability.

Now, while you are doing all this reshaping, there are specific surface finishes to be used in certain areas. The exhaust ports should be quite smooth, finish with a 240 grit. This prevents carbon build-up and subsequent air-flow loss. The combustion chamber should also be smooth, 240 grit once again, so as not to inhibit any turbulance and to prevent carbon build-up. The intake port should be rough, a 60 grit finish is just about perfect. This rough finish on the intake port prevents fuel from clinging to the port walls, the rough finish allows the passing air-flow to pick up any fuel laying on the port wall, thereby reintroducing it to the airstream.

Any finish smoother than what is recommended is not necessary, will take more work and therefore money, and in the case of the intake port will actually reduce performance. Those mirror finishes may look real good, but looks don't always win races.

Many cylinder heads have been resurfaced for many differant reasons, but there should only be one reason to resurface any head. The head is warped. Many heads have been milled (a common term for resurfacing, although it is actually a grinding or broaching operation) to decrease the size of the combustion chamber thereby increasing the compression ratio. This is not a good idea. The maximum any

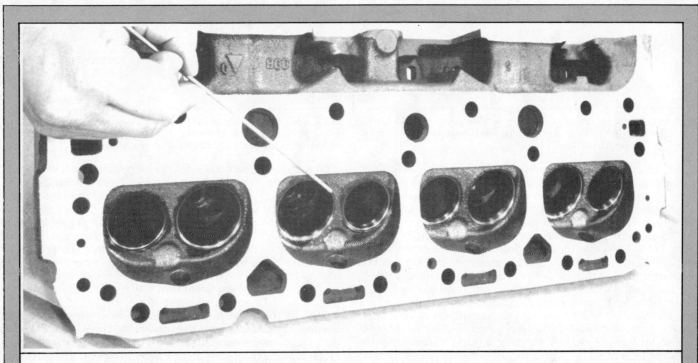

As with ports, valves can be too large as well as too small. Valves must seat same width all around and not be too high in chamber or too low in valve throat.

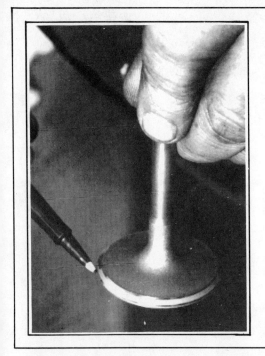
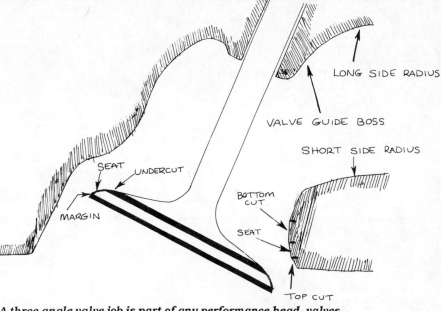

A three-angle valve job is part of any performance head, valves will be ground at an interferance angle with head seat.

head should be milled is .060", and in quite a few cases (eg. Ford Cleveland), the less the better. By removing material, the deck surface of the head, which supports one side of the head gasket, is weakened. With a weakened deck and an increase in compression, blown head gaskets tend to become a common occurance. It is better to increase the compression of an engine by changing pistons, or by using a similar head that has a smaller combustion chamber to start with.

Changing cylinder heads is usually done for a number of reasons, to raise the compression ratio, increase breathing, and so on. Following, is a short summary of the more popular head swaps.

The small block Chevy has had many heads over the years, but the two most popular with performance buffs are the I.94 and 2.02 heads. The numbers refer to the intake valve size. Both of these heads have the same size ports, as do most small block heads, with the notable exception of the very early non-performance heads. This allows manifolds to interchange with practically no problems. The I.94 heads were used on 327 ci four barrel and all 350 ci engines. Heads made in I970 and earlier used smaller combustion chambers, in fact some with small 60 cc combustion chambers will give over II:I compression ratio when used on some 350 ci engines. All late low compression heads have about cc chambers. Most 2.02 heads have 65 cc chambers. One other major difference with these heads is their spark plug location. All I970 and earlier have the spark plug positioned straight out of the casting. Later performance heads were available with angled spark plugs. That is, the spark plug is angled towards the exhaust valve to aid combustion. These were primarily for racing, although many have found their way onto the street. Chevrolet has also introduced oth#r 'racing' heads. In I975 they brought out the Turbo head and now their latest offering is the Bow-Tie head.

With the big block Chevy the standard oval port heads are the best for street use. The big port, high performance heads need lots of camming, carburetion, and stiff gears to work right. Also, because the high performance head has a combustion chamber that is 8-I0 cc larger than the standard heads, different pistons is needed to bring the compression back up. The later open chamber head, available in iron and aluminum, are basically only good for racing.

The 289-302 ci small block Ford Windsor has only one good head swap. Use the heads from a late I960's or early I970's 35I ci Windsor. This head has larger ports and valves, and is worth about 30 more horsepower. You must also use

35Iw intake gaskets and the longer I969 and later pushrods, to make this swap work. Also the combustion chamber is larger than the original heads, so mill the 35I heads .050", and use thin head gaskets to restore compression.

The best heads for the small block Mopar are the I968-71 340 ci high performance heads, with the big ports and the 2.02 intake valves. You can use these heads on any 3I8-360 block as is, but the 3I8 needs an intake manifold change to match up the ports. These heads can even be used on the earlier 273 ci engines, if the cylinder bores are notched for valve clearance. The 1973 and later 340-360 heads use the same ports as the 340 high performance heads but with a 1.88 intake valve. These later heads actually work better on the street than the earlier 340 high performance heads.

If you are using a I967 or earlier big block Mopar, (B or RB block) then use the I968 and later heads. These heads use larger exhaust valves and better ports, and are worth about I5-20 horsepower on the earlier 383 or 4I3 engines. Once again, mill the heads .060" to maintain compression, and mill the intake manifold .075" to realign the ports. This will make up for the 8 cc differance in combustion chamber size.

The I965-66 389 ci Pontiac engines will benefit from using I967 or later heads. The later heads have bigger ports and valves. There is only a 4 cc difference in chamber size which can easily be compensated for by using a thinner head gasket. The late 400 ci engines can use the I969-70 Ram Air IV that have even bigger and better ports, But these heads are rare and quite expensive when you can find them.

Remember, for street use, keep it simple, nothing major as far as modifications go, and don't even think about getting any exotic parts unless you have an equally exotic budget.

VALVE SEAT WIDTHS

INTAKE ....RACING, MINIMUM .030", UP TO .050"
...TITANIUM VALVES .060" (pound out easier)
...STOCK .080"

EXHAUST........RACING, MINIMUM .050"
...STRONG GAS MOTOR .060"
NATURALLY ASPERATED NITRO MOTOR .I00" ...BLOWN NITRO .I25"
...STOCK .080"

Transmissions

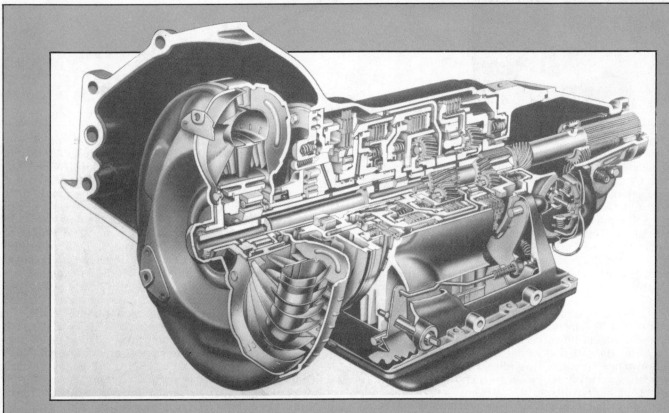

The overwhelming majority of traditional street driven hot rods use automatic transmissions, simply because the modern automatics are so strong. This does not mean the manual gearbox is gone from the highway, but most experts agree that the manual transmission will account for only about 30 percent of street performance gearboxes within 10 years.

While many of the currently used automatic transmissions might liberally be called performance units, most of them are nothing more than stock type transmissions that have been modified with a performance valve body. Stronger shifts, or modified shifting points, is the reason for the change. Even so, a large number of automatics have been completely rebuilt and set up to very demanding performance standards. This applies to the automatic in a fenderless 1931 Model A coupe as well as the automatic in a monstrous off-road pickup.

It is possible to apply some racing transmission technology to the street automatic. Improved internal fluid pressures, better discs, better bearings...these are things that the production automatic may lack, from an economics standpoint. But a street driven vehicle does not need an automatic that will snap the neck vertebra, which a pure racing product can

certainly do. As with other parts of building a real hot rod, selecting "just enough" is the key to automatic transmission plans.

If you are going to buy a modified transmission from one of the several automatics builders, be very honest when answering their questions. They will give you exactly the transmission you need, although you a can be a bit selective about the shifting assembly. Most racing applications can be used on the street, but they can become extremely tiresome in heavy traffic situations.

Heat is the number one killer of automatics, and you need to respect this problem. Really be aware of it if you are going to go the low-dollar route at first and install an automatic from the junkyard. As a basic rule of used-transmission shopping, find an automatic with as few miles on it as possible. Even then, look the car over and see if it might have been abused. If the car has a heavy-duty towing hitch, you might want to skip that trans, unless the car also has a heavy-duty transmission cooler. If the used transmission is a recent rebuild, consider it with a grain of salt. It may, or may not, be good.

You are taking a chance with the torque converter on any

used transmission, because it might not have been replaced. It should have been, but you don't know.

Bottom line: As soon as you can afford to, get a good rebuilt transmission. If you are going for performance, get one from a mail-order company that specializes in them.

From such a company you will have a selection of special torque converters, and this can be very important, especially with very heavy, or very light cars. These converters have been designed for racing use, but street builders have found them to be adaptable to the highway under certain conditions. Again, be honest with the transmission store and tell them exactly what you have, how you drive, and what you think you need.

There are a lot of automatics to choose from, and you can easily get an automatic that is too fragile for your car/engine combination. This is especially true with the current crop of 5-speed autos available. Some of these can be modified to work very well, others are just not worth the risk. Again, consult the transmission specialist. And a special note: For a

couple of years now, some American car manufacturers have been switching over to the metric system, which means that some late model transmissions will use metric size bolts/nuts. Nothing wrong, just be aware of the fact.

Always set your hot rod up to use an automatic transmission cooler. Where this cooler is located, respective to the ambient air flow, and what capacity cooler is selected will be important. Once again, the transmission professional will be your major source of information, because you have to tell him all the parameters. Earlier cars seldom have room for the cooler either immediately in front of, or behind the radiator. So these coolers often end up in places under the floorboards or tucked inside the frame where there is practically no cool air flow. If such a location is absolutely imperative, use a scoop to funnel air. And mount this cooler securely. If you really want to come to grips, put a transmission fluid temperature guage in your car.

Most rodders will not get into rebuilding their automatic, but they will probably be involved with mounting it to the

Automatic transmission were not considered much for performance until B&M Automotive started producing dramatic rebuilds, soon the venerable GM Hydramatic (top left) was the scourge of drag strips, followed soon by the Ford, GM TurboHydro, and Chrysler Torqueflites.

There are more working parts in an automatic transmission than a manual, but with a good cooler and good treatment an automatic can last over 200,000 miles. Special rebuild kits are available if you want to do the rennovation at home.

RIGHT - The Chrysler Torqueflite is a very popular unit to use for swaps, but it has been losing favor in recent years for use behind GM and Ford products. Even so, all automatics can be swapped to different make engines through the use of special adapters.

engine. Take special note: The torque converter will have a slotted end on the one snout that sticks out of it. This is to drive the transmission fluid pump. When the converter is being rotated into place, this slot must align. If you try to bolt the trans to the engine, and there seems to be some reason the trans case does not want to slide right up to the block, you probably don't have the converter pump slot aligned. When things are right, the trans case bolts to the block easily, and then you must slide the converter forward slightly to contact the flex plate. Another note: Make sure you get the automatic flex plate attached to the crankshaft flange correctly. On most engines, they can be turned around backwards. If in doubt, ask the local transmission mechanic. Some converters will have the flex plate bolt holes misaligned slightly, so that you must rotate the pair until the holes all match.

Many chassis of the late 1930s, the 1940s and the early 1950s will accept a late model ohv V8 engine and automatic or manual transmission, thanks to bolt-in center transmission mounts. Here we show a manual/Chevy V8 combination, there is plenty of room for most any type of transmission.

If the automatic transmission has been setting around for a long time, or it is a used item, always change the front and rear seals. Easily done before the transmission is installed, almost certain to leak if they aren't changed.

In street hot rodding, the most commonly used automatics are the Chrysler Torqueflite 727, the Ford C4 and C6, and the General Motors Turbo 350 and 400. When deciding on one size versus the other such as a 350 rather than a 400), the determing factor is usually available space around the frame members. The GM 400 and the Ford C6 should be used whenever there is an abundance of horsepower available.

The selection of a manual transmission for a street driven car is almost always a matter of personal perferance, and almost always a 4 or 5 speed unit is picked. Putting a manual transmission in a car that was originally equipped with an automatic is often no more a job than getting the necessary linkages from the junkyard. But it is time consuming.

There is absolutely no sane reason for going to the expense of installing one of the radical racing manual transmissions in a street vehicle, since the majority of modern manual gearboxes are very strong. It is possible to mate most of the good late boxes to any of the earlier engines, even the Ford flathead V8, by using adapters available from speed shops and mail order sources.

A special note about using adapters, for either manual or automatics. Always use a dial indicator on the face of the adapter after it has been bolted to the block. This will sometimes show an adapter that is not perfectly flat, and a misalignment at this point can be murder on the transmission. A machine shop can save the adapter by grinding it.

Shifting linkage for either the automatic or the manual may not be a problem with cars built after about 1939, but earlier models often do not have linkage room around the floorboards or the frame. This is almost always a matter of

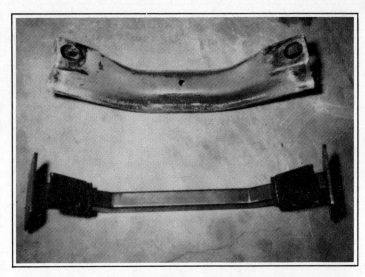

The stock transmission crossmember mount can be cut from most later model chassis and a new bolt-in mount fabricated. It is important that the new mount be strong enough to become an effective member for chassis torsional regidity, use the original transmission mounting insulators if possible rather than mounts from original chassis.

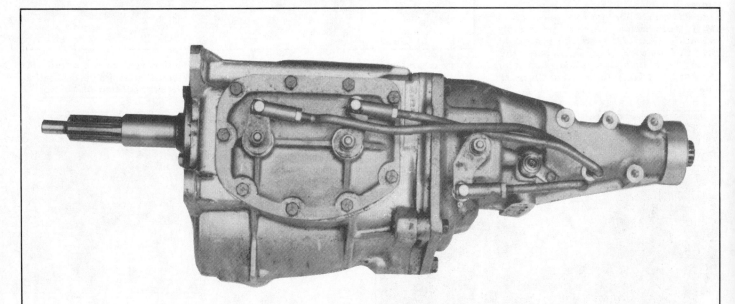

There are many very strong 4-speed manual transmission on the market today, and they have been a part of performance Detroit cars for two decades or more. Some more recent manuals even feature an overdrive 5th speed, which will allow for better highway cruising rpm's, most of these transmissions make provisions for floor shifters.

working out the problem, because so few manufacturers of aftermarket goodies offer special shifters for specific trans/car combinations. Modifying stock linkages to work is not difficult, either.

When using a manual transmission, consider the special clutch pressure plate very carefully. Some of these clutches require a gorilla to operate, making them virtually unusable by women, and extremely uncomfortable for anyone in traffic. Here, once again, when selecting a high performance clutch

be sure and contact the manufacturer and go by the recommendations.

A special note: When mounting the engine/transmission, be sure that the center of the crankshaft pulley and the center of the transmission output shaft are parallel to the centerline of the frame. Since the rearend pinon shaft will (should)be parallel to this centerline, misalignment of the crank/trans center will cause the driveshaft front universal shaft to be out of phase, causing early demise of the u-joint.

One of the big reasons so many rodders use the manual transmission is because of frame/flooring clearance, thinking the automatic is too much trouble. Flooring and frames can be reworked for clearance. Most later model manual transmissions will have plenty of working room beneath any rod or custom floorboard. Do not allow the flooring to touch the transmission of shifting mechanism at any point, since this will cause an annoying sound, and may actually bind the linkage.

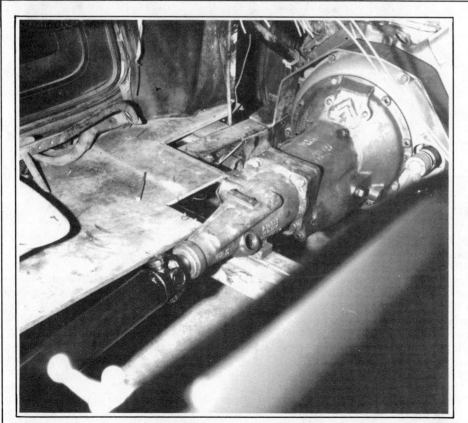

This is an overdrive unit adapted to the back of an early (pre-1954) Ford transmission, such OD units were available on the 1949 and later Ford products and can be used on older Ford products.

Anyone can repair a broken manual transmission at home, without a lot of special tools. However, it is highly recommended that a repair manual be handy, both for diagnosis of what might be broken or damaged, and for reassembly. Trying to remember exactly how everything goes together can be an experience in frustration. Even a broken transmission case can be welded by an expert, but such a case should probably be replaced instead.

CHAPTER 8

Cooling

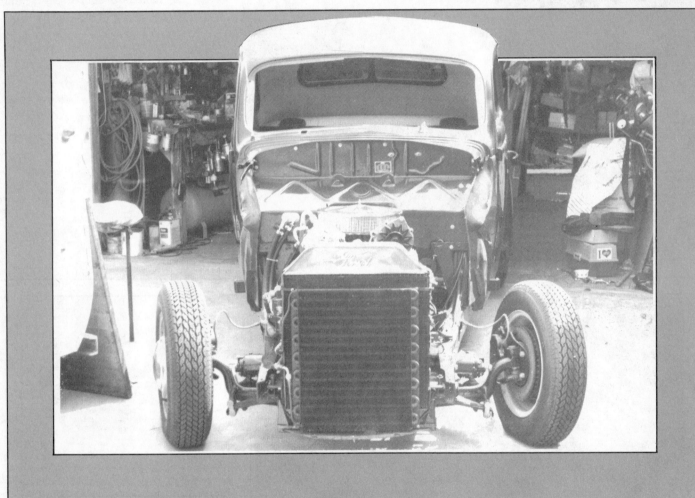

The two least understood things about hot rods, at least for the average rodder, are cooling and electrics. We're not going to get into electrics in this volume, since it requires a book unto itself, but we can cover the basics of cooling.

Interestingly, heat is the thing that is involved with most everything automotive. Heat is the by-product of energy that makes the engine work, and it is the by-product of energy that makes the vehicle stop. Heat is also a problem, in that we want to get rid of the excess, whether it is engine exhaust or bearing heat or brake heat. And since most cars are liquid cooled, we want to get rid of coolant heat as well.

Until relatively recently, there have been no companies making radiators exclusively for hot rodding applications. The car builder could rely only upon the local radiator craftsman. First came several builders of specialty brass radiators, thick-core versions with brass shells. Following in short order were companies that made replacement radiators

for a few of the more popular Fords and Chevrolets...today it is possible to get a custom built radiator for practically every kind of automobile.

The home builder will probably need a special radiator for any hot rod built, even cars manufactured as late as the 1960s, because radiators tend to deteriorate with age. If the car is a later model, the local radiator shop can probably create what is needed, often with nothing more than a thicker core for extra cooling capacity. If you have an older car, and you are lucky enough to locate an original radiator, the local shop can re-core the original and perhaps even include new upper or lower tanks.

The key to engine cooling is volume of coolant and flow rate of coolant. The bigger the radiator, either in thickness (number of tubes and fins-per-inch or in external dimensions, the more coolant it can hold at a given time. The engine water pump will determine the flow rate of the coolant through this particular space.

The radiator is one place where it is very difficult to utilize old equipment, this custom Model T unit includes a transmission cooler tube in the lower a tank.

This Model T radiator, set up for a modern ohv V8, is thinner through the core and has the hose outlets in different places. Custom radiators are not real expensive items.

This small block V8 is in an early 50s MG, the radiator is very much like those used in early Fords and is marginal for cooling the American engine. A good radiator is a rodding must.

Pre-1949 Fords have been notorious for heating up, especially when the engine has been hopped-up. In the great majority of cases, the problem has been too fast a flow rate. That is, the water pumps have been moving the coolant through the radiator too fast for effecient heat transfer to the cooling fins. This has applied to the early tall/narrow radiators as well as the wider units adopted in the late 30s. The usual solution to early Ford overheating problems has been to slow the coolant down, by thermostats in the water outlets (at the heads), by washers in the same place, or by reducing the effeciency of the water pumps, either by breaking off every other pump vane, or drilling holes in each vane.

With any cooling system, start with a completely cleaned out radiator and engine block. This makes sure that there will be no rust or scale in the circulating coolant, and there can be residual rust in an engine that seems almost new, if it has been setting.

So, we assume that you are starting with a clean system. The radiator you use in the car should be at least as big as the radiator needed for the engine used (in its original application). And there can be a difference in engine requirements within the same overall company, an example being Chevrolet versus Oldsmobile, etc. To make yourself feel even more secure, look at the size of radiator that particular car used with air conditioning. This will usually be a matter of a thicker core, or additional row of tubes.

When you start looking into the cooling problem of contemporary ohv V8 engines, it is readily apparent that some are much cooler running than others. An example would be the earlier Oldsmobile, which was hard to get to run hot enough in an older Ford chassis, where the original Ford radiator was used. At the same time, the small block Chevrolet V8 would sometimes overheat with the same radiator.

If you have an older car, without a radiator, start with one of the companies making radiators for these cars. They advertise in Hot Rod Mechanix, Rodder's Digest, Street Rodder, American Rodder, Rod & Custom, and Rod Action magazines. Almost always, these people can create the unit you will need, with a core thickness from 2-4 inches. If you have a special need, such as an air conditioner or a transmission cooler, these manufacturer's can encorporate them right into the early radiator dimensions. This is vital, since there is virtually no extra room between these early radiators and the grille shells.

If you have an old radiator, the local shop can put a new high efficiency core in it, usually with a 3 or 4-inch core, and modify the upper/lower tanks to accept the new engine radiator hoses. The problem you will run into here is the experience of the shop personnel. If they have not had a lot of

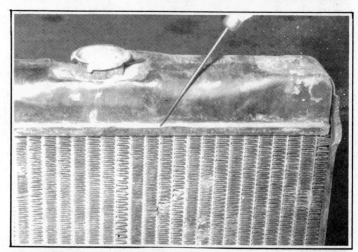

One of the first places the modern radiator will start to fail is along the seam between top tank and core plate, same problem at the lower tank. New radiators often carry over 15psi pressure and will fail at the weakest point.

experience with this kind of radiator designing, you may or may not end up with a unit that will cool your car. One really good reason to go with the commercially available specialty radiators.

When you are working with the radiator people, local or mail-order, they will want to know the kind of engine you are using, how much it is modified (higher compression, higher rpm, and bored cylinders all indicate higher heat), if you will be using A/C, where the A/C condensor must be mounted, etc. All this is usually critical on the older cars, but after about 1939 it begins to sort itself out, since there is more room to use larger dimension radiators.

On older cars, the radiators usually have provision for vibration, so that the radiator doesn't get shook to death. Fords use coil springs on the radiator-to-frame mounting bolts, and other cars use springs between the radiator yoke and the frame. Some modern builders are not using these dampeners, and getting away with it, but there hasn't been enough time elapse yet to know if this is going to be acceptable over the long term.

Most all specialty radiator people use pressure cap designs, but at least one well known expert does not use the pressure system, and there seem to be no problems. The radiator coolant overflow recovery container is very much a part of modern rodding, and it works very well. These can be items scrounged from production cars, they can be specially made units from rod shops, or home made.

Many hot rods will have aluminum somewhere in the system that can come into contact with the coolant. Always use a coolant that will not attack aluminum. Water will definitely erode aluminum over a period of time. Nearly every available coolent today is inert with aluminum, due to the number of production cars using the light metal in the cooling system.

It is very possible to swap radiators in the later model cars, and this is an economical way to get good cooling. The big problem is that a lot of modern radiators are not given to a long life. Really inspect a used radiator carefully before installing it in your car, and it would be a good idea to have the local radiator shop clean and run a pressure test on it.

There are a variety of electric fans now available over the parts store counter, some are better than the others and you need to get the parts salesman's suggestion on what to use. While the higher effeciency air conditioning fans from production cars are ok to use, the electric fans are much more popular. Also, strongly consider the use of a fan shroud, on early as well as late model cars. A shroud will significantly increase the cooling ability of the fan, especially at lower vehicle speeds. And, the electric fan can be disconnected during speed contests, if that is a consideration.

Use new hoses when you are building a car, even if it is only a couple of years old, as well as new engine belts. This is not a place to be scrimping.

The modern car will use either a traditional downflow radiator (right) or a crossflow version, either can be adapted to many fat fender early rods/customs, it is advisable to use a fan shroud with such a swap to maximize air flow during low speed operation. Make sure mounting is solid.

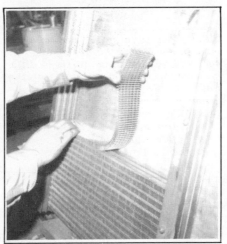

Custom radiators are available in a range of core widths, heights, and thicknesses, generally a 4 tube core is preferrable to a 3 tube but will cost more to make.

When the tubes are inserted into the fins, a tank plate is added to both ends. This forms the basic core, specialty tanks can then be made for any type car.

If you have an experienced professional radiator man in your area, chances are very good that he can make up a core, or order one, that will fit your car tanks.

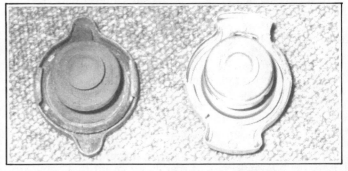

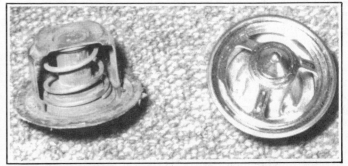

Most radiators now work under pressure, from 5-15 or more psi, so the radiator caps must be kept in good condition and the thermostats should be inspected at least every couple of seasons.

ABOVE - Underside of this A chassis is very typical of early rod cooling practice, with a heater radiator core mounted flat beneath the seat (top right) and a transmission cooler horizontal beneath the frame just behind the battery and transmission crossmember. Because of splash aprons and battery, air flow is restricted. BELOW - Transmission coolers for automatic gearboxes come in a wide variety of sizes and capacities, be sure and consult the manufacturer specs for right size for your application. Mount securely, funnel fresh air to it if necessary.

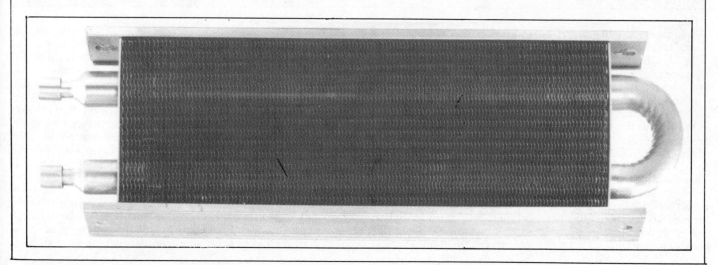

CHAPTER 9

Bodywork

A gorgeous example of the current popularity of high tech and clean look is the 1932 three window Ford coupe that Mal Kieswetter, of Kitchener, Ontario won the coveted 1988 Ridler Award with at the huge Detroit) Autorama.

Two areas where every hot rodder can do virtually all his own work are the body and paint, whether this is metal or fiberglass, exotic or basic paint. Do not hesitate to try body work or paint, but do be advised that most of the new two-part paints are very toxic.

The chemicals attack the lungs, and can even seep through the skin pores. If you are going to do your own painting with the urethane paints (any paint, for that matter), be sure and get the correct protective clothing and masks. And don't think that just because you are painting with the garage door open, or even in the driveway, that you are safe from the problems.

To do your own body work and paint, there are some specialized tools needed that you wouldn't ordinarily have in the box. Write to Eastwood and get their catalog on tools, but you don't have to go overboard on what you order. A regular body hammer (with pick on one end) and railroad dolly will do

most things you need. After you get some experience, you can get into metal shrinking, but that is advanced stuff. The Eastwood panel flanger is a good tool to have, as is the Stitch Welder (fits an arc welder). I'm assuming you have, or can borrow an arc welder and a gas torch. If you're lucky enough to have one of the MIG wire welders from Daytona Mig or HTP, all the better. These are cold welders and don't distort sheet metal like the "hot" welders, An air compressor is really handy, and you'll definitely use a power grinder. A body filler "cheese grater" and an 18-inch sanding board for filler are advisable. The rest of the tools are not essential, just nice to have. You can probably borrow them from a buddy or a professional.

I cannot emphasize enough that the way you get even reasonably good with body work and paint is by DOING. Experience is the only teacher in this interesting part of the hobby. And trust in your sense of feel even more than your sense of sight. If you can feel an imperfection, you can bet you will see it when the car is painted! There is absolutely nothing that you cannot fix or create when it comes to the car body. There may be zillions of hours labor involved, but it can be done. And it can be done over to get it correct.

ABOVE - This radical car was built for Bill Roach of northern California several years ago, the full tubing chassis used a steel Model T roadster body, floor removed to fit over chassis.

LEFT - The mark of a real craftsman is use of body metal file, here the seam between body and bellypan edge roll is being worked.

Old Metal Or New

Metal has a life, and it has a memory. If metal is left to itself, and the natural elements, it will revert to the basics, a process that includes a partial lifespan as rust. When we scrounge up an old car body today, something that is 50 or 60 years old, it simply will not be as easy (or fun) to work with as some thing with "good" metal. Much of our repair of such a structure will be with the unit's foundation, the flooring and support elements. These are mostly unseen pieces that are simple drudgery, but essential.

Inevitably, the question will center around trying to save the old metal, or go with new metal. This is almost always a judgement call when it comes to rust. Is the rust just a surface coating, or is it really a cancer that has affected the structural integrity of the metal? In many parts of the country, particularly in the west, metal will have a thin coating of rust, but will be quite sound. But even here the under structure can be badly decomposed. Very careful inspection is required. What looks good might be nothing at all, a fact that will immediately become apparent if you have a rusted body dipped in a rust removing solution. Sometimes the body almost disappears, because it was almost entirely eaten by rust.

While it is possible to do some temporary patching of rusted panels with fiberglass, it is better to replace badly rusted metal with new metal.

You can get new bodies of metal or fiberglass. There is currently only a very slim variety of metal bodies available, and they cost a bit more than the fiberglass versions. For this book, we will be concerned not with the purchase of a new metal body, but with the repair of an old body with new metal.

If there is any doubt about a body part, make a repair. This is especially true of the lower body and door sections, areas where debris collects, which in turn tends to hold moisture and cause rust. Body sheet metal may range from 20-22 guage on outer skin panels, and from 16-20 guage on substructures. This is not galvanized metal, and it is available from almost every metal supply outlet in the country, big town or small. Chances are very good that any metal you use for a repair will outlast the original metal by several decades.

You can shape a flat sheet of body metal with nothing more elaborate than a hammer and a dolly, but this is also an area where you will only get involved as you gain experience. It is, however, one of the most rewarding parts of the body reconstruction process. So, for the sake of this book, we are going to be working with a combination of metal, old and new.

Buying New Pieces

One of the major problems of building a hot rod, whether it is a 1932 Ford roadster or a 1963 Falcon Sprint, will be in finding good sheet metal parts. Doors come up missing, as do deck lids and hoods. You can usually find these pieces, with enough looking, but the older, or rarer, the car the harder the pieces are to find. And the more expensive. Consider a set of 1932 Ford fenders at the next swap meet you attend. Or an Impala SS hood with scoops.

Some of these pieces you can now buy in metal, most of them you can get in fiberglass. And in the case of a wood body, you can even get new parts. The majority of these parts are handmade, rather than having been stamped out on a huge stamping machine as originally. This means that there can be some minor deviations, and this can lead to problems.

Example: You need a metal deck lid for your Model A and you find a supplier. If your body was originally made to the short side of factory tollerances, and the new handmade lid is to the long side, it doesn't fit right. It is imperative that you supply the maker of any metal body part with the measurements of your particular body. This isn't as important when working with later model fenders and hoods. A few years ago we were getting a lot of metal replacement parts from South America, and they seldom came within a half-inch of fitting. We made do, because that is all we had. Now, the fit is far better, but plan ahead.

Even with patch panels you can't expect a perfect "drop-in" fit. You will need to do some work in fitting, a situation that most professionals have come to expect.

Making New Pieces

You absolutely can make new body pieces, both metal and fiberglass, and you don't have to be a professional to do it. It is possible to make every shape in body sheet metal with nothing more than a hammer and dolly, but there are some tools that can make it a lot easier. Roller flangers, stretchers, shrinkers, mallets, shaping bags, English Wheels... these are names that metal shaping craftsmen are familiar with, but tools that aren't likely to be in the average rod builder's toolbox. Interestingly, you can get practically all of these specialty tools from Eastwood or other tool suppliers.

When you are making a new piece of metal, you might not want to start with a piece of "fresh" metal, but instead you might want to use a piece that already has some features you need. Specifically, there are practically no perfectly flat pieces of metal in a car body. A flat piece of metal tends to "oil can" or flex and make noise. Therefore, a piece of metal that is flat will have one or more beads (called stiffening beads) across the surface to stop oil canning. In car body design, the designers have long since learned that any metal that is flat will tend to look concave, thus there is a slight crown to almost every body panel. This for appearance sake as well as strength. Armed with this knowledge, you can usually find a large body panel on any late model car that can be used for your purposes.

As an example, look at the older Volkswagen van bodies. There are a number of large, slightly curved panels (top, sides) and several tight curves and corners that will work very well on any rod or custom project. You can buy these panels at the junkyard for less than a flat sheet of new metal will cost, and with them you already have curves you need. Just trim to fit and install. Older fenders, hoods, deck lids...all of this is potential metal for a body project. You might want to avoid using the metal from cars produced in the last several years, particularly the small imports, because the metal properties have changed. When you are repairing a modern car, something that is relatively new, you are advised to be sure and do all welding with a MIG machine, because of the metal. Something about the alloy not taking to gas welding, etc. Just keep this in mind when gathering metal for your project.

On my personal projects, I use salvaged metal from fenders for tight curves and hoods/roofs for large flat surfaces. As another example, look closely at a Volkswagen sedan door...it is almost identical to a Model A door, in size and shape, so that the skin makes an excellent skin for older Ford doors. It is possible to use a couple of fenders from older cars to make race car nose pieces, rolled pans, cowl corners, etc. The current interest in filled tops on the older bodies is taking a toll on junkyard station wagon bodies, especially those with ribbed top panels. Some later model vans have wider ribs that might possibly work as top inserts, deck lids from some older cars (such a 1961 Chryslers) have ribs and work as coupe top inserts.

It is possible to make missing pieces for older cars, such as doors and deck lids, by first making up a framework of wood or small tubing. The tubing seems to work best, unless the original body used a lot of wood. This wood/tube framework takes the place of the original inner substructure. As a vague rule, however, when you work on the more "modern" cars, meaning the fat fender cars from about 1935 on, you need to use the substructure. The doors, etc., are just too large.

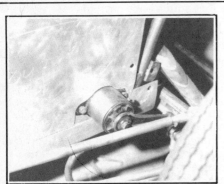

Hood panels are most often made of aluminum, here the panel is carefully trimmed to fit around Houdaille type shock.

Firewall and flooring has been removed from T body, area around wall stiffened with piece of thin-wall tubing.

Full bellypan is used for high speed race cars, may trap too much heat on a car built primarily for street use.

LEFT/ABOVE - Nosepiece of aluminum is made of several small sections hand shaped to fit plywood buck, then welded together to get final unit, grill is also handmade.

T body gets more stiffening with thin-wall tubing welded around perimeter of passenger compartment. Use of tubing on either steel or fiberglass bodies adds considerably to unit strength.

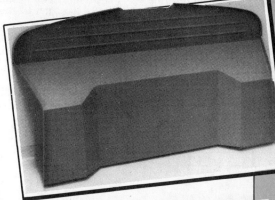
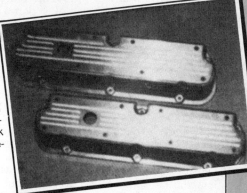
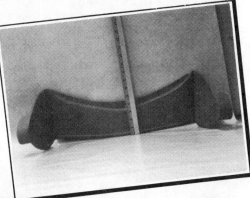
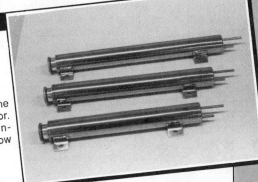

Straightening Metal

This is not a book devoted entirely to body work, so we won't get into the details of straightening metal. Sheet metal has a memory, and it will tend to return to its dominant shape. When a panel is crunched, unless it is full of sharp creases, it will want to return to the original shape if given the slightest chance.

Knowing this, you can often find bent sheet metal parts at bargain prices. But don't get involved with straightening metal until you know the basics, and you get the basics from good books (Eastwood has them, as does Motorbooks, International, Osceola, Wisconsin) and from hanging around with a professional bodyman. Time well spent is that of practicing on bent doors and fenders that the local body shop has discarded. With enough patience and effort, you can "save" just about any bent piece of metal. It is a matter of economics, however, and you have to weigh the time/effort against new panel cost.

One guide here: If you want to repair a crunched piece of metal, try to push or pull the dent in the same plane as the original denting force impacted the metal. Very often, when you do this many of the waves and near creases will be eliminated. Where the metal has creased, it has work hardened, and you'll probably have to work that area back to shape with the dolly/hammer.

Rust Repair

Most rod builders will be more involved with rust repair than with complete panel fabrication. Many inexperienced builders will make the mistake of not removing all the rusted area when making repairs. If all the rot is not nullified, it is a certainty to reappear.

Where the rust is really bad, it can be cut completely away and new metal fabricated. In most cases, the rust will have attacked the inner substructure as well as the outer panel, so both areas must be rebuilt. However, if only the outer skin is affected then there is no need to make new a substructure. A very short term rust repair is possible with fiberglass, but know beforehand that this is not a cure for rust, merely a patch.

With any kind of rust repair, it is wise to treat the rust affected area. This can be done a number of ways. You can have the individual piece, or the entire body, dipped in rust neautralizing chemical. This is usually a part of the paint stripping process. While almost every paint stripping business will claim that there is no residual problems from the stripping, just as many car builders claim that the residue that gets into the body seams eventually works out and causes paint release. Be very careful when taking a body to the chemical vats, because when all the rust is gone there may be very little body left! This is especially a problem with cars that have intricate substructure where the body sides meet the floor pan.

Sandblasting is not a total rust treatment, simply because it only blasts clean that immediately available surface. It does not get into the crevices where the rust is. And, sandblasting is only rust removal, it is not a treatment as such. Still, sandblasting is not to be ignored as a viable way to clean away rust and prepare metal. Be sure that you have a reputable professional involved with the sandblasting process, however, or do it yourself. The large professional services use equipment that will very easily warp and work harden typical body sheetmetal if the blaster is not used carefully. You can get excellent home shop sandblasters from the various magazine advertisers, and while they don't work as fast as the big pro units, you can take the time and do good work. If the sheetmetal has only a surface film of rust, such a home blaster will do an excellent job of cleaning. Heavier rust requires more effort and time. Tip: When blasting, spread a heavy plastic tarp on the ground beneath the work. This way you can save the sand used for additional blasting, and you reduce the clean-up problems. Always use a protective head/mask and gloves when blasting.

Chemical rust treatments are available, and I've used many of them. None of them are absolute cures to the rust problem, but I have found the product Zintex (carry-on of Fertan) to be excellent. This comes from T.C. Cowan (HC Fasteners Company is the same place) down in Texas, and it is a rust converter. Mixed with water, it will seep into every

---

Here is a problem all too prevalent in hot rodding today...original flooring is rusted and must be replaced with new pieces.

New metal floorpans are available from several sources, come with original style beads, or completely flat, your preference.

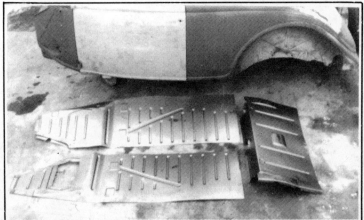

Floors of older cars tend to accumulate debris and water, eventually rust away. While fiberglass is often used as a patch, it is only a temporary fix and best thing to do is cut out floor and add new metal.

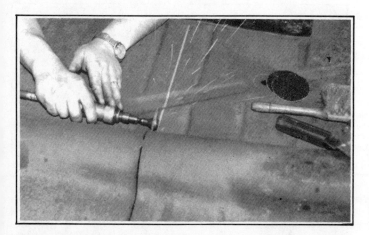

Flooring can be cut away with a torch, but the new carbide wheels made especially for metal make a much better tool. It is essential to use safety goggles, use care to keep tool from binding and breaking.

Where old floor overlaps onto body substructure, drill out original spot welds. If only small section is being installed, this can be cut and shaped at home, larger pieces need to be commercially formed usually.

nick and cranny and kill the rust growth. After sandblasting a piece of metal, it can be coated with Zintex, and wherever the metal turns black, that was where there was some rust. It is amazing how much rust residual stays after blasting or grinding. If a structure is not going to be replaced with new metal, it can be treated with the rust chemical, and in many cases fiberglass matte or cloth can be used to regain structure integrity. Zintex, at least, becomes a kind of undercoating as well and can be painted over. If air does not get to an area of rust, the rust will no longer be active. With a chemical rust converter, the chemical can be poured into all the body seams for a more permanent solution to the problem, and it does not seem to seep out later. A gallon of converter will usually do the average car body, I use it liberally to make sure.

The chemical converter is not a repair, only a beginning. After the converter is used, the panel should be patched. If fiberglass is going to be used, it should be applied to both sides of the rusted area (cloth or matte), because finishing of the panel will remove most of the glass on the outside. If fiberglass is being used to repair a rusted hole in a fender or door panel, the area should be ground clean on the outside before using a converter, then the converter is applied, then the rusted hole edges should be trimmed of "lace" and the opening perimeter should be bent inward slightly. This will allow the repair patch to have a much better purchase to the affected panel. Sometimes, for extra strength, a fiberglass "hair mix" can be stuffed into the hole. This will adhere to the substructure as well as the outer panel, so be cautioned.

After a metal or fiberglass patch is applied, more rust converter should be applied, just to make sure.

When working on any car, old or fairly new, try to cut away all badly rusted substructure and replace it with new metal. This will usually be metal of about 18 guage, and you can get some of the basic bends made at the sheet metal shop, leaving only minor shaping with hammer and dolly necessary. It is imperative the substructure between the floor and the body be in excellent condition, and this is even more important if a new flooring is being installed.

Sometimes, an older body will have had the floor and adjacent substructure removed during a channeling process. If the body is raised to original location, new substructure can be constructed. It does not necessarily need to be identical in cross-section to the original unit, but it should be made so that you gain maximum strength at this vital juncture. Sheet metal can be bent to shape, or square tubing can be welded in place. Sheet metal is more versatile.

You cannot do a good job welding rusted metal. It might appear that you are getting a good strong bead, but usually you are not "biting" parent metal, and the weld will simply break away.

Here new driveshaft tunnel and side pieces have been spot welded together this is strong enough.

These photos are courtesy Bitchin' Products and show some of the use of their flooring repair panels. Larger panels need stiffening beads rolled into them to prevent "oil canning".

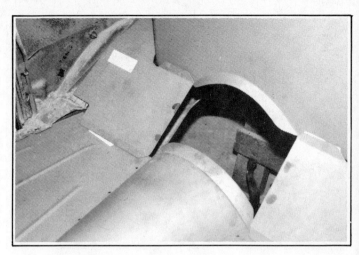

When a new firewall is being built, it is almost always necessary to create new footboards, modern practice is to make them of metal rather than wood. Can be removable, or welded in.

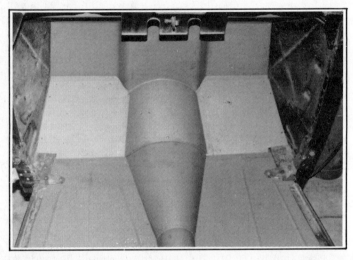

Size of transmission often determines shape and size of flooring humps, slope of footboards will determine comfort for driver and passenger. Larger cars usually have removable footboard/central hump, smaller rods often have everything welded to body.

Here the footboards and transmission hump are spot welded to body at sides, flooring, and setback firewall. It is not necessary to make a full weld around entire perimeter, a series of strong spot welds will work just as well.

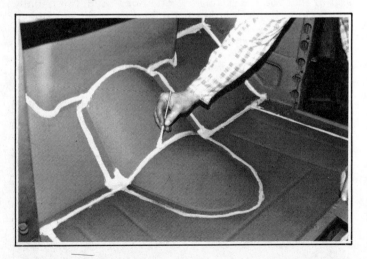

After parts are welded together, the seams should be filled with body caulking compound to make sure there is no engine heat getting into the cockpit. This can be done with removable boards as well. Jute or some other kind of what resisting padding should be used under carpets.

Typical rear fenderwell of an older car, sheetmetal that wraps down and under the substructure has rotted away. This is not a place for temporary fiberglass repairs, there are plenty of manufacturers now making reasonably priced wheel well replacement patch panels.

The rotten metal is trimmed from the body, new substructure must be bent up and welded in place if it is rusted badly. Important step, as this is foundation for the entire body.

Remaining lip of the wheel well should be straightened with body hammer and dolly, even this lip should be cut away and replaced if it is rusted. Note temporary body brace at rear of photo.

Wheel well replacements can be deeper than stock if wanted, an extra 1-inch makes a world of difference when wider tires are used. Edge is trimmed to fit original lip, then welded.

Replacement wheel well panel has stiffening bead rolled in place, if fenders are going to be used attachment bolts or blind nuts should be welded in place with extra support sheet metal.

Patch Panels

Patch panels are available for the more popular car bodies, from Model T's through cars of the 1980's. Generally speaking, these panels are intended for rust repair, but they can be used wherever a small repair panel is needed. As a rule, the older car panels are made by several different small operations while panels for the newer cars come from larger suppliers. Prices are reasonable, usually less than what it would take to create your own panels at home, unless you have some specialized metal shaping equipment.

Most of these patch panels are very true reproductions, there are a few that only approximate the original shape, thus requiring some shaping after installation Suppliers of patch panels usually advertise in the media most associated with their particular product. For old car parts, check with Old Cars Weekly newspaper (general delivery, Iola, WI 54945) or Hemmings. For newer cars, check with your local body shop for a trade journal, or with the club that is associated with the

This is typical of older car door bottom edges. The door skin has cancer, substructure is also rusted beyond use. Both pieces must be cut away and new metal patches welded in place.

141

particular car (Mustang, 1955-57 Chevy, etc). In areas where there is a lot of road salt rust, body shops keep a catalog or two on ready suppliers of panels.

Trim away the old metal so that the new panel will just fit. If you want to make a flange on either the old metal, or the panel, you can do this with a special set of vise grips from Eastwood, or similar flangers. This gives you an overlapping lip. The best connection, however, is a simple butt weld between old metal and patch panel. Once the old metal is cleaned away (usually spot welds around any substructure must be ground smooth), the new panel is held in place and tack welded. Where it fits the substructure there will usually only be a problem of heat warping the panel. Where the patch meets the old metal, tack weld very short sections at a time, letting the metal cool between tack welds. You can do this work with a gas torch, but you need to be very experienced. A Stitch Welder on the arc welder will work, a MIG wire welder works best of all (if you can afford one, which is why the Stitch Welder is so popular). The butt weld between old and new metal is the most important. If you do the weld correctly, it is only a job of light grinding and using a filler. You can heat the weld with the gas torch and hammer weld the seam, but this is also for the more accomplished body man.

If the substructure is not really firm under the patch panel, take the time to repair that area before installing the patch. The results will be much better.

It is possible to attach patch panels with pop rivets, then use fiberglass to cover the flanged connection seam, but the results are not nearly as permanent as with welding.

Door skin has been cut away with carbide cutting wheel, this line should be straight as possible. Skin laps over edge of the subpanel structure and can be pried away after cut is made. Cut far enough up on door to be sure all badly rusted metal is removed.

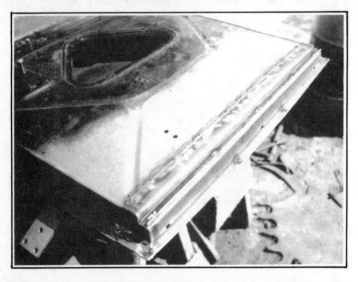

Door inner subpanel is bent up from pieces of slightly heavier metal and welded in place. Curves can be made with an Eastwood shrinker/stretch or with a hammer and dolly (this latter after experience is gained).

Now outer patch panel can be trimmed to fit, butt or lap welded to the original door skin. Edges are lapped over and hammer flat so patch panel becomes same as the original panel. Filler completes job.

Fillers

There are two types of fillers used on body metal, lead and fiberglass. There is an aluminized filler, but this uses the bonding agents of fiberglass.

Leading body sheetmetal is rapidly become a lost art, and it really shouldn't be. When bodies are assembled at the factory, some of the joints need a filler. Lead is used. And sometimes, as the car gets increasingly older, these lead seams will begin to crack. They should be repaired with lead, rather than a 'glass filler, and the original lead should be melted out to make sure that the original seam weld has not broken.

Lead is now expensive, and not readily available, although most auto body supply stores can get it. The metal must be ground perfectly clean, even tiny pock marks in a weld bead must be cleaned for best adhesion. A soft gas torch flame is used to warm the metal, and a leading compound spread on the bare metal (tinning). If the tinning compound does not stick to the metal, neither will the lead, so work until the tin

Lead is the original production car filler, this is a seam in an older body. Sometimes this odl lead must be melted out and new lead used to make the body perfect,sometimes old seams are cracked at this point.

Although leadind is fast becoming a lost body working art, we show how it is done to encourage you to learn how. We show a 1932 Chevy firewall,which needs patching and holes filled. Vertical leading is the most difficult, if you can do it here you can do it anywhere.

is complete. Next, play the soft flame over the lead stick and the metal at the same time, do not overheat the metal or you can get warping! The lead stick will turn from a solid to a soft form within a very narrow heat span, so be ready. Dob the soft lead to the warm metal. When you have a lead mound about 1/2-inch diameter, use a leading paddle to spread it out. It works like butter, keep playing the flame across the lead to keep it pliable. You can work it with the paddle to almost the final shape.

When learning to lead, start on a flat surface. As you get to the vertical surface you will have control of the melting procedure and you won't get so much on the floor.

Once the lead is cooled, it is worked with a file, a special file just for lead, to the shape you want, then finished with sandpaper. Leading is not difficult, but you must have patience. And, you must be willing to do the job over. I use lead as the base on very important areas, where the plastic filler might not be strong enough, and do the final finish with plastic. In this case, I have found it works best to cover the lead with a coat of two-part surfacer. This paint has outstanding adhesion to metal and lead, then the plastic filler is applied over the surfacer. Bites much better.

The fiberglass fillers have improved phenomenally since there were introduced several decades ago, to the point where they have put lead out of business as a filler. During the last handful of years, the fillers have gotten even better, sanding and shaping much easier and bonding extremely well. The superior appearance of the modern hot rod and custom is a direct tribute to modern fillers and paints.

It is imperative to understand that paint does not cover poor bodywork!!!

This is especially true of fillers, and particularly the plastic fillers. Unless you are going to lay the filler over etching primer, rough up the metal, usually a 24-grit disc sander works best. The metal must be absolutely clean of any paint or oils, including that from fingerprints. Use only the best materials you can buy from the body shop supplier, not the economy stuff from your local shrink pack emporium.

When the metal is ready (and warm, since filler doesn't work really well if the metal is cold), mix the filler. Mix on a piece of plastic or an old door glass. Do not use cardboard, as the waxes in the cardboard will absorb into the filler and mess everything up. A stick is used for initial mixing, do not put this stick back into the base filler or it will contaminate it. Use another stick next time. Final mixing of filler and hardener can be done with the plastic spreader you also bought at the parts store. A metal putty knife can be used, but the plastic spreader works better.

Warning: Do not use too much hardner. The excess hardner can bleed through the final paint coats, especially the light coats, and pearls. Spread the filler on as even as possible, but not too thick. It is easy to put on, much harder

Lead is now expensive,the 70/30 tin-lead mix is best. Big bars are harder to work with, lead with star-shaped crossection is best.

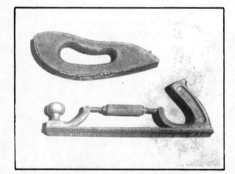

Lead and metal working files are still available, flat and curved blades come in handy for different contours. Keep blades clean and they will last the amateur for many years.

Preliminary preperation of metal starts with thorough grinding clean. The large hole must be filled with sheetmetal,smaller holes can be filled with metal,or MIG welded.

to sand off, and if you get it too thick it can crack easily. If you have an area that requires a bit of thickness, build it up in layers, and sand between coats for proper adhesion. Always blow off sanding dust before applying the next coat of filler. You can use a variety of tools and blocks to get the filler perfect. There is a straight line sander, orbital and jitterbug sanders, and hand blocks. A really trick item is a special block that Carl Brunson uses, which does rapid preliminary shaping, conforming to contours as it cuts. Contact Brunson at general delivery, Driggs, Idaho 83422 for more information. And thanks to Carl for information on the fillers, as well.

On the first coat of filler you can use a cheese grater file to rough shape, if you catch the filler before it has hardened too much. It will be kind of like rubbery cheese. Follow with a rough sanding with 40-grit paper, feel the surface, and sand down remaining high spots. Should metal show up as a high spot, it can be gently tapped down with a body hammer. Blow off the surface dust and apply a second filler coat. Again rough sand to shape with 40-grit, follow with 80-grit, and check again by feel. The hand and fingers will feel imperfections that the eye cannot see. When this roughing stage seems good, apply a thin coat of finishing putty, such as Fiberglass-Evercoat.

Now sand with 100-grit paper, and apply a light coat of primersurfacer. This will be a guide coat. When you now sand the area, the guide coat will remain in any low areas. Expect to do the filler job over as until you gain experience, because getting it just right is a matter of doing it over and over at first.

Lead will not stick to metal that is not tinned, and tinning compound will not flow onto metal that is not ground clean. Use a wire brush to clear detents. When leading holes, they must be dented inward to give more purchase area. MIG welding holes closed is much better, then leading area smooth.

We're showing how to lead holes just to prove it can be done. Here the patch area and holes are being tinned with compound on steelwool which is held by pliers. An extra hand comes in very nicely at this stage.

Use a very long, feathered gas flame for leading, special leading slide-on tips are available. Keep metal surface warm, direct heat to lead, soon as it turns color push it into warmed/tinned metal.

Once lead is "piled" on the metal, it can be heated carefully and shaped with wax-coated wooden paddle. Here paddle is held below pile during heating to keep any lead from melting and falling off.

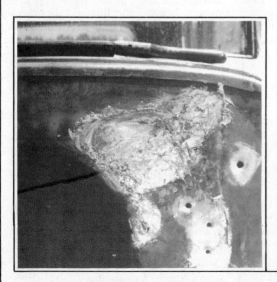

LEFT - Lead is heated and paddled smooth on the metal surface. If it can be shaped and excess wiped away at this stage, there is less filing to do later on. Lead is only as strong as the tinned base.

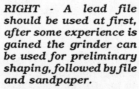

RIGHT - A lead file should be used at first, after some experience is gained the grinder can be used for preliminary shaping, followed by file and sandpaper.

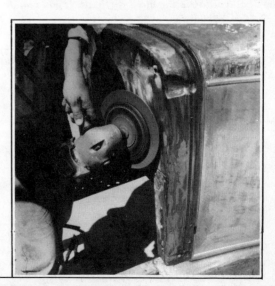

The firewall, as filled with lead. Since heat warpage can be a byproduct of leading, low spots can be pick-hammer worked, minor imperfections can be given a thin coat of plastic filler. Or, entire job can be done with MIG welder and plastic.

Edge of body panel needs strength, so it can be filled with lead and worked smooth, area "inside" the panel can get less strong plastic filler. Here the lead file insure a perfect finish.

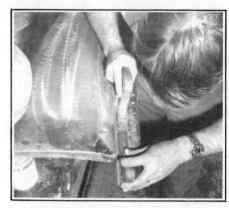

Lead can be used on heavier metal parts, such as the frame rails, but it has lost favor to the excellent modern fillers. However, lead will last far longer than plastic will,

FAR LEFT - As with lead filler, when plastic filler is to be used the metal must be absolutely clean, even the imperfections of a weld seam. Clean with a rotary file. Plastic filler can be applied over quality etching primer.

LEFT - Mix plastic filler exactly as instructions say, do not use too much hardener. Plastic spreaders allow the filler to be shaped during application, greatly reducing amount of sanding needed.

FAR LEFT - While plastic filler is still in the rubbery sa stage it can be rough-shaped with a cheese grater file. This also greatly reduces the amount of final sanding required. Apply filler in several succesive thin coats if build-up is needed.

LEFT - Final sanding is done with various shapes and sides of sanding boards, roll the sanding board to fit contours, ameteur mistake is to sand filler too flat, so that additional filler must be added.

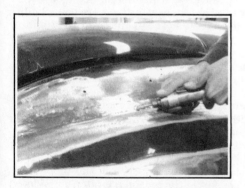

Alignment

Fitting body and frame, and body components such as doors, hood, and deck lid, can be frustration exempli fied. But this is where quality really shows.

If the frame is square and level (no twists), the body should be true when it is installed. All bodies will be insulated from the frame by some kind of pads, except for the unit construction versions. On an open car, it is possible to shim the bolts at the firewall/cowl area to adjust door "hang". This will be especially important on the old roadsters, not nearly such a problem on more modern convertibles.

The cars produced after about 1935 tend to have much better control for the doors and deck lid, so that alignment is mostly a matter of working with the hinges. The first thing to do when a hinge is involved is to make sure the hinge pin is not sloppy in the hinge holes. If it is, replace the pin and weld up/redrill the hinge holes. If stainless hinge pins are wanted, a trip to a well stocked hardware store should secure stainless

bolts of the right diameter...just cut off the thread and round the bolt top. Inexpensive pins. If the hinge can be removed from the vehicle, it is much easier to heat and straighten. As a rule, the lower hinge plate will be bent forward, the upper hinge plate will be bent backward (with front opening doors the directions reverse). It takes only a tiny amount of bend to throw the door completely out of alignment. This is a tedious job, but necessary to get alignment perfect.

Hoods and deck lids can almost always be aligned simply by tweeking the hinges, or by adding washers between hood/deck lid and the hinges.

To check that the door/deck lid fits tight against the weatherstrip (on cars that use rubber weatherstrip), close a strip of paper in the door/lid, then try to pull it out. If it slips out easily, chances are good that there is no seal at that point. Do all alignment before you get too far along with finish body work, then final minor alignment after paint.

Fiberglass

For some strange reason, fiberglass has gained the reputation of being either: (1-A magic material that the most unskilled dork can work with and obtain phenomenal results, or (2-A magic material dreamed up by scheaming demonics in the outer darkness that only practitioners of unknown arts can overcome!

It is neither. Fiberglass is simply useful part of modern life. For the hot rod or custom car, it can be increadibly useful, as a patching material, as a finishing material, as a strengthening material, and as a building material.

For the most part, fiberglass will be used on the metal body only as a filler. However, and this is very important to the less experienced builder, fiberglass can play a vital role in rebuilding an older car that uses lots of wood in the substructure. While the very best method of rebuilding a wood/metal body combination is by replacing all bad wood with good wood, or by building a new metal framework to replace all wood. Both are common practices. However, it is possible to use fiberglass and "save" a lot of bad wood structure.

As an example, suppose you have a 1930 Chevrolet coupe, and most of the wood floor and some of the wood side uprights is badly rotted and broken. It is essentially "all there", but with absolutely no strength. By being very careful to have the body in excellent alignment, the entire floorboard and uprights can be covered with a couple of layers of fiberglass cloth and resin. This will tie the wood together, then the body can be turned upside down and the bottom of the rotten wood can be covered with 'glass. The wood then becomes nothing more than a pulp filler for the fiberglass. No, it isn't the perfect way to do a rennovation, but it is an effective way. And in many cases, the result will be a body far stronger than the original. Also heavier.

When trying to save a body this way, just remember that once the fiberglass has been installed, and set, it is a major job to cut apart and realign something. Be sure the first time, or be sorry!

I should mention a specialty product at this time that seems to work very well with wood. Quite often, wood rot is only at the very bottom of a structure, or the edges. There is a product that is essentially a kind of advanced resin that will actually soak into all dead wood and make it harder than original. Contact RSP at 24 St. Henry Ct, St. Charles, MO 63301 for more information. I use this stuff a lot. Wood

soaked with this resin becomes very hard, and when then covered with fiberglass is extremely strong.

I have seen cases where a metal body that has been badly rusted around the base, but is still "sort of" intact, has been layered on the inside with fiberglass. It may look ok for awhile, but it is going to disappear.

Fiberglass bodies are showing up for a great variety of cars now, and every year the manufacturers learn how to make better and better products. What was once an industry limited to Model T and A bodies now produces 1937 Ford cabriolets, 1938 Chevy converts, 1948 Ford coupes, and even car bodies of the 1950s and '60s. There will come a time, in the not too distant future, when 1957 Chevy converts and Mustang bodies are available. As the metal originals become ever more scarce, the market for fiberglass replicas will grow. For the most part, these special fiberglass bodies are very good. As with every product, however, there are some bodies that are made for the economy segment, and they simply aren't as good as the better units.

There was a time when the purchaser of a fiberglass body got just a shell, and the doors/deck/flooring had to be installed at home. Now, most of this is already in place. Some commercial bodies are strengthened with wood substructure, some with metal. The prices aren't bargain basement, when compared with the cost of trying to save a marginal metal body, the prices are very reasonable.

Yes, it is possible to create an entire fiberglass body at home. This is well beyond the scope of this book, however.

Repair of fiberglass bodies requires only the most rudimentary of home tools, part of the reason it is often considered a "simple" product. A ripped 'glass fender merely needs to have the adjoining pieces aligned, an area either side of the crack scuffed with sandpaper, and new resin/cloth layed on. Far faster than trying to repair a damaged metal fender.

Bodies of fiberglass will start to "check" with age, something many Corvette owners learn. This is a special problem, and it will require extensive repair. Just keep it in mind when buying an older fiberglass bodied car.

Neat thing about using fiberglass for repair, or when building a fiberglass body rod, is that all mistakes can be fixed. Don't get deeply into a fiberglass project without first boneing up on the subject with books.

Top Insert

Replacing the soft top inserts in older coupe and sedan bodies is rapidly becoming commonplace in rodding. This is not a difficult procedure, when done correctly. When done wrong it becomes a bag of snakes.

Essentially, a large metal panel from some donor car is trimmed and added to the hot rod. The key is to match the donor panel curvature to the rod body, and to carefully tack weld it around the edges. Use very small tack welds, alternate side to side, and keep heat absorption of the metal to the minimum. A common mistake is to start welding and keep going. This will cause waves around the perimeter that are extremely difficult to remove, even for the experienced body man.

If possible, do the top insert welding with a MIG unit. Much faster, and keeps distortion to the minimum. While the purist might insist on using body lead to finish off a top insert, the modern plastic fillers are so good that using lead is almost foolhardy.

Photo sequence by Jerry Aaron shows top insert for older Dodge sedan. Original soft top and bows have been removed, wood bows can be left in place as headliner supports.

New top insert can be flat stock curved to fit, or section cut from a donor station wagon or van. Ribbed tops from late '50s Ford wagons are popular inserts.

Top panel is trimmed to fit the old body exactly. Sometimes it is trimmed to fit the opening lip, sometimes it is trimmed to overlap, depending on old car top contour.

In this case, a sliding roof insert was also being added, reason the original wood bows were removed. Top insert sliding mechanism is fit below the insert panel, welded solidly to body.

Top insert panel is tack welded around perimeter, going around the top many times to eliminate any kind of welding heat distortion. This patience is essential, else job may need to be repeated.

The welded seam is then finished off with filler, in this case a quality plastic. Lots of finish sanding is necessary to get the perfect smooth shape that is essential for best looks.

Top Chops

Chopping the top of a hot rod or custom has become almost a necessity. While much of the reasoning for top chopping has been laid at the doorstep of dry lakes and Bonneville racing (improving aerodynamics), the real reason for top chopping older cars goes back to early day magazine and newspaper illustrators. These artists learned quickly that by simply making the tops look "less tall" the car would appear much sleeker. Some specialty coachbuilders took the cue, and the "hammered lid" became a part of the customized car.

Chopping a top is very easy, if it is mostly an all-metal structure.

If the body is mostly wood, with a metal overlay, the top chop can become almost impossible for the amateur. In such a case, the metal should be removed from the wood, the wood reconstructed to the new shape, the metal trimmed accordingly,,and then put back on. Much, much work. There are other ways, but that is left for a later book specifically on chopping tops.

Although top chopping was a designers and coachbuilders trick long before hot rodders picked it up, it gained rodding popularity because of chopped cars running at California dry lakes and the salt flats This "mailbox" slot top chop on 1934 Ford coupe cuts wind resistence, most states have laws governing minimum windshield heights.

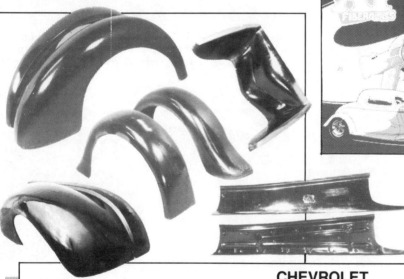

149

Any top can be chopped, no matter how radical the curves involved. The problem is cutting the glass to fit. The older flat glass is not much of a problem, but the new curved and highly tempered glass can be a major problem. In passing, I'll mention only that this problem glass is often cut by sandblasting. The "cut" line is masked off with several layers of tape on either side of the line, then a sandblaste is used to blow away the glass down to the safety laminate. This is cut with a blade, and hopefully the new glass is ready. The problem is that more often than not, the glass will crack. It is a touchy problem, and if you know of a person in your area who can cut this glass, you are miles ahead of your peers. Cutting this curved glass is not much of a problem with street rods (cars built before 1949), but it is very much a part of custom cars, so we'll save the details for our HOW TO BUILD CUSTOM CARS BOOK.

Just how radical can a car be chopped and channeled, this Model A coupe has been on the streets for over two decades, it is just over waist high.

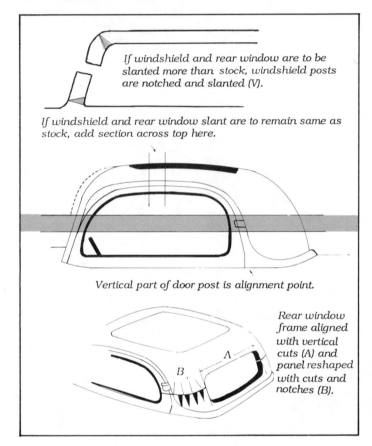

If windshield and rear window are to be slanted more than stock, windshield posts are notched and slanted (V).

If windshield and rear window slant are to remain same as stock, add section across top here.

Vertical part of door post is alignment point.

Rear window frame aligned with vertical cuts (A) and panel reshaped with cuts and notches (B).

A typical top chop on a 1934 3-window coupe. Section is removed to horizontal width of drop. Top door hinge is kept on some cars, may be cut away on '33 or '34 Fords.

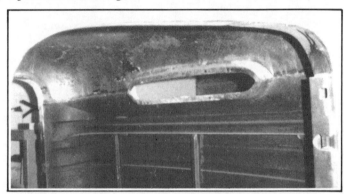

Bill's Custom Louvering in Windber, PA, shared the next series of photos with us of shop work in progress on tops. This early Chevy pickup has a radical cut through rear window for effect.

This later Chevy pickup is not cut as radically, note misalignment of windshield post when door post is aligned (as on Ford coupe at left)

To make alignment, windshield posts must be slanted, or sections added to top, here the cross-insert is apparent. The later model the car, the more this alignment problem, cars with curved door glass really require a lot of alignment planning.

The Chevy pickup with sections added to the roof now has stock slope to windshield. This kind of chop is particularly effective with these 1948 through 1955 GM trucks, coupes and pickups are much easier to chop than the sedans, roadster top bow chopping is different.

To prove a point that anything is fair game for the real hot rodder, Bill's Louvering sends these photos of a Nash four door that has gone under the ax. The result is a vehicle that is truely unique, secret of top chopping is to make it just enough, not too much.

Quite often when a top is chopped the drip rail is also removed. This gives a smooth area, but note that it also may produce a kind of obese look to large metal area between rear of door and back glass. Plan ahead for rear window, it may not need to be cut, or area between glass and deck lid may be cut apart so that extra section is not cut across the width of top.

Replacing Firewalls

Replacing and repairing firewalls really come under one heading. Repair to a firewall is a matter of cutting a patch and welding it in place, then using a filler. This may be a large patch, or it may be as small as a quarter, just to fill a hole. When you start to modify the firewall, then you get into replacing it all, or in part.

The firewall will be made of thicker metal than the body, usually 16-18 or so guage. If the firewall is merely going to be cleaned up, the procedure is straight-forward. But if the firewall must be modified, things get a bit different.

Suppose there is firewall/engine interferance at only one point, perhaps at the distributor of a V8, or the head/valve cover of a six cylinder engine. Only a small portion of the firewall needs to be cut away. A new section can be fabricated and welded in place. At most, the major problem will be reworking the kickboards or transmission hump and perhaps moving the throttle linkage.

If there is significant interference, where the firewall must be setback, you may want to make up a completely new firewall, section the stock firewall, or install a commercially available modified firewall.

If enough clearance is possible just by making a flat firewall, very simple. Drill out the rivets holding the old firewall in place, or carefully trim the perimeter with the torch or carbide wheel. With the old firewall out of the way, measure the opening diagonally and prop the body into alignment if necessary. It is imperative that the firewall opening be "square".

A new firewall can be made up of thick plywood, plywood sandwiched between stainless or aluminum panels, or metal only. Hold a sheet of metal to the firewall opening, trace the outline, trim the metal, and weld it in place. If you need special clearance boxes, they can be added, or if you want stiffening ribs, such beads can be rolled in. Your local sheet metal shop will be your best friend when building a firewall.

Or, you can buy a special firewall for the car, ready to insert and already setback or cleaned up. Bitchin Products, 10707 Airport Drive, El Cajon, CA 92020 makes such firewalls and floorboards, so we asked them for photos of typical ready-made walls. These walls could be used in fiberglass bodies, but most 'glass bodies come with stock or modified walls already in place.

No, we haven't been able to give you a blow-by-blow lead on all the aspects of specialized body work, that will take an entire book, and we'll probably end up doing just such a book. But this chapter will get you to thinking, and above all else, don't be afraid of tackling any kind of body job.

Oh, yes, there was supposed to be paint in this chapter, as well. But, we got to this point and we remembered one of the longest fueds in car building history... that between the painter and the upholsterer. The painter wants the car upholstered before it is painted ("Those trimmers always manage to scratch something, and trying to match pearls and

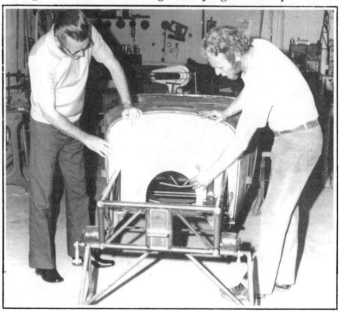

The firewall is often one place where the builder, both amateur and professional, falls down on detail. It may be a really custom aluminum unit, as on the Roach T, or a simple flat piece of plywood, whatever it is it needs to fit the cowl perfectly, and be attached extremely well. There must be no gaps for air to enter the driver's compartment, on either a race car or a street machine.

candies is really tough!"), and the upholsterer wants it painted before he adds upholstery ("Those painters always manage to get paint and overspray on the upholstery!").

Our suggestion: Paint around the door jambs, floorboards, interior, deck lid opening, etc, <u>then</u> take the car to the upholstery shop. Read the upholstery chapter, and then you find Chapter 11, THE REST OF CHAPTER 9, PAINT.

While the bellypan was being created for the Roach Model T, plans for the firewall were being made so that wall would fit body perfect.

This is a typical mid-30s Ford firewall, butchered by someone who needed additional engine setback. Common on older rods.

Same type of car, but with a commercially available firewall (Bitchin.) that includes considerable setback room. Much cleaner.

Most firewalls were riveted in place, or spot welded. Start installation of commercial replacement by drilling out rivets or spot welds.

Where firewall is welded to substructure at footboard area, cut away. Make these cuts as clean as possible, areas are welded to new wall.

On Model As and Ts, the firewall may bolt in place, remove screws and bolts, do not cut the support braces until new wall is tried.

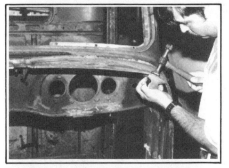

Some straightening of firewall lip may be needed, homemade wall would be welded at this lip for a perfect angle, and filler used if needed.

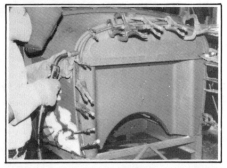

Commercial walls will fit somewhat like originals, use lots of clamps during welding to keep the firewall from shifting in the opening.

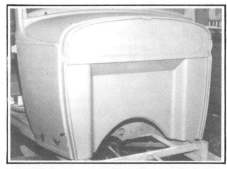

Here is a Model A firewall installed, with minor engine setback. These firewalls look very custom, but anyone can install them.

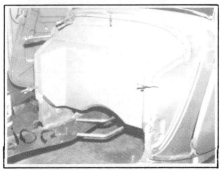

ABOVE - The amount of engine setback included in a firewall will have an immediate effect on footroom, keep this in mind. This is a 1933 Ford firewall, compare it with the coupe at right.

RIGHT - This 1934 Ford coupe firewall has only a minor setback right in the center, for distributor clearance common to the small block Chevy V8. Very careful measuring is needed when ordering a custom built commercial firewall, or when making one at home.

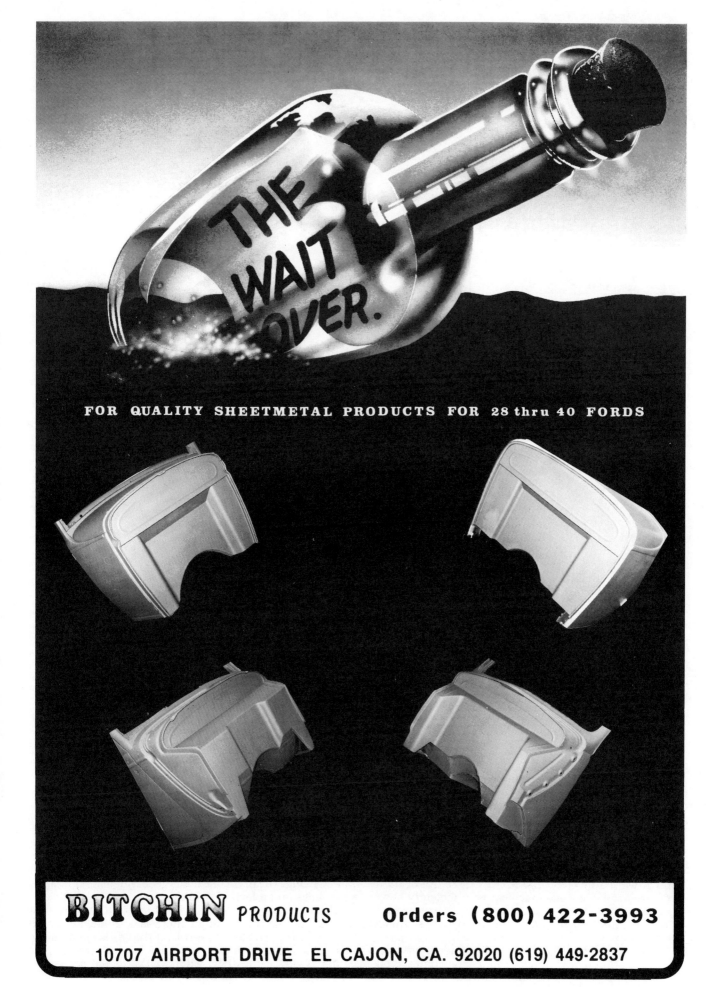

CHAPTER 10

Upholstery

Working with Fabric

It is possible to do the overwhelming majority of work at home when building a hot rod, no matter what the year or what the vehicle purpose. Some of the machine work must be farmed out, and some special equipment must be purchased, but too many builders shy away from other places where they definitely can do virtually all the work. Upholstery is one of those areas.

The modern car will have the interior trimmed in vinyl, or leather, or cloth, and carpeting. Other materials, such as jute and rubber, will be involved to a lesser degree. All of these materials are available from your nearest upholstery shop, those shops in the larger communities will have nearly everything on hand, smaller shops can order most things within a few days.

The tools necessary for upholstery will include a very good commercial walking-foot sewing machine (sometimes available at rental stores), scissors, sharp knives, hog rings and

hog ring pliers, good contact cement, and a strong pair of hands. This last "tool" is one reason some people give up the profession.

Don't expect to read this article and go to the garage for a marathon session of trimming your favorite project. First you need to do some practicing on less important projects. Do a couple of seat covers, or a carpet job, or even a living room chair. Practice sewing, making patterns, sewing, working with padding, sewing, pulling material without wrinkles, and more sewing. The mark of a really good upholsterer is straight sewn lines and a lack of wrinkles.

The materials you choose to finish your car with are strictly a personal choice, although there is a guideline for open versus closed vehicles. As a rule, if the car is open and may be a rained on (which can ruin some fabrics), you may want to use a vinyl or leather, whereas the closed car can use anything. Whatever material you select, be sure and get

154

enough! Quite often you can get great bargains on materials that are being discontinued, or that a local upholsterer may have too much of, but if you don't get enough you may not be able to get additional material when you discover the shortage. Your local upholsterer or materials supplier will usually help you estimate what you need. Add a couple of extra yards for mistakes.

If you are re-upholstering a vehicle that already has trim in place, you can use this old material for a pattern. Otherwise, you can lay large paper/cardboard over the surface to be covered and make up patterns. After you get some experience, you will probably lay the material directly in place and mark it with chalk. This is where that preliminary practicing comes into play, so that you can learn how to cut out the material and sew it up so that it is neither too large or too small. Better large than small, because it can be ripped apart and made smaller.

But even if you will never do your own upholstery, follow along with the photos and you will come to understand what the professional goes through to give you a premium quality trim job, either in fabric as on the author's 1948 Chrysler sedan, or in leather, as on Tom Medley's 1940 Ford coupe.

Material for an open car (opposite page) will probably be selected to resist sun and water more than for closed car (left), careful selection of material can drastically reduce cost of upholstery job.

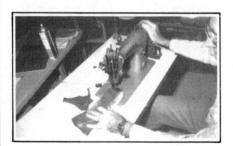

Sewing machines for upholstery are available just about everywhere, the walking foot model is desirable, special foot is needed for sewing right to edge of piping, prices for a good used machine will a range from a low of around $200 to a high of over $1000, this is one tool that can turn a hobby into a profession. For information on good machines, contact Sewing Machine, 7922 Hill Avenue, Holland, OH 43528, telephone (419)866-5558.

LEFT - Rear arm rest is a good place to start. Minor amount of sewing is needed, padding is glued to framework, then material is stretched over rest and edges glued in place. RIGHT - When the arm rest is finished, there will be no wrinkles or tucks in the seams.

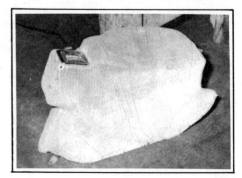

Jim Garrison did custom upholstery before becoming a car show official, here he sews fabric to a backing with foam between. Idea is to make the seams "invisible" by lapping the material over and sewing down the back side. When material is placed back flat the result is a grooved seam. Here the pleats are very wide in near stock fashion.

Material has had the pleats sewn in, is then laid on the seat cushion and corners marked. Side pieces are cut, then sewn to flat pleated section. If in doubt, always make slightly larger so the seams can be taken out and pieces cut down to fit better. With experience this cut-and-try will disappear.

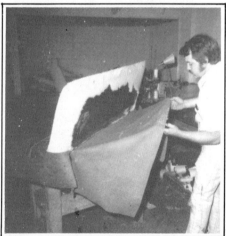

ABOVE LEFT - Align material with center of the cushion, pull top and bottom ends over seat springs and attach to spring perimeter wire with hog rings. Now each end is pulled into place and attached with rings, then rest of cover is pulled taut. Make it tight, because cover will loosen with use. Foam rubber and cotton padding is used to build up the cushion base. ABOVE CENTER - Seat frames are common on many cars, the edges are usually padded with foam or cotton. Fabric is attached to underside of frame, then pulled up and over frame lip, glued in

place. Patterns can be sewn into frame cover but this makes it more difficult to get correct alignment. ABOVE RIGHT - Use the old headliner for pattern, cut and sew sections to fabric "tubing" which is placed on backside of headliner. Steel rods that hold headliner up are inserted in these tubes. Attach center of headliner at front and rear of car, install rods, pull headliner taut front and rear. Wrinkles will be in the material lengthwise at this time, do not make headliner too tight if it is from regular headliner fabric, vinyl would be pulled tight.

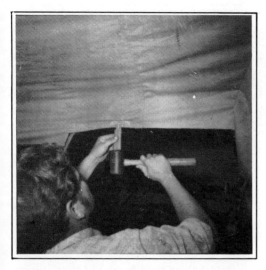

Sides of headliner may attach to body by tacks, or be slipping under a retention strip of toothed metal. Here the headliner material is being inserted under this strip, as it is tucked under the lengthwise wrinkles are pulled out. It takes some practice to get the headliner just right, readymade headliners are available for most older cars through upholstery supply outlets and are a lot less expensive than custom made units.

ABOVE -vinyl headliner is sewn in sections same as fabric and may have the same support rod tubing on backside. On an older car, such as this sedan, it is tacked to the windshield headboard at the front center, then stretched tight and tacked to top wood at the back. BELOW - Once the headliner is in place fore/aft, it is pulled to the sides as with fabric and tacked/stapled in place. These early cars are much more rudimentary when it comes to upholstery, and rely on small panels for covering major attachment areas. Wind lacing around the doors is all that seals out the air drafts.

Once the headliner is slightly taut from front to rear and side to side, it can be lightly misted with water and left to dry naturally. This will cause the material to shrink to a nice taut fit, which is why you didn't pull it too tight to begin with. But if it is too loose, it will sometimes sag in very damp weather at future times. Weather stripping hides the headliner edges around the doors, garnish moldings cover the edges around rear window and windshield.

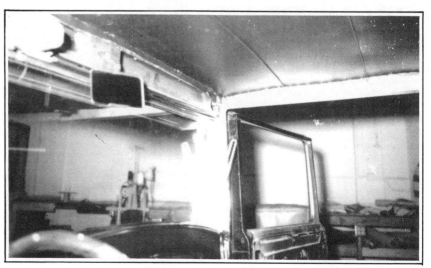

Special upholsterer's "rope" is wrapped with special windlacing fabric and sewn up in long lengths. This is where the special sewing machine foot comes into play, allowing the seam to be tight up against the rope. There is about 1-inch material left over as a tacking strip.

There will be a tack strip around the door opening, or a metal fold-over retention strip. The windlacing is attached before the headliner or any upholstered panels are put in place, bottom ends usually just barely tuck under the scuff plates.

Door panels may have a base of either upholstery cardboard (dense) or very thin plywood. Sewing machine will sew through the cardboard, usually there is padding between the board and upholstery fabric, again the idea is to make as straight a line as possible.

Holes in the door panel are for special attachment clips, you can get clips that will work from any upholstery shop. Holes for door and window crank inside handles are also cut in board. Fabric is cut larger than the board, folded over the edges and glued/stapled in place. If the fabric is pulled too tight it will bow the board, plan ahead and cut the board slightly smaller than door so that when fabric is folded over edge the panel exactly fits door dimensions.

Here is an old door panel alongside the new panel (left). Carpeting is used at bottom of panel where shoe scuffing is probable, note how the simple pattern sewn into new panel makes it more interesting.

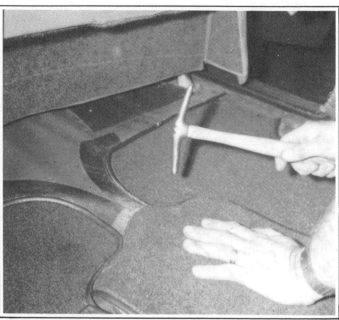

Small panels are made of board and covered same as door panels, they are usually held in place with tiny tacking nails that will go through the fabric and be hidden as the weave closes.

Carpeting is cut to fit, then a trim piece is sewn on. Usually the carpet can be glued in place over a jute padding, sometimes it may be necessary to use special metal nails or screws for difficult areas.

Working with Leather

by Tom Medley

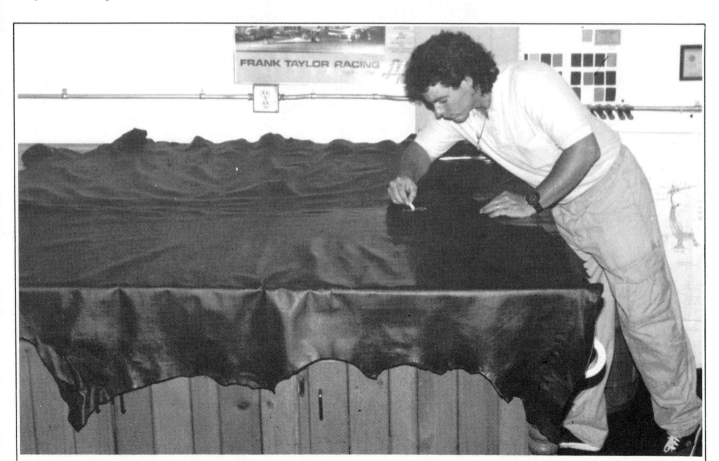

Working with real leather is a whole new ballgame. Conally hides are prefered because they have few, if any, imperfections, cost about $200-$250 per hide. Here a tiny imperfection is identified and will be cut around.

Ideal way to add any upholstery is to paint the body openings before adding trim. The basic tools needed, other than the sewing machine, are rather simple, tack hammer and mallet are especially useful. Leather texture is important selection item.

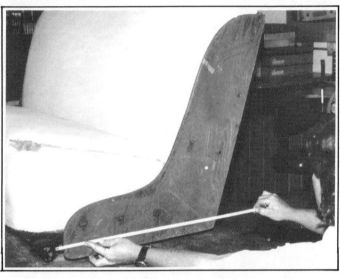

The seat frame will probably be of rough plywood, measure carefully and transfer rough shape to hide. Vat dyed hide is superior to hide that has color sprayed on since it has color clear through hide. Felt or thin foam rubber is cut to fit frame side, covering plywood roughness.

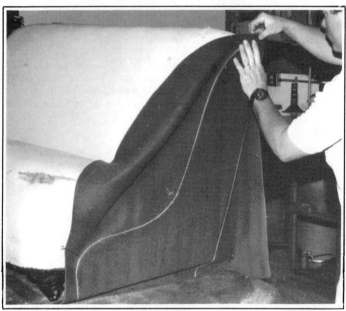

Piece of hide is pinned to the frame, various shapes are drawn on the hide to make sure every little piece is used, due to high cost.

Side panel is trimmed slightly over-size, then padded foam backing is sewn to back of leather, machine will use a large needle, do not force the feed. Special thread is Star Ultra D, a bonded polyester Z-twist at about 16 ounces. Long life, doesn't rot.

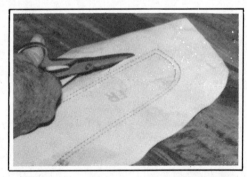

Side panel Padding is trimmed closer after sewing on design. Trim contact cement (#08031 by 3M) is applied to foam backing and plywood, edges are rolled over frame edge and glued/stapled in place. Any krinkles at this stage on back side are trimmed to lay flat.

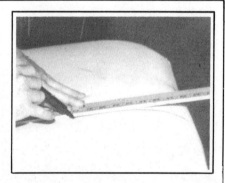

When doing the bottom cushion, start by marking the cushion center, everything will use this centerline as a guide, make the mark across the entire cushion, front to back. A felt tip marker works fine for this preliminary work, make sure you are right on.

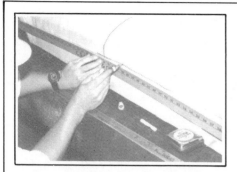

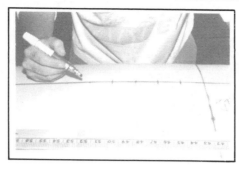

On the back side of the cushion, make a horizontal line just below the top lip. At this point a piece of strong material will be sewn to the leather. This saves leather, and it cannot be seen anyway. It is called the facing.

A few inches back from the front lip of the cushion a horizontal line is drawn. This line will be where a special tiedown will be inserted through the cushion. The smaller marks are spacing for the pleats, so that you come out right on width.

ABOVE - From measurements taken from the marked off seat cushion, the hide is marked out, and edge piece is cut to make welt. FAR LEFT - A piece of leather slightly wider than cushion pattern is cut, then chalked against the cushion lines. Leave enough to tuck around bottom frame and for welt sewing lap. LEFT - The welt is sewn to the front leading cap leather using chalk line as the guide, where cap curves around to sides of seat cushion snip edges to make corner easier. Make this sewn seam exactly where the cushion curves down to front and sides, check next photo for an important tip.

Note here that the center of the front cap piece has a seam down the middle. The cap is made in two pieces because a single large piece of leather is seldom available and this makes better use of the entire hide. This type of seam is called a french seam, check with your local upholsterer to note how such a seam is made as it adds distinctive quality appearance to the job. Welt is positioned on cushion and pinned in place so that top cap can be measured and cut.

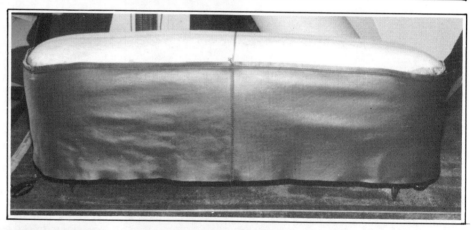

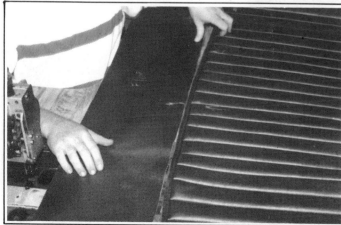

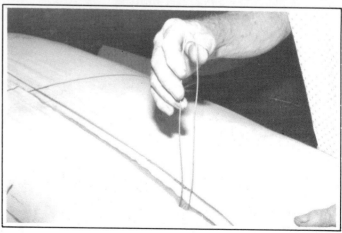

Leather is cut and sewn against padded backing (or pleats can be stuffed individually with foam, using a flat ruler), each pleat is backsewn so that seam doesn't show. A tube piping welt is sewn along front edge of pleated material,

Foam padding is cut along the horizontal line, clear through to the springs, and pieces of wire are slipped through to attach to the bottom of the springs, check next couple of photos to see what all this will accomplish.

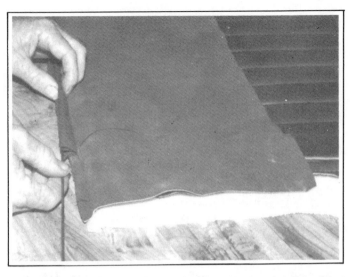

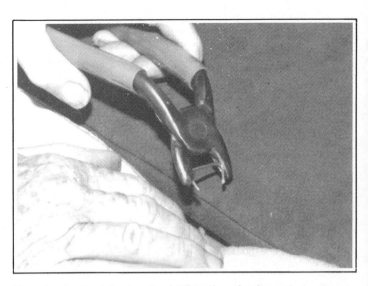

A piece of strong material is sewn in a loop at welt where front part of top cap is sewn to pleats, then a strong length of wire is inserted in this tube. As everywhere, this sewn seam should be straight.

The wire in the tube is attached to the wire loop that was run down through the cushion padding by a hog ring at the center of the top cap, same on wire loops to either side. This pulls cap into slit.

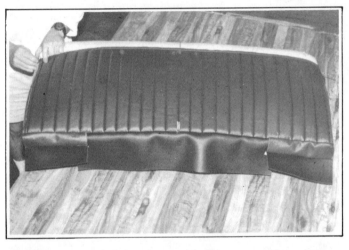

ABOVE - Now pleated cap can be chalked where it will attach to the front cap, and it is trimmed and sewn to the front piece, when slipped over the cushion now it should be a tight fit. The hog rings temporarily holding the cross wire in place are removed before sewing, of course. BELOW - After cross wire is replaced in position and front/side cap is tucked in place temporarily, the back flap is pulled tight and marked so it can be pulled into place all along the edge and stapled or hog ringed in place. Make the seam straight.

ABOVE - After cover is sewn together and pulled over cushion, attach the crosswire permanently with hog rings. Note how this gives a double bulge to the seat, thanks to the slit in the cushion padding. Lower edges of front/side cap is pulled into place and held temporarily with clamps, the idea is to work the cover so that all the seams are straight and there are no lumps. Take your time here. BELOW - Once the cover is in position, as tight as you want it to be, staple or hog ring the entire perimeter to the bottom of the springs.

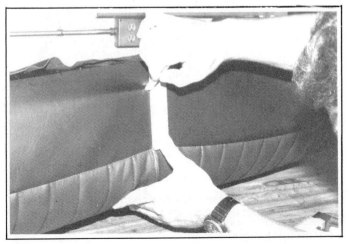

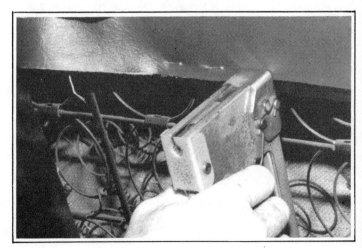

LEFT - Seat back cushion is created same way as the bottom cushion, following chalk marks and cushion marks. BELOW - Pull the back cover into place and attach with staples or hogrings. Since the leather is so expensive it is wise to get as much use from a hide as possible, save all the scraps that are trimmed away during final fitting. When using clamps to hold covers in place, be sure clamps have rubber tips to keep from marring the hide. You must really pull on the leather to get all the wrinkles out during this final fit.

Starting on a door panel, the base can be either upholstery cardboard or, in this case, the thin plywood skin from a hollow-core door, pattern is marked on the wood.

Carpeting is stapled to the wood along top edge where it will mate with the leather pleated piece, use contact glue to keep the carpet in place during work.

Piece of binding is sewn to exposed edges of the carpet and this is pulled around edge of the board and stapled/glued in place.

Door panel pleats are sewn up same as the seat covers, you can piece smaller units of leather together if need be.

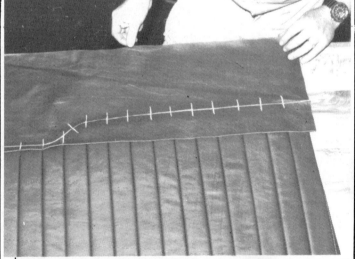

Door panel cover can be sewn directly to the board, since the big sewing machine needle will punch through the board. Go slow and easy, do not push or pull the leather since it will stretch so much, panel is sewn back at edge of carpeting.

Top of panel can have a flat padded section above pleats, it can be shaped a number of ways for design. This piece is sewn to the pleated section with a welt divider, than padding is glued to the back of the flat piece with contact cement. A spray gun is shown, brushes work just as well, put cement on leather as well as foam rubber.

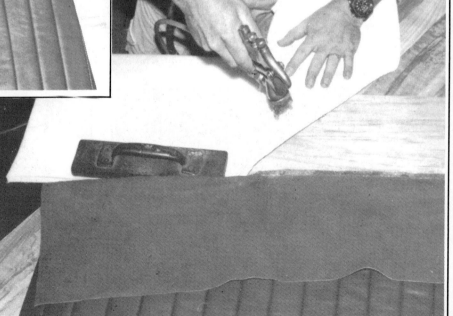

164

Trim the padding at an angle where it is at edge of board so that leather does not stick out too much beyond board, pull the cover around edges and staple, cut corner bulges away so the panel fits tight against the door. Thanks to the folks at Jeff's Top Shop in San Dimas, California for this article. William Jeffrey is the father, Brad is shown, Bill filled in where needed.

Paint

Back in the Bodywork chapter, we mentioned that there was some question in the minds of painters and upholsterers as to which of their services should be the very last thing a rod project received. In all honesty, electrics should fall in here somewhere, probably right after the bodywork, but before the upholstery. Whatever, we have decided to make paint the last step in the rod building pyramid, mostly just to be different from most books on the subject. In fact, it seems that most of the projects that we do will vary...some will get paint before the stitches, some last, and in at least one case, the poor car is still running around in its primer underwear. We have known lots of custom painters through the years, and have learned from them all. But there has been such a tremendous amount of change in the paint technology during the last handful of years, we decided we would ask someone who does both crash and custom work for information. We think this brings us more in line with what is actually being done and is available in most parts of the country. Thanks to Carl Brunson, who has a custom body

shop in our little town of Driggs, Idaho, for the following material.

First, get the car metal clean. REALLY CLEAN! You might even start by washing it thoroughly with some strong detergent and a rag. Follow this with a visit to the car wash (we're assuming the car is a runner. If not, just plan accordingly), where you wash the entire undercarriage, the wheel wells, engine compartment... everywhere. Now is the time to get everything clean, not after you have a new paint skin in place. Next, use a grease and wax remover. Wipe this on and before it can dry, wipe it off. This remover lifts whatever is in the paint pores to the surface, but the stuff will return to the pores when dry, so work fast.

Depending upon how mobile you need the car to be, remove all the outer trim possible. Door handles, bumpers, emblems, etc. Now is the time after it is clean and stripped of trim to really honestly inspect the car finish. Look for tiny dents, rust, existing paint problems (cracking, peeling, checking, etc). The first rule of custom painting is that you can

Start any paint job by a really thorough wash of the car, including engine compartment, wheel wells, and door facigs/jambs. For the best job, remove weatherstripping carefully, then sand door faces/jambs.

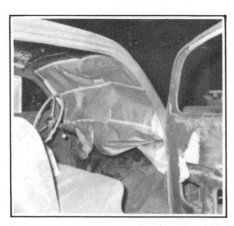

If a full color change is taking place, be sure and mask off areas of the interior where you don't want overspray, including all glass and upholstery. Remove what trim you can, such as door panels.

Attention to small and difficult areas to sand will mean big difference in finish job. It is the preparation that pays off with a superior finish coat, don't cut any corners because of labor.

Edges of doors/deck lid/hood will tend to have small paint chips, these edges need to be sanded completely smooth for best results, do not use any kind of filler on edges, it can break away.

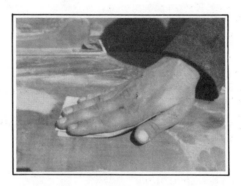

When holding sandpaper by hand, keep the hand flat as possible and curl edge of sandpaper between thumb base and hand to keep paper from slipping. Fingers can make grooves while sanding.

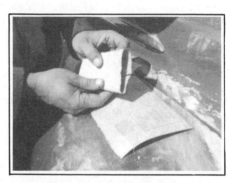

Tear large sheet of sandpaper in half, then tri-fold it as shown. Knock dry paper clean often, change often. Wet sanding will allow paper to go further, but requires careful clean-up of car af-

LEFT - If trim is impossible to remove, be very careful when sanding near it, use finger to keep paper distant. Best is to tape trim off for sanding, then again for spraying.

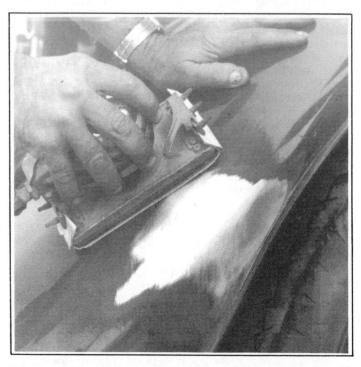

LEFT - Dings, gouges, rips in the paint must be repaired, always blend repair into surrounding panel smoothly. If repaired area can be felt with finger tips, it will be seen in final paint.

When paint is only one or two coats thick, it can be feathered into the surrounding area very nicely at repair edge. The wider this edge, usually, the better the feathering job, finish job with hand block.

<u>never</u> put a quality paint job over a poor one! The top coats are going to be a direct reflection of the undercoats...all the way through to the body work. In essence, the foundation <u>is</u> the paint job.

If the factory or last paint job was a good one, the paint may not need to be stripped to the metal. If the car has had more than about 3 paint jobs, it will probably need to be stripped. If in doubt, strip. It will take more time and effort, but the end result will be worth it all.

Paint stripper is a mess at the best of times, and it can be toxic. The "hotter" the stripper, the more likely it is to be toxic, so be sure you follow the can instructions precisely. Wear protective clothing, and absolutely wear goggles.
To keep stripper out of the seams and panel openings, cover them with several layers of 3/4 inch wide masking tape. After the paint is stripped, remove this tape and sand the remaining area clean. This way you don't have stripper working out of the cracks after the car is painted.

Use rubber gloves and a natural bristle brush, and put on a thick, even coat of stripper. Work in small areas, about a 2-3 foot square, so the stripper does not dry too fast. After the paint blisters, use a putty knife to scrape it away. Keep a piece of cardboard handy to put the paint residue on, much nicer to work around the area then. Work each panel this way and you'll be done before you think possible.

Wash the car body very thoroughly with Acetone, to get rid of any loose paint and stripper. Don't try to be careful with any old body filler, grind it out and apply new filler, if you want to create a truly fine custom finish. As mentioned in the body work chapter, sandblasting can be used on the body, but use extreme care to prevent hydrogen embrittlement of the panels. It is best to chemically strip the panels, and use sandblasting only for door jambs, cowl vents, rust areas, etc.

Refer back to the body work chapter about fillers, also. It is very easy to sand the filler too much, flatten the area, or not sand enough (leave a hump). When you get to the stage with filler where you are doing the finish work, you want to work with the big sanding boards on large flatter areas. You can work the filler to a near shape with power tools, but you will get best final results by using hand tools only. You can make most of these filler blocking tools, from hard and soft wood blocks (no sharp edges), and wood dowels, cardboard tubes, harder rubber tubes, etc. Many of the new sandpapers have adhesive on the back side, so it will stick to any of these blocking tools.

Get the filler and metal as straight as possible, and smooth, before adding primer and surfacer. Do not rely on primer surfacers or spot puttys to make the surface smooth. This is s just asking for trouble later. Keep the paint film build-up as thin as possible, in all aspects of refinishing. Thick paint jobs chip easier and have a shorter life span. Temperature changes cause metal expansion and contraction. The paint also "moves" but at a different rate. Too much filler, primer, putty, and paint and it can all self destruct.

When the body feels perfect, it is time for primer. It is best to let filler cure for at least a day before coating it with primer. Tape off everything you don't want paint on (primer is paint), and wear a respirator mask. The self etching or wash primers are very good. They contain acid and etch right into the metal or filler. This gives a mechanical (sanded) bond and a chemical bond. In every phase of refinishing, there must be one or the other for good adhesion.

These primers give very little fill. A primer surfacer is for filling sand scratches, and is used during block sanding to get an even truer, smooth surface. The acrylic urethane primer surfacers don't shrink as much as the acrylic lacquer types, and give a superior foundation for top coats. Urethanes are where it is at today, and current technology is improving the product until all the toxic problems will soon be eliminated.

No matter what surfacer is used, allow time between coats for it to cure. You will trap solvents in the first coat if you apply the second coat too soon. This causes blisters, and will cause

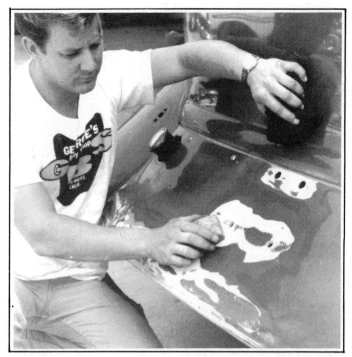

Block sanding the entire area around a repair will insure the best possible blend, results in a spot painting that cannot be seen if color mixs correct.

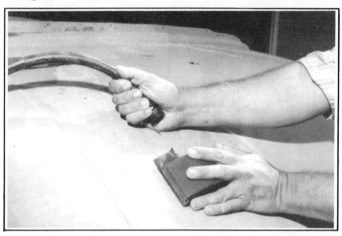

When water sanding, it is essential to keep sandpaper lubricated, whether with steady flow of water, or with detergent/water mix and sponge.

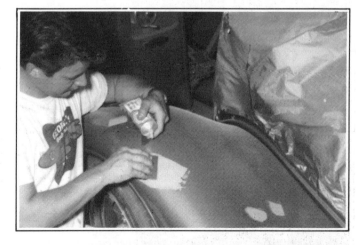

Spot putty, or glaze, must be used for tiny imperfections only, it is not a major filler. Here, plastic applicator spreads it very thin, after sanding most of putty will be gone.

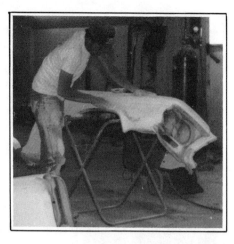

Paint can be stripped with a grinding disc, it is a messy job but does work well. Use a soft disc pad and do not grind too much.

It may be easiest to remove doors/fenders/hood/deck lid for minor repair and stripping.

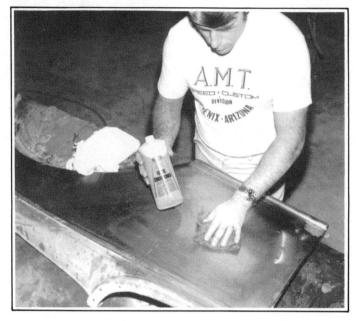

After a panel is stripped to bare metal, the metal must be etched, either with something like Prep-Sol or Met-L-Prep.....

...or, the metal is cleaned with thinner very thoroughly, followed by a grease and wax remover, then etching primer used.

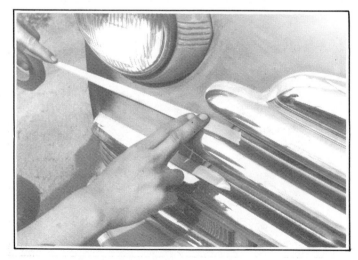

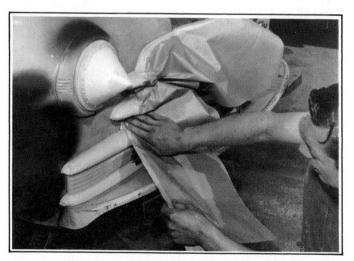

Tape around the edges of all in-place trim, use a razor blade to tuck tape down, best is to trim tape very carefully. Do not allow tape to lay over onto painted metal surface.

All trim, and all open areas are taped off with a quality paper, newspaper is not nearly as good as a tight grain paper, do not leave any paper edges to flap into paint or collect dust.

169

When only an area is being repainted, very carefully mask off adjacent body panels, cover the wheels and tires. Remember that paint will go everywhere and makes clean-up tedious.

shrinkage later. Drying times are important in refinishing, allow plenty of time. At the same time, be sure you very thoroughly read all the application instructions on the product labels, because waiting periods vary.

Do not over apply primer, control film build-up. It isn't wise to use a lacquer type surfacer under urethane paint top coats. The solvents in urethanes are strong enough to soften anything underneath, except urethane surfacers.

Use an old paint gun, and spray on as even a coat as you can. This is practice time for the finish coats. You can mess up here and still sand the goofs out. For most spray equipment, hold the paint gun 8-10 inches from the car. Keep the gun head parallel to the surface being painted, and practice making even strokes across the panel. Pull the gun trigger only part way and you get only air, so that you can practice on curved surfaces before actually applying paint. The more you pull the trigger, the more material will flow from the gun. Start the stroke evenly, easing through the air-only stage, then at the end of the stroke ease off the trigger through air-only. The idea is to keep the gun head an exact distance from the panel, the spray pattern even, gun not tilted, and make smooth and constant speed passes across the panel.

Carl starts at the bottom of panels on the sides, and works his way up. On the flat surfaces of roof, hood, and deck lid, he starts at the panel middle and works toward the outside. You may discover a work pattern that suits you better. In any case, overlap each pass over a panel about one-half the gun fan pattern. This gives gloss, but not too much texture of the surfacer. No gloss means you are moving too fast, or holding the gun too far from the surface.

A small air guage attached to the gun will indicate the correct air pressure. A piling up of material, or runs, means you are too close, or going too slow. You will find that painting becomes a kind of dance, weight shifting from one leg to the

This would be an ideal paint booth, with double doors, plenty of light, excellent circulation fans, and heat lamps. You'll probably have to work with much less.

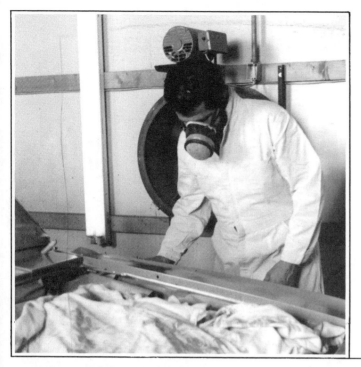

A premium respirator mask is imperative with painting, dual mask and full clothing for urethanes, air suit is best of all.

You must have a quality paint gun to get quality work, if you do several cars in your lifetime, invest in a good gun.

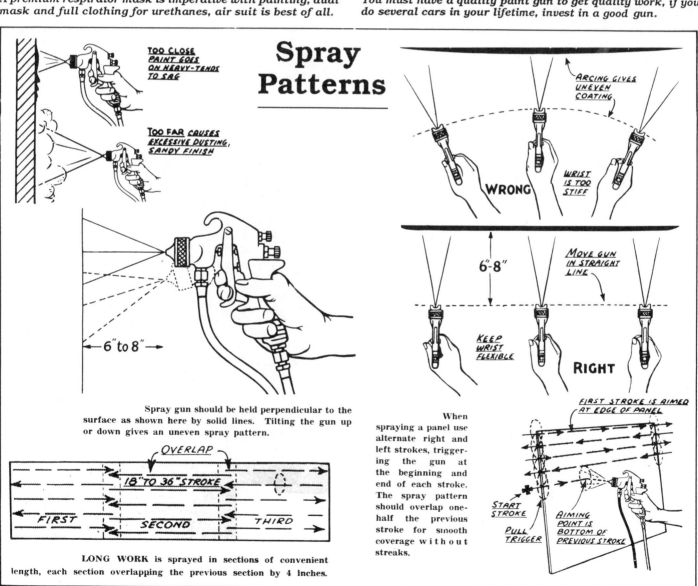

Spray Patterns

TOO CLOSE PAINT GOES ON HEAVY-TENDS TO SAG

TOO FAR CAUSES EXCESSIVE DUSTING, SANDY FINISH

ARCING GIVES UNEVEN COATING

WRONG

WRIST IS TOO STIFF

6"-8"

MOVE GUN IN STRAIGHT LINE

KEEP WRIST FLEXIBLE

RIGHT

6" to 8"

Spray gun should be held perpendicular to the surface as shown here by solid lines. Tilting the gun up or down gives an uneven spray pattern.

OVERLAP

18" TO 36" STROKE

FIRST   SECOND   THIRD

LONG WORK is sprayed in sections of convenient length, each section overlapping the previous section by 4 inches.

When spraying a panel use alternate right and left strokes, triggering the gun at the beginning and end of each stroke. The spray pattern should overlap one-half the previous stroke for smooth coverage without streaks.

FIRST STROKE IS AIMED AT EDGE OF PANEL

START STROKE

PULL TRIGGER

AIMING POINT IS BOTTOM OF PREVIOUS STROKE

171

Spray Gun Troubles and Remedies

What causes air leakage from the front of the gun?

(a) Foreign matter on valve or seat.
(b) Worn or damaged valve or seat.
(c) Broken air valve spring.
(d) Sticking valve stem due to lack of lubrication.
(e) Bent valve stem.
(f) Packing nut too tight.
(g) Gasket damaged or omitted.

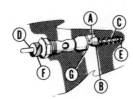

What causes a jerky or fluttering spray?

Air leakage into fluid line due to:
(Applying to both suction and pressure feed)
(a) Lack of sufficient material in container.
(b) Tipping container at excessive angle.
(c) Obstructed fluid passageway.
(d) Loose or cracked fluid tube in cup or tank.
(e) Loose fluid tip or damaged tip seat.
(Applying to suction feed only:)
(f) Too heavy a material for suction feed.
(g) Clogged air vent in cup lid.
(h) Loose, dirty or damaged coupling nut or cup lid.
(i) Dry packing or loose fluid needle packing nut.
(j) Fluid tube resting on bottom of cup.

How should guns be cleaned?

A suction feed gun and cup should be cleaned as follows: Loosen cup from the gun and while the fluid tube is still in the cup, unscrew the air cap about two to three turns, hold a cloth over the air cap and pull the trigger. Air diverted into the fluid passageways forces material back into the container Empty cup of material and replace with a small quantity of solvent. Spray solvent through the gun to flush out the fluid passageways
Then remove the air cap, clean as directed above and replace it on the gun. Wipe off the gun with a solvent-soaked rag, or if necessary brush the air cap and gun with a fiber brush using clean-up liquid or thinner.

What causes fluid leakage from the fluid needle packing nut?

A loose packing nut, worn packing, or dry fluid needle packing. Lubricate packing with a few drops of light oil. Tighten packing nut to prevent leakage but not so tight as to grip the fluid needle. It becomes necessary to replace the packing when it is worn.

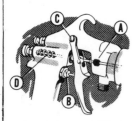

What parts of the gun require lubrication?

The fluid needle packing (A), air valve packing (B) and the trigger bearing screw (C). A drop or two of oil should be put on the fluid needle packing occasionally to keep it soft. The fluid needle spring (D) should be coated with petrolatum.

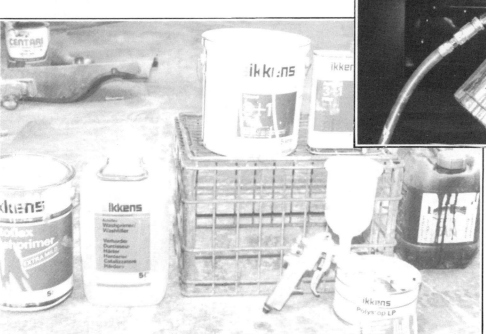

Cleaning And Lubricating The Gun

How should the air cap be cleaned?

By simply immersing it in clean solvent and drying it by blowing it off with compressed air. If small holes become clogged soak the cap in solvent. If reaming is still necessary, use a match stick, broom straw, or any other soft implement Digging out holes with wire or a nail may permanently damage the cap.

What causes defective spray patterns?

(a) Top heavy pattern caused by:
  (1) Horn holes partially plugged.
  (2) Obstruction on top of fluid tip.
  (3) Dirt on air cap seat or fluid tip seat.
(b) Heavy bottom pattern caused by:
  (1) Horn holes partially plugged.
  (2) Obstruction on bottom side of fluid tip.
  (3) Dirt on air cap seat or fluid tip seat.
(c) Heavy right side pattern caused by:
  (1) Right side horn holes partially clogged.
  (2) Dirt on right side of fluid tip.
  (3) On twin jet air cap, right jet clogged.
(d) Heavy left side pattern due to:
  (1) Left side horn holes partially clogged.
  (2) Dirt on left side of fluid tip.
  (3) On twin jet cap, left jet clogged.
(e) Heavy center pattern caused by:
  (1) Too low a setting of the spreader adjustment valve.
  (2) With twin jet cap, too low an atomizing pressure or material being too thick.
  (3) With pressure feed, too high a fluid pressure for the atomization air being used or the material flow is in excess of the cap's normal capacity.
  (4) Too large a nozzle for the material used.
  (5) Too small a nozzle.
(f) Split spray pattern due to air and fluid not being properly balanced.
Reduce width of spray pattern by means of the spreader adjustment valve or increase fluid pressure. This latter adjustment increases speed and the gun must be handled much faster.

Normal Spray Patterns.

Remedies

For (a) through (d):
Determine if obstruction is on air cap or fluid tip. This is done by making a test spray pattern then rotating the cap one half turn and spraying another pattern. If the defect is inverted (Fig. 38), obstruction is on the air cap. If not inverted, it is on the fluid tip. Clean the air cap as described on page 13. Check for fine burr on the edge of the fluid tip (remove with 600 wet or dry sand paper) or for dried paint just inside the opening (remove by washing).

For (e) through (f):
If adjustments are out of balance, readjust atomizing pressure, fluid pressure and spray width adjustment until the desired spray is obtained.

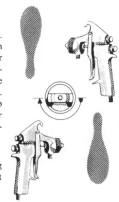

35. What causes fluid leakage from front of the gun?

Fluid Needle not seating properly due to:
(a) Worn or damaged fluid tip or needle.
(b) Lumps or dirt lodged in fluid tip.
(c) Packing nut too tight.
(d) Broken fluid needle spring.
(e) Wrong size needle.

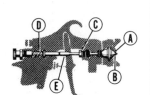

other as you move the gun along, keeping the strokes even. Pay attention and a smooth pattern will evolve.

Over the primer, spray a thin guide coat (contrasting color of primer), this should be very thin, even kind of splotchy. Remove the tape, and let the car cure for several days, if possible. In the sun is best of all. All primers and paints shrink as the solvents dry. If you sand too soon, the base will still be curing and you may end up seeing 100 grit sanding marks in the finish.

After the primer/surfacer is cured, it is ready to block sand. This is all hand work, and it takes time. Start with 280 wet or 150 dry sandpaper on a long board. Sand in long strokes, a kind of X motion that produces a cross block effect (same as on the fillers) Use this long board on longer areas and switch to smaller hand blocks for smaller areas. The shape of the area to be block sanded determines the shape and size of the block.

When block sanding, feel the area as you go along and watch the guide coat. Don't make grooves. Block a section of a panel about 8-12 inches square at a time. Sand forward, backward, up, and down until the panel is sanded clean of the guide coat. If you sand only one spot too much, you stand a chance of creating a low spot. Keep extending the sanded area into the unsanded area, feathering everything smooth.

After the panel is sanded with 280, remove the 280 grit marks with 400 wet or 320 dry sandpaper. If you want, you can spray on a very thin guide coat again and use a rubber block, except for the edges which should be done by hand. This second guide coat will show any grooves made by the long board, or scratches from the 280 paper.

It is super important to have a perfect panel at this point. If the panel isn't perfect, apply more surfacer and block sand again. This is the only place to use spot putty. This product is for minor scratches or imperfections, IT IS NOT A FILLER!

Clean up all sanding residue (mud) in the seams and cracks now. After it dries, it can really be tough to clean away. Wash the car with lots of clean water. Use a compressed air hose/blower in one hand, and plenty of lint free rags in the other. Dry the car. Blow dirt and water from behind any molding, weather strip, seams...everywhere water can collect. Smart to wear safety glasses at this stage. Blow and wipe dry, blow and wipe dry. Dirt is your enemy now, so get the car spotlessly clean.

Roll the car into the clean paint room. If you put the car up on jackstands, you can remove the wheels. Disconnect the battery. This grounds the car to prevent static electricity from attracting dust. You should have special painting clothing, lint free, including a cap. You don't need a hair in the top coat! There are some inexpensive plastic paint suits from the supply store that really work great for this.

If you have removed most of the trim, there will be very little final taping necessary. Just remember that it is relatively easy to remove paint from chrome or rubber, but if you lap the tap onto the to-be-painted metal surface, you will find touch-up's difficult. So, go around all taped trim pieces with a razor blade, either tucking the tape under the piece, or trimming it off.

Cover all large areas with paper. It is easiest to run tape around the edges of these areas, then add the taped paper. Use only quality paper and tape. Solvents will bleed through cheap tape and newspaper. Never leave a loose edge of paper...air pressure can/will blow it into the fresh paint. If the tape doesn't stick well to a rubber weatherstrip, try mixing some clear lacquer with thinner. Dip a rag in this solution and wipe the rubber. The tape will stick to the clear film left behind.

Use plastic drop cloths to cover the engine and interior. If you have a detailed chassis, tape paper from the chassis edge and attach this with tape to the paint room floor. Paint goes everywhere, especially urethanes.

If this is a color change, or a project car, you'll need to do the door jambs, the deck lid opening, around the hood edges,

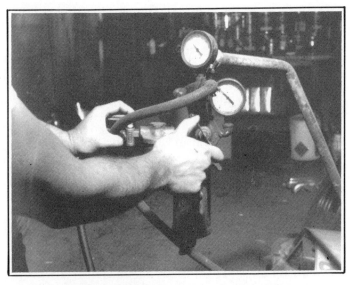

ABOVE LEFT - Air pressure determines how well material flows from paint gun, in addition to main system regulator, a small guage at the gun is advisable.

ABOVE - After surfacer is sprayed on metal, follow with a thin coat of different color. Block sanding guide coat shows high/low spots. LEFT - Door jambs, trunk opening, cowl and hood areas can all be sprayed with finish color first. Car can then be sent to the upholster shop, or pieces reassembled and car is ready for final coats of paint.

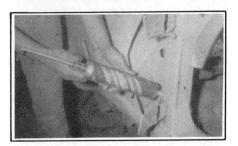

Use body caulking compound everywhere a seam need sealing. This is a resilient caulk, and can be painted over.

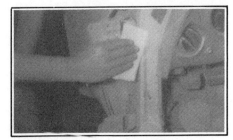

For premium job, doors/decklid/hood are removed, and all the hard to reach areas are sanded

ABOVE - Edges of the hood need to be filled and sanded if the car is going to get a show-judge type finish. This takes extra time, but it pays off in the long run.

FAR LEFT - Carl Brunson finishes inside edge of ISCA show winning Corvette belonging to John Moore. Car won many best paint awards.

LEFT - Engine compartment is very carefully taped off and covered with paper and plastic, this tape job is checked again just prior to spraying on the paint.

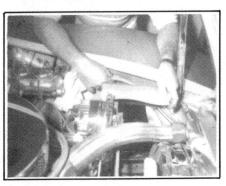

174

Corvette owner John Moore checks out possible paint schemes and available colors from Colors, Inc., out of Minnesota. Look at paint chips under lights and outdoors before selecting.

Moore confers with Brunson and striper Brooke Passey while the graphics are being laid out. For this kind of championship paint, everything must be better than perfect, no glitches.

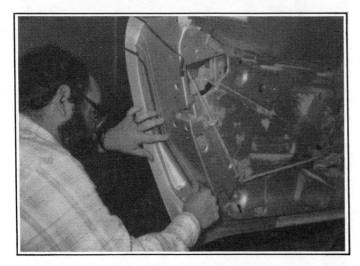

Passey lays out the graphics design inside the door, on the jambs, even into the fender wells. There is a tremendous amount of taping required for the more complicated graphics jobs.

etc. This will turn into a day's work alone. A show quality paint job requires these areas to be as nice as the outside. That means block sanding and all the rest. If the inner fenders, inside the doors, hood and deck undersides are to be painted, it is nice to do this with the pieces off the car. If this isn't possible, after these area are "cut in" with paint, let the paint dry and then tape the areas off. This will keep the final outside paint from blowing into the cracks and causing a dry edge.

Door jambs are a hard area to prep and make look good. This is one of the areas car show judges look to determine Best Paint awards. Be sure to paint under the door, and the hinge area. You can prep it by sanding with fine sandpaper, then with a scratch pad (3M #7447). Wash the area good with grease and wax remover. These are areas that only a few people are likely to see, but they are part of the paint job.

After painting the jambs and other openings, sand off any overspray on the outside panels, and wipe the surface clean with a final wash. This is not grease and wax remover, but a mild cleaning solvent to clean off fingerprints (yes, fingers will leave a grease) and any other potential problem residues.

Now, the car is ready to seal. Clean your hands, put on cap and paint clothes, and the best respirator mask you can get. Total fresh air systems are the best, particularly with the urethanes. More and more information is showing that most of the two-part paint systems now available can be tremendously toxic. The bad stuff can even seep through the skin. Protect yourself from the paint...no paint job is worth poor health.

About a half-hour before you are going to use it, open the tack rag all the way. This airing out helps to prevent any of the rag residue from rubbing off onto the car. Fold the tack rag loosely, and tack the car, using the air hose at the same time. Do not press hard with the tack rag, just push it over the surface. Turn the rag often, and refold to get a fresh surface. A neat trick is never to cross the body openings (doors, hood, deck lid). These cracks can knock particles of dirt from the tack rag, dirt which will later blow into the paint. Tack three times at least, the last time without air.

Now you can seal the car. Sealers keep the solvents of the top coats from penetrating into the undercoats. Skipping this step can result in a dull finish, because solvents get trapped in the undercoats and try to dry out after the top coat is dry. The sealer also prevents sand scratch swelling. Primer sealers will take care of any small bare metal sand-throughs (at the edges). Only urethane sealer can be sanded without resealing. The final paint will bond to sealer if applied when the sealer has dried according to the manufacturer's instructions! It is important to know these instructions. Apply the sealer in a good, even coat.

Until you become a really advanced professional, do not play around with the reduction and drying time instructions from the paint companies.

Mix the paint very well. With metallics, be sure to stir all the settled paint off the can bottom. Use the reducer recommended for the temperature range you are painting in. Reducers play a key role... if the reducer is too fast the paint doesn't flow out, too slow and the paint will probably run.

Do not paint or prime under about 68 degrees. Paints are not designed to dry in colder temperatures. While mixing two-part paints, wear the respirator. Mix in clean cans, use a paint strainer, and fill the paint gun cup 3/4 full. Too full and the can can drip paint out of the vent hole (even with the so-called "dripless cups"). Brunson uses a DeVilbiss MBC #7 gun with a #30 air cap, and a Binks #7 with a 36 SD air cap. These are expensive tools, but they last a lifetime. I have had two DeVilbiss guns for over 40 years now, and they were used when I got them. An air guage is attached at the gun for correct air pressure (which is whatever the manufacturer recommends).

Turn on the paint room exhaust fan during all stages of blowing, tacking, and painting. Leave this fan on until the paint is "dust free". Get dust and paint vapors away from the newly painted car. If you turn the fan off as soon as you are done painting, you loose air flow around the car and the paint has a hard time "vaping out". Remember that trapped solvent means a dull finish.

Put the first coat of color on medium dry. The usual practice is to start on the roof, starting in the middle and working back towards the edge. Keep the hose over a shoulder and off the surface. Do both roof sides. Brunson then does the passenger door, passenger quarter panel, deck lid, and then the passenger fender, back to the driver's quarter panel, door, both sides of the hood, then the driver's fender. This system seems to eliminate any dry edges. Putting on the first coat "dry" gives a "tack coat" that the next coat will bond to better, helping to prevent runs.

Follow this tack coat with a full wet coat, with a 50 percent spray pattern overlap. Let this wet coat dry to "tacky", which means the point when you can touch tape and leave a finger print, but not get any paint on your finger tip. Test the last area painted.

The tack coat and two or three wet coats are all that is needed for most paint jobs. Metallics need to be "dusted" to even the metallics out. While the last coat is still wet, over reduce the paint some and turn up the gun air pressure. Pull the trigger only part way, and dust a light, even coat on the surface. If it is really warm, use a slow reducer to over reduce the paint.

After all graphics are sprayed on, the overlay paint edges are very carefully sanded to remove burrs, then the striper can lay on fine lines to make the graphics/flames/whatever stand out even better.

When spraying very large cars or vans, it may be necessary to have two painters working simultaneously, starting with the top and hood. When reaching over a panel, be sure and hold the air hose away from the surface, and be sure that no paint drips from the paint gun.

The newer basecoat-clearcoat finishes look super, and are not hard to apply. The color coats are easy to put on, and always dry even looking, with good coverage. Put the clearcoat on with the tack coat-wet coat system. If you want a super finish, the kind you are seeing from the high-tech builders, let the clear dry overnight and color sand it smooth the next morning. Use 500 and warm water, with Ivory liquid to lubricate the sandpaper. Dry the surface with air (thoroughly), and respray with another coat of clear. This makes the paint look a mile deep, very wet, and has little texture.

If a run shows up in the finish, and everybody who swings a paint gun gets them, it is not the end of the world. Non-clearcoat metallics are trouble, and will require some respraying, but solid colors and clear coats don't. If the run is in an area that will be hard to block sand, spray more paint on to cause the run to "move" to an area easier to sand. This is really a trick that the very experienced pro uses all the time. It is actually possible to move a run right off the bottom of a panel! With solid colors and clears, only, of course. Watch for these runs while you are spraying, because after the paint has had a set to "tack up" it is almost impossible to move a run.

When the run is in a sandable area, next day use a hardwood block and wrap it with 600 grit sandpaper. Use Ivory liquid and water, and lots of light and careful sanding. This will sand the flow edges out. Use very light, even strokes... do not press hard. When the run is almost out, switch to 1500 grit paper, sand out the 600 grit scratches, then use 2000 to remove the 1500 grit scratches. Polish with a fine compound, such as Glasirut, followed with Mequire's #7. The same system will work to remove dirt, but use only 2000 grit sandpaper.

If the entire car is to be color sanded and polished, use something like 2000 Mikka sandpaper. This takes out the texture. It takes a long time to sand, but the polishing goes easier. Use a lower rpm polisher and something like the Glasirut polish. Use a sheepskin pad and go over the car on the last time around. This sheepskin, and clean Bright's #27 Liquid Ebony will remove all swirl marks. Finish up with Meguire's #7, and do not wax for 60-90 days. This way you don't seal in any residual solvents. Wax Shoppe's Super Glaze makes a good finish after this waiting period.

These are tricks that Brunson has picked up over the years, many of them new to journalism. As an "old time" painter, I've followed along and find that working the new two-parts system is not nearly as difficult as I thought. Probably the hardest part for me was getting used to the improved respirators and full coverage clothing.

One final caution: Don't think that just because you are going to do "just a little painting" that you can get by without the safety equipment. Your lungs work "just a little" as much as a whole lot. Mess around incorrectly with this paint, and they may end up not working at all!

Spraying acrylic enamels and acrylic lacquers follows essentially this same pattern, although they are less costly. We have been hearing rumors of the pro's using urethane clears over lacquers, but we haven't been able to try this system yet, so we can't comment.

You can do your own paint job, but you will need a paint booth. Fortunately, most smaller community body shops will let you rent their booth over a weekend. But don't plan on using their paint guns or equipment other than air. For obvious reasons, a good painter is very jealous of his tools. You will become that way as well, because once you do your first paint job, you are hooked with this part of Building Real Hot Rods.

ABOVE - Small pieces can be painted with the modern spray cans, practice until paint is applied smoothly. BELOW - replace all weatherstripping with quality weatherstrip adhesive, don't spare the glue.

After all the taping has been removed, clean up all the trim to get rid of overspray, very tiny areas can be misted with fresh paint without remasking if you are careful.

ABOVE - Carl Brunson shows off his custom coupe that took on an entire new character when unique "bustle back" paint scheme was applied. The key to the very best paint schemes include a lot of planning beforehand. BELOW - We dug this photo out of the archives to show that radical paint styles survive the test of time. Surrealistic flames do not have to be same on both sides of the car, however, and this pattern-painted top has long been out of favor.

AUTO RESTORATION TOOLS AND TECHNIQUES

GUARANTEED TO SAVE YOU TIME AND MONEY. PRODUCTS DESIGNED FOR HOME AUTO RESTORERS TO GET PROFESSIONAL RESULTS. 30-DAY MONEY-BACK GUARANTEE ON ALL EASTWOOD TOOLS.

SPOTWELD IN 6 SECONDS

Fix body panels with original type spotwelds. Gun attaches to 50 amp A.C. arc welder. Can weld in corners. Over 50,000 sold. Perfect welds for patch panel work.

4325 Spotweld Gun **$39.95**
4321 Spotweld Electrodes (10) . **$ 9.95**

REMOVE OLD SPOTWELDS

Cuts away old spotwelds without damaging panels. Lets you remove spotwelds from top panel—leaves lower panel intact for reuse. Attaches to standard ¼" drill. Saves hard-to-replace body pieces.

3219 Spotweld cutter **$12.95**
3220 Replacement cutter . . . . . **$ 4.95**

ENGINE PORTING KIT

Porting improves engine performance. Smooth off the rough head castings to increase engine airflow—this gives power. Kit includes 48 120 grit rolls (round and tapered), 2-4" and 2-6" mandrels and instructions. Use with high speed grinder. Carbide burr to remove a lot of material.
2242 Porting Kit **$24.95**

FIX WINDSHIELD CHIPS

Repairs chips in outer layer of windshield. Unique resin penetrates under surface for permanent repair. Sets in a few hours. Save hundreds in windshield replacement costs.

1909 Windshield repair set . . . **$16.95**

ECONOMY SPRAY GUN

Quality at low price. Spray varnishes, urethanes, lacquers. Detachable forged head and air nozzle. Includes aluminum cup. Uses 1 hp or larger compressor; std. ¼" inlets.

5653 Economy Spray Gun . . . **$49.95**

BODYWORK MADE EASY

Learn how the pros straighten dents. Used by bodymen for over 40 years. Over 100 photos, 126 pages.
6602 Key To Metal Bumping **$6.50**

SANDBLAST WITHOUT SANDSTORM

Spot blaster contains sand in special recycling bag. Efficient; great for small areas or where neatness counts. Uses 1 HP compressor.

9557 Spot Blaster **$59.95**
9561 Special Abrasive (3 lb.) . . **$ 9.95**

HOLDERS GIVE YOU A 3RD HAND

Holds panels tight for welding. Just drill ⅛" hole and insert. Eliminates rivets and "C" clamps. Comes with two, 2 side style holders and compression tool.
1286 13 Piece Holding System . **$29.95**

RIVET FLUSH TO METAL

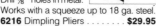

Dimpling pliers puts a countersunk recession in sheetmetal to keep smooth panel look. Drill ⅛" holes in metal. Works with a squeeze up to 18 ga. steel.
6216 Dimpling Pliers **$29.95**

DO YOUR OWN ALIGNMENT

Same money from the alignment shop. Checks toe-in, toe-out—even wheel wobble—from your driveway. Simple instructions show you if adjustment's necessary. Tool pays for itself with first use.
2692 Wheel Alignment Tool . . . **$29.95**

POWER WASHER ZAPS GRIME

Uses solvents, cleaners, or degreasers for cleaning action. Can siphon liquids or connect to hose. Attach to 1 HP or stronger compressor. Works great.
8629 Grime Blaster **$39.95**

DASHBOARD REPAIR

Fix impossible-to-replace dashboards. Kit complete with colors, grain patterns, and instructions. Easy to use.
3764 Dash Repair Kit **$13.95**

METAL NIBBLER

Cut away corrosion with our nibbler. Works from a hole small as ¼". Easier to use than standard shears. Perfect for autobody sheet-metal.
6281 Metal Nibbler **$28.95**
6284 Repl. Blades (pkg. 2) . . . **$ 9.95**

FLANGERS FOR FLUSH WELDS

Cam action jaws produce an offset flange so replacement panels fit flush. Just takes a squeeze to make a flange. Works with metal to 18 gauge.
6286 Panel Flanger **$29.95**

BUFFING KITS RESTORE METAL

Polish metal parts in your own workshop. Kits work with standard bench grinder or electric motor. All kits complete with compounds, wheels, and instructions. Even beginners get professional results.
2606 Stainless Steel Kit **$26.50**
2604 Aluminum and Brass Kit . **$17.50**
2612 Combo Stainless/Alum. Kit . . **$34.95**

CAST IRON GRAY

Paint duplicates the look of freshly sandblasted metal. Helps keep cast iron parts like wheel cylinders, suspension pieces, etc. look factory fresh for years.
1258 Spray Gray **$4.95**
2 or more each . **$4.50**

GAS TANK SEALER

Stops rust and seals dangerous pin hole and seam leaks. Unaffected by octane boosters or alcohol. Must remove tank from car. 1 qt. covers 8-10 gallon tank.

1611 Tank Sealer (qt.) **$19.95**
1613 Tank Etch (cleaner) . . . . . **$ 8.95**

STITCH WELDER

Joins autobody sheetmetal with MIG-like results. Works from standard A.C. arc welder (set at 80 amps or less). Over 30,000 sold! Complete instructions. Use Eastwood welding rods for best results.
4369 Stitch Welder **$59.00**
4377 Welding Rods (3 lb.) **$14.95**

A RUST REMOVER THAT WORKS

A chemical rust remover that attacks rust but not good metal. It's reusable, non-toxic, non-flammable, non-caustic. The safest and best rust remover we've used.

3430 Oxi-Solv (16 oz) . . . . **$ 8.95**
3432 Oxi-Solv (1 gal.) **$24.95**

RUST PREVENTION COMPOUNDS

Anti-Rust: Seals areas in hard-to-reach places, like rocker panels and doors.
2712 Anti-Rust 11¾ oz. aerosol **$5.95**
2722 Anti-Rust quart **$8.00**

Cold Galvanizing Compound: A primer for all metal surfaces. Fights rust.
2709 Cold Gal. 16 oz. aerosol . **$6.50**
2714 Cold Gal. quart **$17.95**

Rubberized Undercoating: Seals out moisture, dust, noise, heat. Dries fast; paintable.
4055 Undercoating 17¾ oz. aerosol . **$6.95**
4353 Undercoating quart **$6.95**
4059 Undercoating gun (for qt.) **$21.95**

HIGH TEMP MANIFOLD PAINT

Keeps exhaust manifolds like new. Stainless pigments bond to surface, last for years. Cures with heat. Good to 1200°F.
1256 High Temp Paint **$13.95**

Prices in this ad supersede those of previous Eastwood ads. © 1988 Easthill Group, Inc.

Eastwood

TO ORDER CALL TOLL FREE **1-800-345-1178**
Outside U.S. (215) 640-1450 *30 Day Money Back Guarantee*

Send me the following: Code *1C41RMHB*

_____ Items (s) # _____ $_____
_____ Items (s) # _____ $_____
_____ Items (s) # _____ $_____

☐ **Send me your free catalog**
☐ VISA ☐ MasterCard ☐ C.O.D. (Add $2.75)
Credit _____ Expiration _____
Card _____ Date _____
☐ Check enclosed
(PA residents add 6% sales tax)

Packing and Guaranteed Delivery Charge
$ 1.00 to 20.00 = $3.50   40.01 to 50.00 = $4.95
$20.01 to 30.00 = $3.95   50.01 to 75.00 = $6.00
$30.01 to 40.00 = $4.40   75.00 and up = $6.50

SHIPPING $_____
TOTAL $_____

Name_____
Address_____
City_____
State_____ Zip_____

The Eastwood Company ● 580 Lancaster Avenue, P.O. Box 296, Malvern, PA 19355

FREE! EASTWOOD CATALOG FILL IN COUPON.

179

More photos from the past, because it just might be that the wild paint schemes of tomorrow could be splatters, or lace designs, or cobwebbing, or any number of different patterns.

They may be worked into the overall design differently, but there is very little new. The Pontiac below shows that entire paint jobs were needed to win shows, even two decades ago.

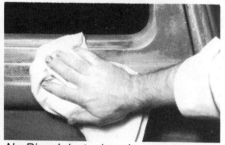

CHAPTER 12

Examples of the Art

1935 CHEVROLET 3-WINDOW COUPE
Bill Batchelor, Idaho

I t would only be appropriate to close this volume one of HOW TO BUILD REAL HOT RODS by giving two out standing examples of real hot rods. One is the product of a self-taught bodyworking professional, the other is the work of a hot rodder, self-taught. One includes enough of the so-called high-tech look to fool the most expert, the other flies in the face of everything that is considered state-of-the-art. And the one which might be considered a "California Car" isn't, and the one which wouldn't be considered such, is.

Let's start with a look at a Chevrolet that is as slick as any high dollar pro-built car on the road today, but something that was built on a reasonable budget and proves conclusively that anyone can build a quality ride if they are willing to learn and work.

Bill Batchelor is a former career Air Force type who retired to the western Idaho town of Mountain Home. Not what you would think of as a mecca of hot rodding, yet it turns out this small community near the air base is a seething cauldron of hot rodding. Hot rodding of all years. Because of his building talents, and willingness to help others get their cars on the road, Bill has become something of a rallying point for street oriented rodders. All the while working away in his home garage getting this 1935 Chevy coupe ready for driving. Yes, it is show quality, and it has won its share of exposition awards. But it is also for driving, and out west a simple little drive to the hamburger stand might take 5 hours and 250 miles!

This is a car combining lots of Bill's talents, as well as a practical amount of mail-order parts. We think it represents what is probably the current state of affairs with the "average" hot rod builder, with costs kept within reason. Some builders might produce a similar machine for less, some for more. Doesn't matter, because this is a <u>real</u> hot rod in the best sense of the word!

LEFT - Batchelor found his project in a farm barn, and paid the "huge" price of $1750 for the privilege of completely rebuilding it. It is still possible to find hot rod building projects like this, if you are willing to take something a little out of the ordinary.

RIGHT - General Motors cars will likely have a lot of wood in the body through the 1936 model year, if this wood is in good condition it can be renovated, there are wood kits available for most GM cars.

ABOVE - It is far easier to work on a clean car, so Batchelor started by hauling the Chevy down to an available steam cleaner and spraying the entire under-carriage.

RIGHT - Before the body was removed from the frame, the top was chopped 3 inches and the soft top insert replaced with a piece of metal. Windshield posts are V-notched, slanted as part of the chopping procedure.

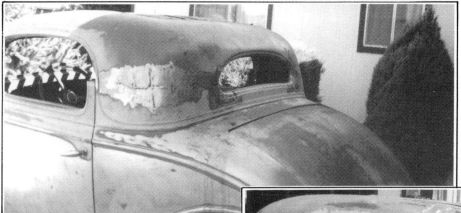

Panel alignment at top quarters is by vertical slits in metal, the door posts are used as basic alignment guide on such bodies. Do the metal work right and there is very little filler needed.

ABOVE - Plastic filler applied in thin film where top has been rewelded. Filler is used in door jambs as well.

BELOW - Entire body was stripped of old paint and best quality primer and surfacer was applied.

Windshield posts were slanted slightly to compensate for misalignment, as was front of door. Clean area at front of top was original factory lead seam.

With the top finished, the body could be removed from the frame, a body dolly was made of scrap iron and small wheels, very convenient for the home shop where workroom is minimal.

The stock Chevy frame was very strong to begin with, still it would get considerable modifications from Batchelor. This is when that earlier steam cleaning is fully appreciated.

Bill used two engine stands as rotating mounts for the frame, installed a Sbarbaro center crossmember with driveshaft and mounting points for the Sbarbaro 4-bar rearend locating links.

The Sbarbaro dropped tube front axle uses Aldan coil/over shocks and springs, notice how much the front crossmember has been trimmed away. Special crossmember strengthens frame at engine, gives engine mounts as well.

Frame and suspension components were painted Martin Senour Ureglow Red, cross-steering gearbox mounts against the engine crossmember.

The 8-inch Ford rearend also uses coil/over springs and shocks, with a panhard rod to control sidesway. Shocks mount to extra crossmember.

185

While Bill was building and painting the chassis, friend Jim Bledsoe created a strong 331-cubic inch small block Chevy engine that hauls the mountains but still gets good mpg.

The 350 TurboHydramatic transmission has plenty of working room in modified chassis, trans mount drops out the bottom for service. Shifter and parking brake levers mount atop the polished trans case.

A stainless steel gas tank was welded up for the stock position. Though the original X-member is missing, the frame still has a great resistance to twisting, complimented by the tight coupe body.

ABOVE - The body was placed back on the chassis for component fitting and individual parts such as the grille and shell started to get paint.

RIGHT - Fenders and running boards are fiberglass items from Superior Glass Works, wheels are from Enkie. The cars stance is just right.

LEFT - Fender apron on non-Fords keep builder from going too low in front, note engine fits compartment without firewall setback.

BELOW - Stock steel hood is set on for a trial fit, if front end is not made too low the car can be roadworthy throughout the country.

ABOVE - Fenders were removed before the body got final color, note that all glass is still not installed, that comes after painting.

LEFT - Rear frame cover has the license recessed, gas filler door installed, and taillights frenched in place.

187

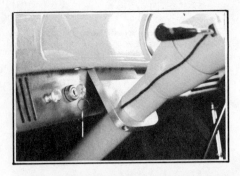

LEFT - Tiny things make a big difference, such as sanded pieces of metal to hold hood lacing in place.

FAR LEFT - Homemade auxiliary panel below stock dash has slits for air flow column mount is aluminum plate. Air conditioner is AirTique.

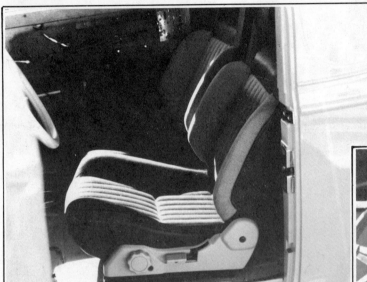

LEFT - Celica adjustable seats were found to fit almost perfectly, could have been used without recovering.

BELOW - Vent windows have been eliminated, VDO gauges are used in Carriage Works dash panel insert, Vega steeing is topped with a Grand Prix wheel.

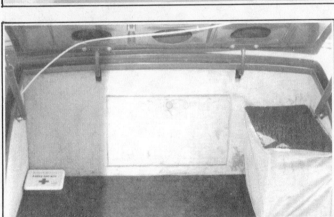

TOP - Board at front edge of trunk has access door for hidden storage area, a neat trick for any street driven car that is a show winner.

ABOVE - The fiberglass deck lid uses a remote cable operated latch.

ABOVE - Aluminum plate was used to make up exhaust pipe clamps, so far the resonance has not proven objectionable to passengers.

INSET - Gas filler door for rear panel is from a Volkswagen.

This is a very smooth car, and although it has a final cost about that of a contemporary new car, it will hold value, probably increase.

ABOVE - The car does not run bumpers, in current fashion, small headlights are Deitz aftermarket items. While a lot of fiberglass replacement parts were used, original metal could have been retained.

RIGHT - The big/little tires and the dropped front axle make this one Chevy coupe that seems to be right on the ground.

1923 FORD ROADSTER

Bob Accosta, California

Bob Accosta has been associated with hot rodding for a number of decades now, so it is no wonder that he has created a <u>real</u> hot rod of the more traditional sort. The kind of car that people think they remember as having graced the driveways of every 1950s California home.

We first saw the car at the Goodguys West Coast Nationals rod run at Pleasanton, California, earlier this year. Bob parked near our Hot Rod Mechanix magazine booth at the fairgrounds clock tower, and the car immediately drew a crowd of appreciative rodders. Later, we presented the Tex Smith Real Hot Rod award to Bob, because this car was the very epitome of the award meaning. Yes, there were hundreds of superbly built cars at the run, but for the most part they were clones of each other. Bob's T stood apart from the crowd.

Well built, well finished, but in every respect it encorporates what hot rodding is all about.

Which is no surprise, because Accosta has been around rodding since the "golden years". At 64, Bob is now retired, and this roadster is the first project he tackled after leaving the daily grind. Years ago he had a 1933 Ford two door sedan, back in the 1950s when closed cars in California weren't all that popular. He is a member of the elite Oakland National Roadster Show hall of fame, so he knows what this hobby is all about. Starting with a body and frame that had been in the garage rafters for 25 years, he spent 1 1/2 years on the project. This roadster would never be construed as a high-tech billet aluminum piece, yet it cries real hot rod from every lightening hole!

Accosta had the 1932 Ford frame and 1923 Model T body for 32 years, he paid a princely sum of $75 for the pieces originally, then the stuff hung in the garage rafters for 25 years, Bob ended up making a roadster "like they usta do", and it's a beauty.

The 1932 frame rails were narrowed to fit the T body, note how tiny pie cuts were taken from frame lips in many places so the curve is smooth.

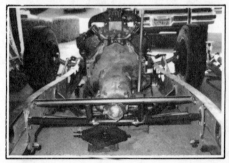

ABOVE - The frame was boxed in the central area, a new K-member of tubing was made up. Center part of bottom tube unbolts for trans service. Keep in mind that all this was done at home.

LEFT - After reworking the frame curvature, the rear horns are much closer together than originally, so that they now tuck inside the narrow T turtle deck, rearend is a Ford item.

Another look at the tubing K-member, by adding two extra tubes that run aft it is really a sort of abbreviated X member, very strong and very simple.

The idea is to get as long a panhard (sway) bar as possible, so rearend brackets lean outboard, bar has single adjustable end which is a good idea.

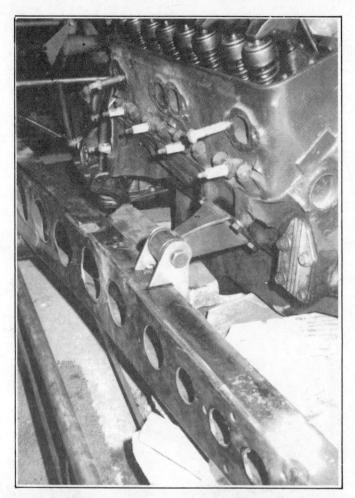

TOP - Very simple engine mount uses insulator at extreme end of motor bracket, this positions weight directly over inner edge of frame rail and helps reduce rail twist tendancy.

ABOVE - The new narrowed tubular rear crossmember bolts in place, since the frame was punched full of holes it was essential that all stress points be boxed.

LEFT . All the brackets were kept as simple as possible including those for the coil/over shocks. Patterns can be made of cardboard, stiff paper, or tin/aluminum sheet before cutting brackets from plate. When in doubt, make brackets of thicker material.

ABOVE - Since the round tube Ford production type axle is used, a dropped spring perch is best way to get car lower, this "suicide" perch is strongly gusseted.

LEFT - The old style hairpin radius rod locaters are used for the rear axle, made of thick wall tubing with Heim rod ends at the very strong frame bracket.

ABOVE - Look closely to see that special spring shackle perch is different this allows free spring alignment regardless of caster, such bolts are commercially available.

There are over 300 lightening holes in the chassis components, and while this might not improve vehicle performance, it certainly makes it look like a very serious race style car. Note at the left how the frame horns tuck up into the turtle deck area, and below how the body is only slightly channeled over the frame.

ABOVE - The entire flooring is made of aluminum, engine turned on the underside just to impress whatever rodder might be crawling around under there. Note how substructure of body/flooring at edges has also been pie-cut for curvature. ABOVE LEFT - Small piece of sheet metal has been formed as frame cover just aft of the body and below deck. LEFT - The Vega steering leads to a column that is supported at the lower end by a bolt-on bracket that looks like swiss cheese, note master cylinder immediately behind.

Photo above shows fiberglass mold being made of top rear part of deck, at right the mold is used to make a rolled pan that exactly duplicates the deck. Ingenious.

The fiberglass deck pan is mounted to small square tubing bracing that bolts to the deck lid, the battery box inside the pan is in a box that bolts to the frame horns, round holes are for 1950 Pontiac taillights.

Homemade brake pedal mount and arms are liberally drilled, extra wide pedal and dual arms make this an extremely strong unit, note pedal notch for steering column.

The aluminum flooring started with flat stock trimmed to fit on frame inside body, trans hump patterns from brown paper.

Note tubing body supports in cowl/dash area. Trans hump is formed of aluminum, there is still plenty of foot room.

Trans hump is riveted to the flooring and firewall is opened up to accept the steering column, steering wheel is Grant.

Emergency brake lever is floor mounted adjacent to the trans tunnel for foot room.

Two 7 1/2 gallon gas tanks are mounted between frame rails beneath the seats, each has separate filler.

Tank lines feed to a single pump, then one gas line runs along frame to the engine.

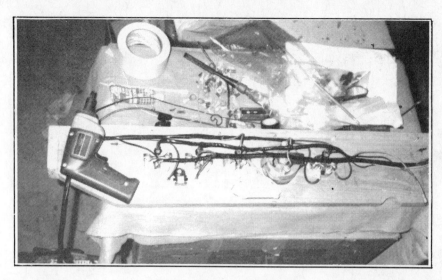

Bob did all the wiring at home, including that for the wooden dash, friends and relatives were called in for help, including application of the black lacquer on the body, and black Imron on the chassis.

VDO guages are spaced along the wooden dash, each instrument is grounded. Entire body is reinforced with thinwall tubing, making it very solid for the oak dashboard.

Bob placed all the "extra" electrics under the seat, this is one of the ways to maximize use of very limited space available in the older style rod bodies.

Bob made up an alternator bracket froom plate stock, puts the alternator to the lower right hand side of the engine, ok for the California climate.

The small block Chevy engine is a 283-inch version with 3 carbs, Sanderson headers, cooling comes from a Brass Works radiator, the transmission is GM 350 TurboHydramatic.

This "small" engine might well have been the killer motor of the mid-1950s, even the fuel block for tri-carb setup has been made at home, keeping the costs down.

With the seat in place, only another hot rodder would know that the radio and other electrics are underneath.

This bare bones look accentuates all the holes in the chassis, this is a classic case of hot rod.

BELOW - All hot rods go through stages of construction, here the roadster awaits the final phase of upholstery in black/silver vinyl. Small band of red and yellow flames circle the cowl, brakes are discs front and drum back, front shocks are homemade friction.

LEFT - The finished car already knows northern California roads very intimately, Tires are 15-inch TA's on the rear and 14-inch Michilen up front, hub caps are stock 1941 Ford items.

BELOW - This is why it is so important to keep things simple and uncluttered, those old Pontiac taillights are still hard to beat for basic rod styling.

So what is a hot rod? It is any kind of vehicle that has been modified to improve performance or appearance.

A hot rod is a street rod, and a custom car. It is a drag race car and a Baja off-roader. It is a NASCAR roundy-rounder and an ISCA show stopper. Most of all, a hot rod is the very spirit of individualism, whether it is in Los Angeles or Sydney, New Jersey or London, Paris or Stockholm, Iowa or Mexico. There are hot rodders wherever there are machines.

A hot rod may be built for less than a thousand dollars, or it may cost several hundred thousand. It may be in primer or violent custom colors. It may have a diminutive 4-cylinder or a 32-valve monster motor. It may be fast, or it may be slow. It can be all things, just as long as it is a reflection of the builder or owner.

But to be a REAL hot rod, it must be honest to itself. It can't claim to be a Bonneville record holder and never pass over the salt. It can't pose as a drag racing rocket and never roll on the drag strip. It cannot be considered a show car if it is never in a car show. When a personalized car can, and does do, what it was designed and built to do, then it is a real hot rod.

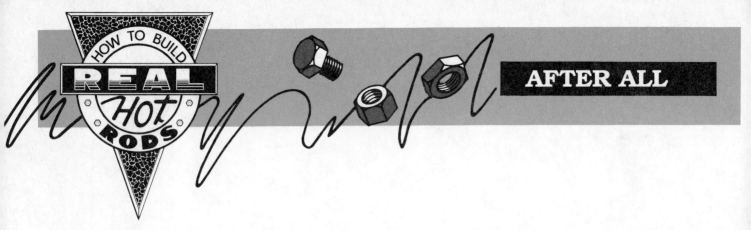

To prove a point, I present a project roadster that we have been building and reporting on in the pages of Hot Rod Mechanix magazine. This is a 1931 Ford roadster body on a frame made of part 1932 Ford frame, part home-made frame, part 1937 Ford frame, and part 1927 or so Dodge frame. It uses a 1969 Pontiac overhead cam six cylinder engine, turbo transmission, SuperBell front axle, and Volvo rearend. We expect the final cost to be around $1500, including paint and upholstery. Lots of so-called experts say we can't do it. But we have been doing it for over three decades now. And so has an army of home builders around the country and world.

This is what Hot Rod Mechanix magazine is all about...building real hot rods. Yes, HRMx looks at race cars, and exotic stuff from the world's automakers, and high-tech, high dollar cars of all kinds. But only as idea platforms. As design exercises. What most of us will drive on the street is a far cry from the ultra-machines we see in many magazines and at rod runs/car shows. Fantasy is fun, but reality is everyday!

LeRoi Tex Smith
Publisher/Editor

DICK MENDONCA
1930-1978

This book is dedicated to a friend who will never read it with mortal eyes. Dick Mendonca was never a "big name" in hot rodding, although his car enthusiast friends were legion. He wrote a few articles in magazines, and published photographs, yet he was not a journalist. He belonged to the Bay Area Roadster Club of northern California, yet he was not an avid events organizer. He drove his 1929 Ford Model A roadster pickup all over the country, but always kept cars and life in total perspective. He didn't do every bit of work on his car, but he did most of it. The car was practical, yet an outstanding example of what this hot rodding art can be. Most of all, Dick Mendonca was a <u>Real </u>hot rodder!

"Real hot rodding is not Mega-Bucks...
it is Mega-Ingenuity."

Dave Lukari
USA, 1988

TEX SMITH'S
HOW TO BUILD
REAL HOT RODS

by LeRoi Tex Smith

Motorbooks International
Publishers & Wholesalers ®
Printed in USA